Memoirs of Duke De Richelieu, Volume 1

You are holding a reproduction of an original work that is in the public domain in the United States of America, and possibly other countries. You may freely copy and distribute this work as no entity (individual or corporate) has a copyright on the body of the work. This book may contain prior copyright references, and library stamps (as most of these works were scanned from library copies). These have been scanned and retained as part of the historical artifact.

This book may have occasional imperfections such as missing or blurred pages, poor pictures, errant marks, etc. that were either part of the original artifact, or were introduced by the scanning process. We believe this work is culturally important, and despite the imperfections, have elected to bring it back into print as part of our continuing commitment to the preservation of printed works worldwide. We appreciate your understanding of the imperfections in the preservation process, and hope you enjoy this valuable book.

The Regent and his Mothe

Courtiers and Favourites of Royalty

Memoirs of the Court of France
With Contemporary and Modern Illustrations
Collected from the
French National Archives

BY
LEON VALLÉE
LIBRARIAN AT THE BIBLIOTHÈQUE NATIONALE

Memoirs
of
Duke de Richelieu

IN THREE VOLUMES
VOL. I

Paris
Société des Bibliophiles
New York
Merrill & Baker

224064

Edition du Grand Trianon

Limited to
One Thousand Sets of which this is copy

No. 539

Copyright, 1903, by Merrill & Baker

MEMOIRS OF
MARSHAL DUKE DE RICHELIEU

BY
M. F. BARRIERE

THE DUKE DE RICHELIEU.

ARMAND DE VIGNEROD DU PLESSIS, Duke de Richelieu and Fronsac, is one of the most remarkable figures of the eighteenth century. Grand-nephew of the celebrated cardinal, he is born prematurely at Paris, March 13, 1696. Such are his weakness and constitutional debility that, to save his life, he has to be reared in a box of cotton! This little sickly, puling creature is nevertheless to astonish the world, and will not die till the age of ninety-two, after having achieved a highly active and very stormy career.

His father marries him against his will, at fourteen, to Mademoiselle de Noailles; then straightway presents him at Versailles and at Marly, where the ladies of the court nickname him *the little doll*, and begin to dote on him. But the outbreaks of the young duke soon compel the father to request of the King his son's imprisonment in the Bastille. There, during fourteen months, Richelieu has for his solitary diversion the daily visits of his young wife and the lessons of the learned Abbé de Saint-Remy. He takes the instruction, but he accords his wife none of the intimate privacies she has the right to, and which she tries vainly to obtain from him.

When war breaks out, Richelieu asks to serve in the Musketeers, and goes through the campaign in Flanders with Marshal de Villars, who, to reward him for his fine conduct, commissions him with carrying to the King the news of the army's success.

During his sojourn at the court, Richelieu has a public duel with the Marquis de Gacé, son of Marshal de Matignon; for the second time he is shut up in the Bastille, where he makes close acquaintance with the young Arouet. Happily his detention is short; he is set at liberty.

But there soon occurs the conspiracy of the Count de Cellamare, which has for its aim the transfer of the regency of France to Philip V., King of Spain. Richelieu allows himself to be drawn into the plot, which is unluckily discovered. Cardinal Dubois and the Regent for the third time incarcerate the duke in the Bastille, and give rigorous orders concerning him. A little later, nevertheless, they release him, and content themselves with exiling him to Conflans, at the Duke of Noailles', his uncle.

The end of the regency is marked by a great financial event. Law has launched his famous System! All Paris is a prey to stock-jobbing; and when the complications arrive that lead to the crash of the System, ruin strikes almost the entire population. Like the rest, Richelieu has gambled, has speculated; but by an exception most fortunate for him, he escapes the general shipwreck, and is one of the rare individuals whom the System profits by a very great fortune.

Now appointed ambassador to Vienna, he sets out for Austria, where he astonishes the people by his magnificence. He spends his immense fortune in princely fashion. He cultivates intimate relations with the richest and most brilliant noblemen of Austria. He conquers the court by the elegance of his manners and the resources of his wit. He gains the friendship of the Emperor Charles VI., and finally decides Austria to form an alliance with France.

When the War of the Polish Succession begins, Richelieu at once resumes military life, and contributes to the winning of the battle of Fontenoy. He next marches to deliver Genoa, besieged by the English. His conduct is so brilliant that Louis XV. confers on the duke the baton of marshal, while the senate of the Genoese Republic votes him, with the sum of a million crowns, the erection of a statue in one of the squares of Genoa, and inscribes his name in the Golden Book of the Republic. Then placed in charge of the expedition to Minorca, he descends on the island, outstrips the English, and in spite of their desperate efforts, seizes Port Mahon. Finally, in the German campaign, he makes himself master of Hanover, which he ravages and ruins from end to end.

We have just viewed Richelieu as a good diplomatist and a fortunate soldier. These are enough for his glory. The literary career also tempts the duke, who at twenty-four profits by the death of Dangeau to force the doors of the French Academy. He hardly knows how to spell, but he has wit, and he is the grand-nephew of the founder of the illustrious society; which, seeing in him a powerful protector rather than a brother member, votes in his favor.

In the domestic politics of the kingdom, Richelieu also plays one of the principal parts; for he is everywhere mixed up with the affairs of the country. Called to the Royal Council, he always votes against anti-religious innovations; he always defends the Church, its traditions and its beliefs. His acts sometimes arouse violent protests among those under his jurisdiction; especially when, as governor of Guyenne, he commits such monstrous abuses of power that the Parliament of Bordeaux prints and posts up a decree which orders the officers of bailiwicks and seneschalships to address themselves to their attorney-general, and forbids their obeying the governor's injunctions. A martinet to the utmost, used to making everything bend before his will or his good pleasure, Richelieu flies into a terrible anger at this, and swears that he will destroy the parliaments, those assemblies which dare to address remonstrances to the King, refuse to authorize the subsidies demanded, and issue decrees against the high functionaries of the state! In his efforts the duke is seconded by Madame Du Barri, by D'Aiguillon, by Maupeou. He finally succeeds in extracting from Louis XV. the edict which crushes the parliaments. His joy is extreme, and he experiences one of the greatest satisfactions of his life the day when he is charged with bearing and reading the *lettre de cachet* which dissolves the Paris Court of Aids. He penetrates into the session hall; and when the president, M. de Malesherbes, protests against his action, the duke draws his sword and cries, "My orders are my soldiers!" then calls in his black musketeers and compels the councillors to leave.

But Richelieu's joy is of short duration, for events hurry forward. Louis XV. dies, and with him disappears the work of Maupeou and Richelieu. Louis XVI., the new sovereign, is the enemy of the corruption of the old court. He wishes reforms, and he recalls the parliaments, which, now grown more powerful than ever, are to open the revolutionary era. Richelieu dies August 8, 1788, the day of the convocation of the Assembly of Notables at Versailles,—that is to say, just soon enough not to assist in person at the disappearance of royalty and of the governmental principles he has served during his entire existence.

In the life of the marshal there is one very characteristic side of which we have not yet spoken. We know that the eighteenth century is distinguished by the lightness of its morals, that woman then played one of the most considerable parts in the history of France, and that the scandal of the most shameful connections checked neither princes, nor the upper clergy, nor kings. In the midst of this brazen riot, Richelieu, from his first youth to his last year, appears as the most tireless soldier of love. This *Céladon*, who lived under three reigns, makes it a title of glory to have married three wives. The first, Mademoiselle de Noailles, dies young without having obtained, despite her advances, those intimate satisfactions of which her fickle spouse is so prodigal for other women. Richelieu marries at a second wedding Mademoiselle de Guise, whom he loves, but to whom he remains faithful hardly six months. And when the marshal, at eighty-four, marries for the third time, with Madame Roth, the widow of an Irish colonel, age has not calmed the passions of the old duke, and the third consort quickly bears her share of the conjugal infidelities. Nevertheless, in spite of their too well justified griefs, these three wives preserve for their husband a love which is never interrupted; and like their rivals, the irregular companions, they manage to content themselves with the small share of affection which their

THE DUKE DE RICHELIEU.

lord and master deigns to accord them! How great was the power of enticement of the latter, all Paris had the evident proof under its eyes during the duke's captivity; for at the hour when Richelieu was authorized to take the air on the height of the Bastille rampart, there was seen every day the throng of his mistresses, who, in the hope of obtaining a glimpse of him and addressing him some signs of affection, promenaded far and wide at the base of the sad fortress! None of his contemporaries obtained so much success with the weaker sex; no one counted more love conquests, and Richelieu took the tender victims indifferently in all ranks of society, as witnessed by these lines of Voltaire: —

> "Wearied awhile of musket fire,
> Forgetting Germany entire,
> You will admit, as o'er-true tale,
>   The fleeting favors you display
>   Fall on the first that comes your way,
> Modest or prude, or fair and frail,
> The wise or silly, haughty, soft,
>   Whoever falls within your lines;
>   But if you still retain a trace
>   Of pity for your neighbor's case,
> Spare, on the road you walk so oft,
>   The beauty that my heart enshrines."

LÉON VALLÉE.

Table of Contents.

CHAPTER I.

From birth to seven months of age.—A pretty attendant.—Sponsors.—Admitted to the court at fourteen years of age.—Conquest of a person of high rank.—Marriage to Mlle. de Noailles.—First sojourn in the Bastille.—His wife vainly endeavors to reconcile him there.—He leaves the Bastille and departs for the army of Flanders.—Siege of Marchiennes.—A beautiful Italian woman offered as a prize to the conquerors.—Siege of Fribourg.—Details.—Flattering commission with which the Duke of Fronsac is charged.—Treaty of Utrecht. 1

CHAPTER II

The Duke of Orleans.—His fickle propensities, and numerous mistresses.—Sorcery: How Richelieu discovered it.—Rivalries between a mother and her daughter.—Diamond earrings. 25

CHAPTER III.

Death of Louis XIV.—Various events.—Joy of the people.—Onions scattered along the route of the funeral procession. 45

CHAPTER IV.

The intrigues that marked the commencement of the regency.—How the Duke of Orleans obtained it. 51

CHAPTER V.

The Abbé de Saint-Pierre.—The pretext under which he was excluded from the French Academy.—His books poorly written; his morals not above reproach. . . . 61

CHAPTER VI.

The general favor with which the administration of the regent was received at first.—The roués.—The quick repartee of a commissary of police to the brother of Louis XIV.—The society and entertainments frequented by the regent.—The Duchess of Orleans, his wife: the Duchess de Berri, his daughter.—An adventure at the Luxembourg.—The house of Condé.—Sojourn and fêtes at Sceaux. . . . 68

CHAPTER VII.

The regent and Mme. de Berri, his daughter, at the opera.—Masked balls given there.—Passion of Mlle. de Charolais for Richelieu.—Rendezvous that the princesses gave.—Nocturnal fêtes at the home of the Count de Gacé.—His duel with Richelieu, who is imprisoned in the Bastille for the second time.—Mlle. de Charolais visits him there. . . . 84

CHAPTER VIII.

Struggle of parliament against the nobility.—Memoirs of same.—Open war between the legitimate and legitimated princes.—Other differences between members of the high nobility and the peers.—The decree of the States-General pronounced. . 94

CHAPTER IX.

Jansenism at the court of the regent.—Mlle. of Orleans, Abbess de Chelles.—Her life as an artist at Savant and as a woman of the world under the veil.—Her interview in the guise of a convert with the Cardinal Bissy.—The princesses, daughters of the regent.—Morals of the court.—Rivalries between the prince and the Duke de Richelieu.—Two women fight a duel on account of him. 102

CHAPTER X.

The man with the iron mask.—Different conjectures.—What Richelieu knew of him. 119

CHAPTER XI.

The conspiracy of Cellamare.—Richelieu imprisoned in the Bastille for the third time.—The price of his freedom. . . 152

CHAPTER XII.

Richelieu at Modena, under the guise of a book-colporteur.—His interviews with the duchess.—He is surprised by the duke, but throws him off the scent.—His return to Paris.—Reception and dress at the French Academy.—Details of gallantry. 164

CHAPTER XIII.

D'Argenson was made keeper of the seals through the influence of Dubois and of the roués.—His birth.—He was at first lieutenant of police.—Indispensable to Mme. de Maintenon he is feared in Paris.—Leads the Duke of Orleans from that time on.—His tastes for convent life.—Relations between him and Richelieu who, in the guise of a nun, enters the Abbey of Tresnel.—The pleasant existence that D'Argenson enjoys there. 175

CHAPTER XIV.

Dubois wishes to become cardinal.—Tencin charged with the commission of negotiating with the Court of Rome in his behalf.—The promise that he exacts from Cardinal Conti before nominating him pope.—The regent kicks Dubois.—He becomes cardinal.—His reception in the council.—The haughtiness and insolence with which Marshal de Villeroy treats Dubois in his own home.—The exile of Villeroy. . . 190

CHAPTER XV.

The licentious festivals mentioned by Mlle. Tencin, praised by Dubois, and celebrated in the presence of the regent at Saint-Cloud. 211

CHAPTER XVI.

Picture of the ministry drawn by the regent himself, after the regency. 217

CHAPTER XVII.

Greek orgies beneath the windows of Louis XV. at Versailles. 222

CHAPTER XVIII.

How the police made use of prostitution to govern the capitol during the regency.—Adventures of the celebrated Fillon.—An experience of a president's wife. . . . 226

CHAPTER XIX.

Death of Dubois.—Strange peculiarities.—The Duke of Orleans prime minister. 232

CHAPTER XX.

Portrait and death of the Duke of Orleans.—Monsieur le Duc, Prince de Condé declared prime minister. . . . 239

CHAPTER XXI.

The results of the Spanish queen's ambition to rule in France.—Abdication of Phillip V.—Reign of Louis I., his son.—The unseemly conduct of the daughter of the regent, Queen of Spain.—Phillip V. reascends the throne. . . . 243

CHAPTER XXII.

The ministry of Monsieur le Duc, of the House of Condé.—Character of the prime minister.—Customs of the time and anecdotes of the court. 249

CHAPTER XXIII.

Rivalry between the Houses of Orleans and Condé.—Continuation of the picture of public morals. 253

CHAPTER XXIV.

The sequel of the rivalry of the Houses of Orleans and Condé.—Marriage of the Duke of Orleans. 256

CHAPTER XXV.

Richelieu ambassador to Vienna.—He was first taken for a spy.—He challenges Riperda, Spanish Ambassador.—His useful and gallant conduct towards the Countess Badioni, Mistress of Prince Eugene. 261

TABLE OF CONTENTS.

CHAPTER XXVI.

Public reception of Richelieu in Vienna.—Adventure of the sleighs with the Princess Lichtenstein.—The sequel of the adventure.—He causes the cardinal's cap to be given to the Bishop of Fréjus.—He is made chevalier of the order of the Holy Ghost before being eligible on account of age.—He concludes his negotiations and returns to Paris. . . . 270

CHAPTER XXVII.

The dismissal of the Infanta.—How Mlle. de Vermandois lost the crown.—Louis XV. married to the daughter of Stanislaus.—The irritation of Spain. 290

CHAPTER XXVIII.

The house of the queen is prepared.—Different word-paintings.—The young queen is astonished at the presents that France makes her. 299

CHAPTER XXIX.

Attempt of the queen and M. le Duc to get rid of Fleury.—Triumph of the prelate.—Character of the Duke de Mortemart.—Facts about the court.—About Mme. de Prie and M. le Duc. 301

CHAPTER XXX.

Exile of M. le Duc, prime minister, and of Mme. de Prie.—Character of the king and Fleury. 320

CHAPTER XXXI.

Character of M. le Duc.—How the women De Prie, Duvernay, and Dodun deceived the prince. 330

CHAPTER XXXII.

Picture of France at the beginning of Fleury's ministry.—The court.—The king.—The queen.—Beauty of the king, his timidity in the presence of women.—Character and expressions of the queen. 338

CHAPTER XXXIII.

Curious details about the princes and princesses. . . . 348

CHAPTER XXXIV.

Portrait of Cardinal de Fleury.—His character. . . . 355

CHAPTER XXXV.

Courtiers disgraced and the reasons therefore.—M. le Duc does honor to his retirement.—The Court of Madrid.—An illness of Louis XV. 361

CHAPTER XXXVI.

Polet confessor of Fleury.—Barjac, his valet-de-chambre.—His conduct toward the nobles who demeaned themselves to flatter him. 371

LIST OF ILLUSTRATIONS
VOLUME I.

	PAGE
THE REGENT AND HIS MOTHER. Frontispiece.	
AUTOGRAPH OF THE DUKE DE RICHELIEU.	
THE DUKE OF ANJOU DECLARED KING OF SPAIN	36
LOUIS XIV BLESSING HIS GRANDSON	46
MARRIAGE OF MADAME DE MAINTENON AND LOUIS XIV	48
THE ROYAL PALACE AT MEUDON	76
DUC DE RICHELIEU VISITED IN PRISON BY THE ROYAL PRINCESSES	92
THE MAN WITH THE IRON MASK	120
THE REGENT NAMING CARDINAL DUBOIS PRIME MINISTER	190
PORTRAIT OF THE YOUNG LOUIS XV EXHIBITED TO THE ROYAL FAMILY	342
THE POWER BEHIND THE THRONE	372

à Bordeaux ce 7 juin 1766

Vous ferez très bien de faire tendre en taffetas muy Sallem en taffetas ennui muy enuuues et jusques que je te uues ey tiens cequel tous nves et en bon etat

Celle uy de Richelieu

Memoirs of the Duke de Richelieu.

CHAPTER I.

From birth to seven months of age.—A pretty attendant.—Sponsors.—Admitted to the court at fourteen years of age.—Conquest of a person of high rank.—Marriage to Mlle. de Noailles.—First sojourn in the Bastille. His wife vainly endeavors to reconcile him there.—He leaves the Bastille and departs for the army of Flanders.—Siege of Marchiennes.—A beautiful Italian woman offered as a prize to the conquerors.—Siege of Fribourg.—Details.—Flattering commission with which the Duke of Fronsac is charged.—Treaty of Utrecht.

WHEN we recall the kind of life he led and his long career, it is difficult to realize that the Marshal de Richelieu, privately baptized the 13th of March, 1696, was born after pregnancy of seven months. It is to nature that he owed his robust, and at the same time, delicate constitution, which long resisted the assaults of time and passions which would quickly have destroyed an ordinary temperament. From the very day of his birth he struggled against death and was so delicate that he had to be enveloped and protected in a box of cotton. Believing that new born babes, when they are as feeble as was the case with him, have need only of a benign warmth, his father ordered the doctors away from the frail body, commanding them to allow nature to take its course. And it was to nature alone that he owed his existence.

For the little duke gained new strength from day to day and gradually drove away the apprehensions which his untimely birth and the ill-health of his mother had created, though a convulsion which seized him one day nearly caused his death. On this occasion he was actually abandoned for dead, but an unexpected event saved him. A female attendant whom curiosity had attracted to the vicinity of the child perceived a change in what was thought to be the corpse; it commenced to give some slight signs of life; she called for help; they returned to the little duke who had been left for dead and he was very soon livelier than ever. From this time on he never was sick. This crisis appears to have brought about an advantageous change in his constitution; he became very much stronger and in a few months his health became so rugged as to prevent any further fears for him. It is fitting that a man who became so renowned in after years should have had something singular in the history of his infancy.[1]

He was baptized in 1699, being held over the baptismal font by the king and Mme. the Duchess de Bourgogne.

Mme. de Maintenon, who was under certain obligations to the Duke de Richelieu and who, being at that time Mme. Scarren, visited him frequently—a circum-

---

[1] They say that the female attendant was very pretty and in after years the marshal was very often rallied about this circumstance; this seemed to foreshadow the power which beauty would have over him and he never denied it. It is not at all surprising that he passed his whole life in performing acts of homage to beauty.

stance which excited considerable unfavorable comment at the time—was very well pleased at being able to serve the son of her former protector. The baptism was celebrated with pomp. The child already gave promise of intelligence and beauty.

His early education was quite neglected; his father, who was but slightly educated and who had always given himself over to his own pleasures, could not devote attention to his instruction; and it was intrusted without surveillance to the care of a tutor who did not have the requisite qualities of an instructor. Moreover the child was willful and preferred play rather than study, a preference in which he was seconded by his tutor, who, wishing to retain his position, continually boasted of the progress of his pupil, in spite of the fact that he really was very backward.

Presented at the Court of Louis XIV., in 1710, he had an opportunity of enjoying a few of the dazzling days that marked the end of that great king, and of learning the professions of war under his most skillful generals. Mme. de Maintenon continued to regard him as her protegé, even when he appeared least to merit her affection. Several letters of Mme. de Maintenon addressed to the old Duke de Richelieu acquaint us with the exact position of the young Duke de Fronsac at the Court of Louis XIV. at this time. He had only been presented a few months when Mme. de Maintenon wrote to his father, who rarely visited Versailles, informing him how well the young man had succeeded. "I am delighted, my dear duke," she wrote to him, "that I am able to say to you that the Duke de Fronsac was remarkably successful at Marly. No young man ever entered into society under more pleasant circumstances; he pleased the king and the whole court; whatever he does he does well; he dances very well; he plays honestly; he rides a horse perfectly; he is polite; he is not at all bashful; nor is he forward. On the contrary he is very respectful; he jests and converses fluently; in fine there is nothing wanting in him, and I never have heard any untoward comments made concerning him. I realize on this occasion my relation to you, for I have an extreme pleasure in hearing him praised and in being able to bear such favorable testimony of him. You will believe, sir, that this is most sincere, for you know that I am not given to flattery. Mme. the Duchess de Bourgogne has paid your son great attention. Yesterday I sent for him to visit me and I am greatly affected by what I saw. I spoke to him of his marriage and of Mlle. de Noailles. Both in regard to the prospective event and in regard to her personality, he replied with candor far beyond what I could have expected. He is a veritable prodigy. Enjoy this happiness, my dear duke, and believe me, no one wishes you happiness as much as I."

As a matter of fact it was rumored in the court that the young Fronsac was receiving marked attentions from the Duchess de Bourgogne. There were also rumors of many other conquests. In order to circumvent these love-affairs, and to fix his affections, a marriage was determined upon. Not until a short time previous to its consummation did they succeed in gaining his consent, employing means which are usually made use of only when one wishes to obtain a favor from a child. Contrary to his own inclinations, he married Mlle. de Noailles in the month of February, 1711; as a husband, he was obstinate and unyielding. No children resulted from this marriage.

This compliance on his part, to the wishes of his father, of Mme. de Maintenon, and of the king, who urged this marriage, contrasted with his stubborn resistance to the yearnings of his wife, who adored him, caused him to recognize the fact that there was in his nature an element of submissiveness as well as a strain of recalcitrancy which it would be of value for him to carefully analyze; but he was still too young to be able to reconcile these opposing qualities.

Mme. de Maintenon had charged detectives to shadow him, to carefully note all his movements and report to her, and she was soon pained to learn that his marriage had in no way altered his mode of living. He was characterized by that frivolousness and lack of determination so common in the youth of his age; he gambled, lost considerable, and greatly irritated his father, whom Mme. de Maintenon sought to mollify by attempting to correct the son. About this time she wrote to the duke:—

"Monsieur, le Duc de Fronsac left my apartments overcome with sorrow at his own waywardness and deeply regretting that he had grieved you. He dared not present himself to you, but was going to write you to-morrow requesting an interview; he desires that my letter be received by you before his. He assures me on his word of honor that he has gambled but once, and that he has made but one journey, which cost a thousand louis; he gave me his word several times that he would never play except with ready money and that he would wager none but small amounts. He spoke to me in a most intelligent manner, and expressed sentiments which, if sincere, should make us sanguine for his future. He realizes the misfortune of having lost in a moment the esteem acquired in a lifetime. I assured him that if he would never disgrace himself again, this one mistake would be pardoned out of consideration for his youth, and that he would find his reputation entirely re-established. I told him that I would inform the king of this promise; also that if he failed to keep it, he would surely complete his own ruin. I assured him that he would not be abandoned at the age of fifteen years, and that you would endeavor by every means in your power to help him; furthermore, that the king would interest himself in this endeavor. To all this he replied gently and politely, showing a deep tenderness for you. This, my dear duke, is what I have accomplished. Proceed in *your* endeavor, and above all, trouble yourself in this matter no more than seems necessary."

In spite of the surveillance of Mme. de Maintenon and his father's resentment, the young duke continued to live as before, both in Paris and in Versailles; he passed from conquest to conquest, and at length reached the point where it was impossible for his escapades to be more serious in their consequences. Even the king was tormented by suspicions. We must confess, however, that as yet, his liaison with Mme. la Duchesse de Bourgogne only resembled the flirtations of a callow youth.

After that, invited to dress balls at Marly, and to the repetitions of those dances which took place in the presence of the king, he was in the habit of preparing for the fête in the private chamber of Mme. la Duchesse de Bourgogne, where several young dancers were accustomed to congregate in a most familiar way. In this position, Fronsac, remembering the customs of his paternal home, could not feel that degree of respect suitable to such an assemblage. Whatever he did was approved, a good deal as a stranger in a private house praises a spoiled, though amiable, child. One day all the families having prepared the costumes of their dancers with great magnificence, his costume seemed ordinary, even shabby in comparison to those of the others; and as several of his comrades mentioned the fact intending to humiliate him, he replied that it was a mother-in-law's coat. As a matter of fact he did have a mother-in-law famed for her thriftiness. His repartee passed from mouth to mouth as was customary at that period, and it soon was said at court, when one was not magnificently dressed, "*que c'etait un habit de belle-mere.*"

Another incident occurred somewhat more favorable to him. Mme. la Duchesse de Bourgogne one day opened a ball with the Duke de Berri and the Duke de Bourbon, and as she was of French birth—according to the custom of her time—she was permitted to dance with no one but princes or dukes. During one of the first days of the carnival, after her first minuet, the princess invited the Duke de Brissac to join her in the dance, and, though it was customary for the gentleman to return that compliment to the lady who thus favored him, the Duke de Brissac, after the minuet was finished, left Mme. la Duchesse de Bourgogne and sought another lady.

It could be easily seen from her astonishment that the Duchess de Bourgogne had arisen to receive him, not dreaming that Brissac could forget her. She was, however, obliged to take her seat again, which gave rise to a ripple of suppressed merriment. The Duke de Brissac continued, nevertheless, to dance with the lady he had chosen and who afterwards danced with Fronsac; but when the latter had finished his minuet, instead of returning to take the lady whom he ought to have taken he addressed Mme. the Duchess de Bourgogne, and, grasping her hand, said, "Madame, will you permit me to make amends for the mistake of my friend, Brissac?" Mme. de Bourgogne accepted, and the apparent ease between them, which under different circumstances would have passed for a great impropriety, caused general amusement. This incident was well received at the court and rendered the young Fronsac so celebrated that he was everywhere invited to dine and to sup for the purpose of eliciting from him some new witticism.

The Duchess de Bourgogne, who was dauphine after the death of monseigneur, was adored at the Court of Louis XIV. The Duke of Savoy, her father, and one of the most clever princes of his time, had given her most careful instructions as to the best way to succeed in the conquest of all hearts. Now, in order to accomplish this it was first necessary to please Mme. de Maintenon; to seek out everything that might be agreeable to her; and above all to submit to her every whim. Mme. la Dauphine's character was fitted for this very undertaking; she was intelligent, shrewd, attractive of manner, and, in fact, possessed all those qualities which assured her success,— although the wife of the heir apparent to the throne,— in living at peace with Mme. de Maintenon. And indeed she was admitted to the most private functions of the king and his favorite. She was the prime mover in all amusements, balls, recreations and all the pleasures of the court. Nothing was done without her and she gave life to all parties by her vivacity, ease and constant attention to the entertainment of all.

The princess was not really beautiful, but she had a pleasing countenance. Her lower lip was large, a characteristic of the Austrian house, all of the members of which had this peculiar feature, which was frequently to be noticed also in families allied with them in marriage; her hair was chestnut and the features of her face irregular, but mobile; her eyes were fiery and her glances were as quick as lightning. Her teeth were somewhat decayed, but she was the first to joke about this fact, although she was secretly pained by the mention of it. She had a beautiful complexion, and her neck, though short, was well formed and graceful (according to the testimony of the contemporary author who makes this statement in his memoirs.) Moreover she was well proportioned, majestic, full of grace and attractiveness, unable to endure affected women.

Paris soon learned of that which was commented on at Versailles; they knew that not loving his wife, the young duke bestowed great homage on the Duchess de Bourgogne; it was reported that a third person had surprised them in a tête-à-tête which was immodest and out of place, and that, terrified, Fronsac had slipped under the bed. In addition to this, a few days afterward, they very truthfully told the story that they had discovered a very magnificent miniature photograph, which he had accidentally dropped. The Duke de Richelieu, becoming alarmed at the results which rumors of this sort might produce and yielding to extreme anger, even to the point of striking him, went to Mme. de Maintenon and the king, and insisted that the latter sign an order for his confinement in the Bastille. This was done, and he entered the Bastille for the first time, April 22, 1711, accompanied by his own father, who threatened to let him rot there, unless he amended his ways.

Fronsac knew by the event, that the king, Mme. de Maintenon and his father had had a serious council over his conduct, and that three principal reasons had determined them in throwing him into the Bastille; the first, in order to silence the jokes associating him with the princess; the second, to deprive him of every opportunity of meeting her; and third to oblige him to love his family.

Louis XIV. loved the name and the house of Richelieu on account of the cardinal, whose government had prepared the way for his reign, and he suffered a great deal in seeing himself obliged to deprive a child of Fronsac's age of his liberty; he showed a desire to ameliorate the horror of the prison by seeking out some virtuous ecclesiastic, who might consent to share imprisonment with him and serve him by his counsel and example. The Abbot de Saint-Remi generously devoted himself to this service, and the duke never forgot the sacrifice. He busied himself with the duke, in the gloom of the prison, by translating Virgil, which work was afterwards published by the abbot.

Detained in the Bastille, the change he underwent, from the court to a prison, produced in him a revolution which few people ever have an opportunity of experiencing. From the lap of pleasures and love escapades, he saw himself suddenly plunged into gloomy solitude and given over to regrets and the need of love, which those who are free cannot realize. He had to submit, however; any complaint, any show of resistance on his part would have produced a bad effect, and would have delayed the forgiveness of the king, of Mme. de Maintenon, and of his father: therefore he assumed in the Bastille a well sustained air of serenity in order to influence, if it were possible, the lieutenant of police, and the other jailors to whom he first spoke of nothing but his passion, and contented himself with ridiculing their double-iron doors and their great bolts, made to enchain crime, but incapable of conquering love. He continually requested of these sombre men news of several charming women of the city and the court; but it is with the

Bastille as it is with the rest of the world; the wooden bridge once passed and raised, all intercourse is interrupted, and, according to the laws of the prison, there could no more be communication between Paris and the unfortunate inmates of the Bastille, than there could be between the living and the dead.

He was soon familiar with the obscure rules and regulations observed in those dungeons; he learned to moderate the impetuosity of his former life and to obey an order at once, to follow punctually certain usages of the jail which are considered necessary for the good government of prisons. Afterwards the memory of the Bastille caused disagreeable circumstances in his life to be less insufferable than they otherwise would have been. Many of these circumstances would have been almost unbearable to him if he had not experienced this trial. The monotonous uniformity of prison regime was what tried him most and a thousand times the unrelenting jailers grieved him.

All of these objects, the sombre faces, the hideous grimaces, the whole interior of the Bastille, had he remained alone, would have changed the character of the Duke de Fronsac, at that time more fit to enjoy than to think; but there remained to him the society of the good abbot who had voluntarily shared his sufferings. The abbot was a Jesuit and lived at a time when the members of his fraternity obtained many *lettres de cachet*. The fact that he kindly volunteered to suffer with Fronsac, all that he suffered, bound them in a close friendship; but one day the Jesuit disappeared. Fronsac gave himself up to an inconsolable sadness; he abandoned himself to dark projects and to gloomy thoughts. He was thoughtful if not utterly desolate, when one fine morning he saw his wife, whom he had not yet learned to love, appear at the door of his prison. The good angel that flew from heaven to earth to deliver Peter was not more radiant when he came to loosen his bonds.

The Duke de Fronsac was bewildered, and his wife who perceived this wished to aid him in regaining self-possession by overwhelming him with compliments and caresses; but the duke remembered that Louis XIV. and Mme. de Maintenon sometimes gave orders to their courtiers to love their wives and he thought that they had sent her to the Bastille to tell him that he must love her because the king willed it, and it appeared to him that in reality the king added to this order the tacit threat of absolute disgrace, which fact left him in a cruel and desperate uncertainty of having to suffer a long imprisonment if he did not love her, whilst an early deliverance with some recompense would follow if he began to love his wife as they intended that he should.

In this perplexity the prisoner soon decided on a course of action; he received Mme. de Fronsac with the respect due to a messenger of the world's greatest king; never was an ambassador received with so much veneration. His wife uttered many expressions of regret at seeing him still visited with the displeasure of the court. In reply, he congratulated her upon the favors *she* was permitted to enjoy. She then recounted the news and they exchanged compliments; and Mme. de Fronsac, returning to report her mission to the king and Mme. de Maintenon, acquainted them with the fact that she returned to the court as she had left it. Fronsac was therefore abandoned once more to his gloomy solitude and to all the internal and devouring passions that can torment a heart at once sensitive and susceptible to love.

It was in the fourteenth month of his sufferings that the king remembered him and acknowledge himself conquered. The voice of the public, touched by his youth and oblivion, made itself heard, ladies began to speak in audible tones, both in Paris and at the court, and above all, those who knew by experience what must have been his suffering in the Bastille, made such strong protests that the king, the favorite and his father, weary of punishing him, yielded. All three determined to bring him out into the world and send him to Spain under De Noailles, or Marshall de Villars, who commanded in Flanders; for it was customary at that time to expatriate prisoners just leaving the Bastille and allow them to come to their senses gradually.

Light and liberty overwhelmed the Duke de Fronsac at first, just as it affects a caged bird when it escapes; but in a short time he recovered himself and left to join the army of Flanders, with the intention of causing his dark humiliations to be forgotten by the glory of some brilliant act of bravery.

Villars was in command of the French army in Flanders. His successes at Denain gave new courage to dismayed souls; a slight hope of peace dawned, and the renown of this victory, having spread abroad throughout France, successive ages preserved the name of Denain to history as the cherished name of Fontenoy was preserved. M. Senac de Meilhan, commissary at Haiñaut, had a monument erected on the field of battle which recalls to passersby that eventful conflict. It bears this simple inscription: "Denain, 24 Juillet, 1712."

In order to achieve complete success in this campaign, it was necessary for us to take the city of Marchiennes, built on a flat, marshy location, surrounded and defended by impassable marshes and approachable by two roads only. It was the great depot for munitions of war, for supplies, for heavy artillery, and was the centre of trade of all the surrounding countries. The mistress of Prince Eugene, a lady of Italian origin, held a court there, and as she feared the sound of arms and the movements that follow in their wake, she hid herself in this city, which she believed impregnable.

Marshal de Villars, aided by excellent captains and surrounded by a band of brilliant youth, who were given to mutual emulation, commanded the Count de Broglie to lay siege to Marchiennes, and informed Contades, Richelieu and other aides-de-camp, whether as a joke or seriously, is not known, that he would give them the mistress as a prize if they took the place. All these young men being dominated by the passion for glory, as well as that of love, agreed that the first to get possession of the beauty should be considered the bravest, and as a consequence they determined to distinguish themselves in the siege of Marchiennes.

Preliminary and unexpected successes prepared the way for its surprise. The Count de Broglie, at the head of a detachment of soldiers, got possession of the Abbey d'Anchin, which sheltered five hundred of the enemy who were compelled to surrender unconditionally.

On the 25th, Marchiennes was summoned to surrender, but the beauty besieged in the place absolutely refused to yield, having as a protection a garrison of six battalions, eight hundred courageous men, and an immense muddy moat, surrounding a city which seemed to rise out of the bosom of a marsh, across which, it was impossible to move without becoming mired.

Villars arrived and asked this band of youthful soldiers if the beauty were not capable of increasing their natural zeal. Contades, for a long time a widower, having conceived a romantic passion for the mistress of the prince, had a burning desire to get possession of the place in order to make use of the right of conquest. All those who were in the secret, not concealing from each other the desire of a double victory, answered the general, stating their feelings in regard to it.

On the 30th, at about five or six o'clock in the evening, Sieur de Berkfer, brigadier commander of the garrison of Marchiennes, signaled for a parley, and surrendered unconditionally, being unable to obtain any better conditions, in spite of his fierce resistance.

The capture of Marchiennes cost France a loss of six hundred men killed and wounded and the enemy nine thousand, among whom were four hundred officers; and the number of men lost at Denain, or during the present siege, reached a total of fifteen or sixteen thousand men. On the 29th, Prince Eugene raised the siege of Landrecies and bore away his beautiful Italian mistress, who succeeded in reaching him safe and sound, having escaped recognition by the besiegers, to the great regret of all the youth in the service of Marshall de Villars, who had abandoned her to them as a recompense for their courage. Marchiennes captured, the siege of Landrecies raised, and the fortifications of Denain, Saint-Amant and Marchiennes destroyed, we marched toward Douai to attack it; Douai is situated upon La Scarpe and the enemy had occupied it since 1710, having taken it from the king in spite of the fortifications with which we had surrounded it. The besieged defended themselves with courage, resorting to the stratagem of opening their sluices and inundating the trenches during the night. The fort of La Scarpe, which we attacked under the orders of Villars in true military fashion, seeing itself nearly hemmed in and cut off, requested us to accord it four days of truce in order to receive orders from Prince Eugene as to the surrender of the place; but Villars, always bold in conception, when a grand coup or master stroke was necessary, placed himself at the head of his brave grenadiers and asked their advice as to what was to be done, knowing well the heroic courage of which they were capable. "Let us go on," replied several soldiers; "let us continue the siege." In a short time the enemy surrendered unconditionally and thirteen hundred of them were conducted to Amiens.

The king, retaining his cautious reserve in dealing with Marshal de Villars, who had saved his kingdom, and as if to keep him in the same position of dependence as his other subjects, promised him the command of his armies in Germany. Villars, secretly displeased with this caution on the part of the king, affected much indifference. Nevertheless, he obeyed the orders of the king, who as a matter of fact, was as loath to intrust his troops to Villars, as Villars was to obtain the command of them. We shall tell the story of the siege and capture of Fribourg only, which was a part of this brilliant campaign.

The attack was first made on three sides by the Count du Bourg, the Marquis d'Estrade and Baron d'Aspheld; in the city the count repulsed two battalions, and the marquis and the baron after a bloody encounter, accomplished as much. Richelieu arrived there with Marshal de Villars, and this general placed himself at the head of a few hundred grenadiers, directing the operations, having at his side the young duke. The approaches of Roschoph are very precipitous, but the general was surrounded by an ardent band of young heroes who urged him on and aided him with all energy. The Prince de Conti and the Prince d'Epinay in particular showed great emulation and courage in the pursuit of the enemy, who, losing their standards, fled into the city of Fribourg.

Marshal de Villars, with whom Richelieu remained, determined to place himself at the head of thirty battalions and to attack a defensive work which he considered a most essential strategic point. The enemy making a sortie from this side of the city, they engaged in a murderous combat which lasted two hours. Richelieu was wounded in the head by a stone and bore the marks of the wound the rest of his days, and almost at the same time, Marshal de Villars was wounded on the hip. The troops on both sides did not stop at this encounter and we saw in this sortie two thousand men distinguishing themselves by desperate courage, die before our eyes. When after continued and assured successes, a soldier finds some resistance, it is perfectly natural that he should become impatient and that he should bravely fly into danger; it is then that it is necessary to guide this new-born courage by directing the operations with some definite end in view.

The work was carried, and those who guarded the outposts were all put to the sword. We lost a hundred and twenty-three cavalry officers and engineers; the regiment of Alsace, that bore the brunt of the entire fire in the attack which was made on its left, lost its four captains of grenadiers and six hundred men. Villars wished to excuse this regiment from further service, but the officers and soldiers who survived would not consent to this and continued to distinguish themselves. A suspension of hostilities was asked for; Marshal de Villars who granted it, made use of the interval to bear away the dead, which having lain for several days, emitted a sickening odor and offered a dreadful spectacle.

The interior of the city, which they attacked, was

given over to despair; the clergy, the old men and women tried to exact a promise from d'Arch, the governor, not to continue the resistance to the point of risking the ruin of the city; they feared, with reason, that if the city were taken by assault citizens could not expect any quarter. The besieged, continually annoyed by the pleas of their women folk, even went to the extent of asking our general permission to allow the most prominent ladies to go out of the city; but Marshal de Villars, who feared lest Venus might turn his brilliant band of young heroes away from the occupations of Mars, would not listen to this suggestion. His plan was, in case the governor signaled for a parley, not to accord any capitulation unless the forts were surrendered. White flags were seen raised above the ramparts, as a sign of peace, and two magistrates hurried out to meet our general with letters from the governor, which acquainted him with the fact that he had retired into the forts leaving Fribourg to his mercy.

Upon entering Fribourg a spectacle was seen; the magistracy in ceremonial robes, beautiful women, who had retired into this place, believing it to be a place of safety; children and old men kneeling, implored our clemency. Villars promised that their lives would be spared, but he demanded a million for the preservation of the city from fire and pillage, which the right of war gave to the soldiers, and told the governor, intrenched in the forts, that if he fired a single shot, he would put all the inhabitants to the sword. The next day he notified the governor that he was to care for his own wounded and sick and in order to compel him to do it, he pointed his cannon toward his position, without being exposed to a single shot. The governor, within his fortifications, replied from the heights that he could not believe that the Christian religion would justify us in allowing so many poor unfortunates to die of want. Villars sent as his reply, wagon-loads full of wounded, sick and dying which were abandoned to the mercy of the governor, and our general summoned him to surrender the forts, under penalty of seeing the ladies of the city, the children and the old men, arrive with the rest of the sick, and assuring him that they would perish if he did not allow them to retire into the stronghold. Then the ladies, in tears, said of De Villars that he did not have the mercy of Alexander, even if he had his talent, and some swore that they would perish by their own hands. This wanton cruelty displeased even the king and the Court of Versailles, who called these acts *les douceurs de Villars*. But he offered a plausible reason for his conduct ; for if the besieged enemy had provisions, it ought to care for its wounded and sick, and if it did not have provisions, it ought to surrender. Villars gave until the next morning for reflection ; and the baron, asking for five days' suspension of hostilities, in order to receive from the Prince of Savoy permission to surrender, sent bread to the women of the city, whom Villars had caused to be imprisoned in the convents because they had been abandoned to the brutality of the soldiers and even of the inhabitants. The officers were sternly prohibited from visiting them, and Villars had them blockaded on every side, in order that they might not give any assistance to the city, so that the garrison of the place, obliged to care for them, saw their provisions diminished day by day.

While waiting, sixty pieces of cannon and thirty-six mortars were placed in a position to rake the forts; and the time accorded for the purpose of receiving a reply from Prince Eugene having expired, Villars received conditions of capitulation, which he rejected. The besieged, on their part, had received orders from the Austrian general not to excede their powers, whilst Villars wished a complete and glorious success, or the complete destruction of the place. Happily the king sent a courier to him acquainting him with the fact that a treaty of peace had been made with the emperor, which hastened the end of the siege. Villars consented to articles, which he would not have acceded to without the above news. Capitulation was therefore accorded the 16th of November, 1713, and the same day the two generals, so stubborn, so bitter, and so inhuman in war, invited each other to dine. The Austrian Governor, who was sick, not being able to come, sent one of his chiefs to represent him. The garrison marched out with the honors of war. Villars left Count du Bourg to command the place; the French officers were allowed to set the women free from their prisons in the convents, reassuring them that a Frenchman is not ferocious in times of peace, though stern in war. Never did the sex appear more interesting. Villars, who left hastily for Strasbourg, gave Richelieu orders to carry the news of the surrender of the place to the king.

Flattered by such an agreeable commission, he fairly flew to Fontainebleau, where the king was at the time, to bring him the glad tidings. He had left the court under a sort of disgrace to go to the Bastille, and he returned with the honors of war and in a sort of triumph gained over his father. He was immediately presented to the king to whom he showed his wound; but as this monarch bore himself in a majestic way before him, he was disconcerted, knowing by experience what the power of such a sovereign was. All the horrors of the Bastille appeared before him, and doubtless the king perceived his embarrassment, for he encouraged him to speak. Having regained his composure, Richelieu told him of the operations before Denain, the capture of Marchiennes, and the annoying escape of the mistress of the Prince of Savoy (which greatly amused the monarch); he told the story of the campaign so concisely that it apparently pleased the king. The king asked several questions, which were promptly answered without the slightest embarrassment. He used the language of military life as if he were a veteran, and he had the satisfaction of hearing the king use these words: "The sight of your wound effaces the disgrace of the *lettre de cachet*, which I issued against you. Bear yourself like a man, for I believe you are destined for great things."

His triumph was complete; he even believed that the affair of the Bastille was already forgotten by every one; but he soon learned that successes can reawaken the oldest affairs at court when there has been some disagreement with a favorite. He lived henceforth on friendly terms with everyone, yet observing the utmost reserve; he observed those who controlled affairs at Versailles, and it taught him no longer to play the child; from this time on he was dominated by an ambition inspired by the words of Louis XIV., when he said to him that he was capable *de plus grandes choses*. This monarch understood men, understood talents and character, and the duke had a better opinion of himself when the king had made his estimate of him.

The Duke de Richelieu had scarcely arrived in the presence of the king at Fontainebleau to announce the capture of the forts, when Marshal de Villars and the Prince Eugene began their conferences at Rastadt. The malignity of certain courtiers was responsible for the rumors, that the two generals were conspiring to put obstacles in the way of peace in order to make themselves men of importance and for mercenary motives and this odious rumor even reached the ears of Marshal de Villars and Prince Eugene, who were neither annoyed nor surprised and who told one another of it; but in the end they both proved their good faith, and early in January they sent to their respective courts the drafts of a treaty which were returned to them approved and which they signed the 17th of March, 1714.

CHAPTER II.

The Duke of Orleans.—His fickle propensities, and numerous mistresses.—Sorcery: How Richelieu discovered it.—Rivalries between a mother and her daughter.—Diamond earrings.

THE young Duke de Fronsac so often opposed the actions of M. the Duke of Orleans and played so important a part in events in his reign, that it is necessary for us to first thoroughly understand the character of this prince.

The Duke de Chartres, afterwards Duke of Orleans and Regent of France, son of monsieur, the brother of the king, nephew and son-in-law of the monarch whose daughter he married, had a natural taste for the beautiful and all that was related to the fine arts. He was a musician and a painter; he carved in a wonderful manner; he had an exquisite taste for architecture; sculpture, physics and all of the sciences. He sought out men of merit; he was kind, of even temperament, always having pleasant things to say to them. He was naturally drawn on by his tastes towards new objects, unknown systems and great enterprises; he loved liberty and glory and naturally inclined toward the profession of arms, he was ambitious to distinguish himself, a lifelong admirer of good King Henry IV., and extremely pleased when told that he resembled that monarch in character and appearance.

In addition to these qualities the Duke de Chartres had

a very amorous tendency, which the Abbot Dubois countenanced, during his tender years; a circumstance that made him entirely successful in getting control of the mind and the will of his master and in reducing him to a sort of captivity from which his affability did not permit him to escape. In this shameful apathy, Dubois, in order to dominate him thoroughly, early inspired in him the love of change in pleasures. His love liaisons were never of long duration, and for the same reason he never devoted himself to difficult conquests, nor to women who demanded great assiduity. In this regard he set the pace for the nation during his regency and rendered morals more loose and loves less decent, or rather he abolished all preliminary conventionalities of love, depriving women and society of the customs of our ancient gallantry, which had particular charms and which Louis XIV. knew so well how to preserve. The young women whom the duke loved were almost all transitory mistresses who appeared for the moment, but were soon displaced. He took them from all ages and all ranks and commenced in his earliest years to make conquests in a small way, having seduced Leonore a child like himself and a daughter of the Concierge of the storeroom of the Palais-Royal, an event which caused the greatest scandal, on account of the tender age of the girl as well as the prince. The king's brother was greatly grieved by it and the king punished the offender by forbidding him to appear before his presence until called for. Madame after having reprimanded him took the girl under her protection and she was afterwards married to Charencay, son of a lawyer of Riom in the department of Auvergne.

From this first gallantry the Duke de Chartres was constantly falling in love. From the daughter of the Concierge he passed to La Grandval, a famous actress. Madame this time circumvented the new liaison deeming this comedienne too old for him and too corrupt for such a young heart. They had the young prince leave for Italy to serve under Marshal de Catinat, who was then in that country.

This determination on the part of the late king was really a kind of reward rather than a punishment; it emboldened the young prince still more and strengthened his passion. In passing through Lyons he won the heart of a young lady, de la Massonniere, whom he seduced. He corresponded with her during the war and on his return, having found a very pretty child as the result of his amours, engaged Mme. de la Massonniere to come with the mother and child to Paris. They reached there some days after his arrival and this kind of kidnapping caused such a scandal in Lyons that the old father Massonniere, who could not persuade his wife and daughter to return to him, died of a broken heart.

The mother and daughter reached Paris eight days after the arrival of the prince, who, they found, had in a fickle manner devoted himself to Des Marre, a famous comedienne, whom he deserted a few days after for Florence, a beautiful danseuse of the opera. The result of the former conquest was the birth of a child who afterward became the Abbot Saint-Albin, and who was cherished by the mother of the prince. He told every one that she only found her likeness in the illegitimate children of her son; she was a mother to all of them, loved them as the others, and in fact cared for them better.

La Florence continued her relations with a registrar in the city although she was loved by the prince, but Des Marre being supplanted shadowed her rival, revealed her infidelities and in her turn supplanted Florence, without giving up Baron, whom she loved passionately. 'The Duke de Chartres believed himself to be the father of a daughter, as the result of this liaison and he had the child educated in a convent at Saint Denain as a nun; but the young lady never wishing to take her vows, the Duke of Orleans married her to Segue, then a musketeer. He loved an abbess, daughter of the Duke Saint-Aignan. This abbess passing through Fontainebleau was confined and Saint-Aignan hearing of it, but ignorant of the fact that it was his own daughter, recounted the strange adventure to the king, who already knew of it. A royal smile justified the courtiers and favorites of the court in bursting out in laugther; Saint-Aignan knew nothing further of the circumstance.

Although the Duke de Chartres married Mlle. de Blois, a legitimate daughter of the king, he never ceased his attentions to other women; but convinced of the infidelity of Des Marre, the lover of Baron, whom she even preferred to a great prince, beautiful and generous though he was, he became smitten with Mlle. de Sery, maid of honor to Mme. of Orleans, his mother.

Mlle. de Sery was a young lady beautiful, virtuous, witty, and be it said to her credit resisted his pleadings for nearly two years. She was the only woman whom the prince pursued in this persistent manner, for he was fonder of easy conquests; but having shown her his violent passion, she finally yielded to his desires, and as if to be consistent with his past fickle conduct, he at once caused her great sorrow by seeking another favorite, by whom he had two sons.

The first was the grand Prior of France, General of Galleys and possessed rich abbeys; the younger died. The passion of the Duke of Orleans for Mlle. de Sery was permanent; he bought her a country place and she took the title of Countess d'Argenton; then he abandoned her because she had a liaison with the Baron d'Oppede which was carried on in such a public manner, that Louis XIV. became offended by it and in concert with Mme. de Maintenon did what he could to allay the passion which the Duke of Orleans still had for her. Then the prince again returned to Des Marre and having become regent, he exiled Baron, her lover.

These mistresses, who practically reigned and who were openly avowed, never succeeded in preventing what were called *passades*. Already the Duke of Orleans had become accustomed to nocturnal and secret gatherings where the freest remarks on the principles of Louis XIV., and his devotion to his favorite, were frequently made. The confessor of the king, his ministers and generals, were also discussed. The king appeared not to notice these scandalous orgies, for it would have been necessary to have punished severely too many persons. A year before his death, however, he made an example of one man and the Abbot Servien was punished for the scandal he had caused.

It would be difficult to recount the various love affairs of this prince, or even to give a simple list of the women he loved; he sought them even from the ranks of bourgeoisie, but only a small number among the nobility. The women of the vicinige of the Palais-Royal, most exposed to his observation, never escaped his attention if they were comely. Indeed this quarter was soon abandoned by honest mothers who wished to preserve the honor of their children, and gradually there were left in the environs only those beautiful females who were not averse to his attentions.

Eventually this licentious life displeased Louis XIV., so much that he took a decided aversion to his nephew, especially when towards the end of his days, Mme. de Maintenon had gained complete sway over him. The monarch doubtless could reproach himself with very many short-comings, as far as love intrigues were concerned, but as they were hidden, and as he had known perfectly well how to conduct his court without scandal, and had always given orders concerning everything that went on about him, even directing the affairs of his natural children, he was exacting concerning the affairs of his nephew. As a matter of fact, great dignity reigned in the midst of the greatest disorders. We do not find in our annals a period in which the court knew pleasures without restraint and without offence. The king, endowed with exquisite delicacy, would have feared that a breach of decorum in his own house might belittle his person, and indeed the dignity of his character was such that he never allowed himself to laugh in the presence of any one.

The libertinism and above all the independence of the Duke of Orleans, his nephew and son-in-law, must inevitably have deprived the latter of the favors of the monarch; he was the only one of the Royal House of whom the king said that he was unable to make something, whilst in reality he was the only prince who was perfectly natural; the only one who had an individual character and who would have refused to receive that courtier-like veneer, that Versailles gave to those who went there. And again he was not employed as much as his courage, military talents, his successes, and his birth demanded. Moreover he distinguished himself in the army by his superior talent, by great personal popularity, and by the minute attention he paid to the individual soldiers, among whom he was a favorite, a fact which eventually effected a complete estrangement with Louis XIV., who was jealous of the distinguished talents of princes of his own rank, fearing lest they should diminish the consideration due his own talents.

At first the king employed him in his personal service at the seat of Mons. The following year he was charged with the command of the reserve corps at the battle of Steinkerque, where he was wounded. In 1693, animated with the desire to distinguish himself, he led the troops he commanded on into the very midst of the enemy, who five times came very near capturing him. At the battle of Neerwinden he bore himself bravely.

On his return to Paris he busied himself with science and pleasures only, neglecting to do homage to the king and his favorite, and never ceasing to joke about the court, in his nocturnal meetings with his companions in debauchery. In 1706 he was present at the siege of the city of Turin which must surely have been captured if Marchin had not presented an order to stop the prince in an action which would have decided the fate of this capital. A quarter was forced by the besieged; the duke, who hastened to that part of the battlefield was wounded by two shots and was repulsed. The rout of our troops was general and the mistake of Marchin was irreparable.

It was said and is yet claimed that the court intrigue, which had as its object the declaration of the marriage of Mme. de Maintenon, had obtained this order from the king through secret plotting of the favorite. It would have been concluded without doubt that being favorable to the marriage the duchess would have obtained the concession of sparing Turin as a return favor; but the duchess, although Italian born, had French sympathies, justly preferring her wifely and motherly duties to the ambitious aims of her father—a father, indeed, whom a cruel state necessity led to pursue his own daughter in France, and who was one day to be the sovereign, and to dethrone him who was already sovereign in Spain.

Louis XIV. had so exalted an opinion of himself

that his whole life was devoted to increasing his own dignity and greatness. Fostering this weakness of the king, Mme. de Maintenon caused him to raise his natural children above the rank to which their birth entitled them and to place them in a position superior to that of the legitimate princes of all his royal predecessors. He had destined his male offspring, legitimate and illegitimate, to princesses of the blood, and princes of the blood were given in marriage to his natural daughters. Marianne married the Prince de Conti; Mlle. de Nantes the Duke of Bourbon, and the Duke du Maine, Louise de Condé. All these marriages were quite readily concluded, but that of the Duke de Chartres offered the greatest obstacles, on account of the more indomitable character of the prince and the objections that the mother of the duke made to it.

These objections were great owing to the fact that she brought to France the German principles, so uncompromisingly opposed to mésalliances. The king who seemed to ignore the oppositions which were raised against his wishes in the matter, determined to arrange the affair himself and to win the prince over. In order to succeed in his purpose the abbot, Dubois, was employed, who, having reared him and initiated his pupil in the art of debauchery, still furnished means of satisfying his passions, and had complete control of his mind. For these various reasons, he was a useful ally to the king. Dubois, won over, pointed out to him in detail the prospective anger of the king which would follow the refusal of his daughter, and obtained from the Duke de Chartres the consent necessary to this alliance. But Dubois who had insisted on complete understanding of the will of the king before commencing a negotiation which might ruin him, determined to receive his orders directly from the king; and when, after his success, the king asked of him what he desired in the way of a favor which would show that he was satisfied with his services, the king with a single glance caused the ambitious man to blanch with fear and to become disconcerted, when he asked for a cardinal's hat. Dubois did not lose courage and future events demonstrated that he never forgot his ambition to become a cardinal.

Nevertheless, in spite of the complaisance of the Duke de Chartres, who consented to marry the legitimate daughter of the king, this monarch never felt for his nephew, now become his son-in-law, any particular affection and he detested him after the famous anecdote of Spain which we shall relate. The Court of Versailles seemed never to have forgotten it and it had great influence in after years in shaping the conduct of the king with reference to the Duke of Orleans.

Skillful in the profession of war, the duke had rendered inestimable services to Phillip V., King of Spain, when this king occupied a tottering throne. Assailed by all the powers of Europe, he was on the point of fleeing from the kingdom of Spain. The Duke of Orleans had reduced Valencia to his obedience; he had subjected Saragossa; he had captured Tortosa and Lerida, dubbed La Pucelle, because the genius and the strength of the greatest generals who had laid siege to it, even the great

Condé and Harcourt had been disappointed in their attempts to conquer it; finally he had restored for a short time the fortunes of Phillip, which were on the point of collapsing.

In spite of these expeditions the king found himself in such a crisis that the grandees of Spain despaired of keeping him on the throne and persuaded the Duke of Orleans that he ought to ascend the throne in his place according to his rights; they led him to consider that the general hatred of Louis XIV. in Europe being the principal cause of the war, this hatred would die out if he occupied the throne. For then Louis XIV. would no longer have any desire to govern it. They pointed out to the Duke of Orleans that this crown belonged to him by right of birth, and by being lost to Phillip V. he ought to contest for it with the arch-duke and the house of Savoy. They told him that it was the wish of the Spanish nation and of the grandees and that this revolution would be very advantageous to France as she would see a prince of the house of Bourbon wearing the crown. They added also that he would succeed in drawing a large party to his standard in Madrid, should he consent to ascend the throne of Spain.

The Court of France soon had definite knowledge of this conspiracy; the knowledge, which was most authentic and most damaging to the Duke of Orleans, was that which was given by the Princess des Ursins, who held the prince under continual espionage; formerly she had been very intimate with him, but she had become his implacable enemy. She sent from Madrid to Louis XIV.

treaties signed by the Duke of Orleans, whose authenticity was recognized in a council held to determine this fact. When it was found that the duke aspired to dethrone the grandson of the king, all those present turned pale with anger against the prince, author of the conspiracy. The Duke of Orleans acknowledged his signature, but he protested that he had never signed such treaties; he said that he had left blank signatures with his agents and that these having been surreptitiously obtained by the Princess des Ursins, favorite of the King and Queen of Spain, they had tried to gain her favor by filling out these blanks with a treaty, of which he had not the slightest knowledge, knowing well that the princess was his avowed enemy. The Duke of Orleans confessed that he had conspired, *cabalisé*, as he expressed it, but he explained this affair by saying that inasmuch as the King of Spain was about to lose his throne it was but right for him to obtain an inheritance to which the Duke of Savoy would be called to his prejudice. Renaud and Deflandes, secret agents of the Duke of Orleans in Spain, being implicated in this plot, were imprisoned. All France was incensed against this claim, however, natural and just it may have been, and Spain aroused by the machinations of the Princess des Ursins was equally incensed. The party favorable to the Duke of Orleans in the kingdom of Spain were silent and the whole court resounded with loud complaints against the Duke of Orleans.

At Versailles the council of the king which inspired the rumor was intensely excited; some wished to

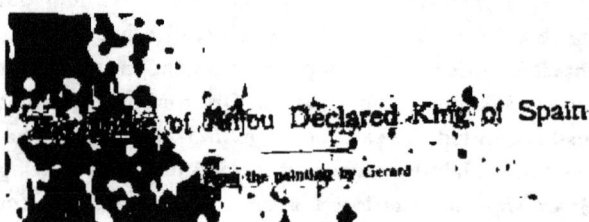

of Anjou Declared King of Spain
From the painting by Gerard

condemn the Duke of Orleans, others wished to imprison him for life. Mme. of Orleans, natural daughter of the king, threw herself on her knees before her father in the greatest consternation, for monseigneur, father of the King of Spain demanded his death. After mature deliberation a vote was taken. The advice of Pontchartrain was that the Duke of Orleans was not as guilty as he was said to be and explained the matter with such conciseness and clearness that he showed that all princes would have done the same as he in a similar case, adding that it was only an imprudence on the part of the Duke of Orleans, and that it was the part of wisdom and justice, to overlook it. The king, who already believed as Pontchartrain, was determined to avoid a harsh punishment, yielded to his advice and carried it out, at the same time, however, cherishing in his heart a secret animosity against this prince who had conspired and had imagined possible future misfortunes, always odious to a king, accustomed to seeing the humiliation of his enemies and the success of his arms.

Sometime afterward they arrested at Poitiers a Franciscan Friar disguised as a cavalier and accused of having desired to bribe the cook of the King of Spain to poison this monarch and his entire court. Chalais, sent by the Princess des Ursins, conducted him to the Bastille, heavily ironed. He had with him different poisons, which had been found on his person, the malignity of which was ascertained by experiments made on chickens, and this other strange event also was cited to the hurt of the Duke of Orleans.

It was said that this friar, realizing that he was about to be captured, cried out, "I am lost!" Chalais had a long and secret conference with the king, and the frightful news was soon disseminated that they had captured one of the poisoners of princes. This capture made all the partisans of the court jubilant and disconcerted the small number of the partisans of the Duke of Orleans, who were imprudent enough to seem to be affected by it. The Duke of Orleans alone continued his customary manner of life without manifesting any embarrassment. The friar, closely watched, was thrown into the Bastille and d'Argenson, who examined him and who reported this affair to the king, took occasion to demonstrate to the monarch that his nephew was entirely innocent; this demonstration was made with all the skill and address of which he was capable; his conduct in this affair resulted in a great reward for this service, rendered under such delicate circumstances, when the enemies of the Duke of Orleans might have easily advanced to fortune by making false charges against the conduct of the unfortunate prince. This reward was given in after years when the Duke of Orleans had become regent. The friar, being questioned, was pronounced a man capable of any crime; for while being conducted by Chalais to Segovia where he was confined, he said all manner of horrible things against the house of Austria. He had replied to d'Argenson with the impudence of a criminal, that these poisons were genuine poisons when administered alone, but being administered with suitable drugs, were very good remedies, and by their use he had cured a number of sick people; he said that he was an expert in medicine and was fond of alleviating the sufferings of the poor, but the judges having sent couriers to the places where this monk claimed to have cured sick people, they found that there was no truth in his statements. Ten years after he had been imprisoned in a fortress, he loudly complained that he had been abandoned by those who had been instrumental in starting him on his criminal career, but he never accused the Duke of Orleans. It is believed that d'Argenson preserved in a casket—at the house of Pomereu, one of his confidants, during the regency of the Duke of Orleans— the reports of the examination of this monk. This is a circumstance that it would be well for the reader to remember, for d'Argenson guarded these papers as documents which might some day make him a man of importance, and, as a matter of fact, they aided him, during the regency, in rising to a high degree of favor. In spite of the innocence of the Duke of Orleans the result of this affair was, that this prince was more and more suspected of having plotted for the wholesale poisoning of the royal house of Spain with the idea that, commanding a French army in that kingdom, he could easily assume the crown as being a nearer heir than the Duke of Savoy.

A new incident which caused a good deal of excitement in Paris seemed to the enemies of this prince, sufficient to confirm the desire to reign, which was attributed to him, or at least sufficient to show a great fickleness of thought. There came to this city a little

Provencal gentleman, called Boyer, who claimed to be a great magician. The Duke de Richelieu, having examined him and put his magic to the test, saw in him nothing more than an impostor, as are most of that profession. This man, having been presented by Mme. de Senneterre at the home of Mlle. de Sery, mistress of the Duke of Orleans as a magician, the duke, being very fond of magic, requested him to demonstrate his skill. They called for this purpose a young lady, who was said to be a virgin, and who looked into a glass of water for the purpose of divining future events, which they were curious to know, and especially concerning the fortune of the Duke of Orleans and of the King, Louis XIV.

The substance of the thing which this girl afterwards publicly declared she had seen, was the death of the king, whose funeral she depicted. She also added that she saw the Duke of Orleans with the royal crown on his head. This prediction was enlarged upon by his enemies, who did not fail to say afterwards, that if the duke were to become regent, there never would be a king who would govern France with so much officiousness. Mlle. de Sery, who rehearsed this anecdote to the Duke de Richelieu, begged him to talk to this young seeress who said moreover that since the time of the above mentioned event the spirit, which had enabled her to see these things, followed her everywhere, in such a form as to cause her great fear. We do not care to ignore these anecdotes, for they show both the opinion of the times and the malice of evil-minded persons who divulged them for the purpose of injuring the Duke of Orleans. For some days nothing was spoken of but his magic; but the prince became interested in it rather on account of lack of employment, than through any faith in it. However as it was known that he mingled with those who claimed to have intercourse with spirits, that he was accustomed to go in person amongst Bohemians and visit all those charlatans who made a profession of prophesying, and who are usually impostors, this conduct lent credence to the anecdotes which had reference to his curiosity; the king, himself, was informed of the story of the glass of water and determined to ignore it. However, it made a deep impression on his mind and on the mind of the princes who were to inherit the crown and especially on the heart of the dauphin, who did not like the Duke of Orleans, and at whom he afterwards looked askance as a person full of ambition and wild fancies.

Another thing that was displeasing in the Duke of Orleans was that he had so little discretion in his deportment, and displayed a certain imprudence in boasting of things which propriety would have made it advisable to screen from the eyes of the public; for example he accompanied his mistress abroad publicly to the comedy, to the entertainments of rope-dancers, and permitted himself to be seen at the opera in a box in which it was said there was a bed.

It is known that the king had two daughters by Mme. de Montespan; he had married the elder to the Duke of Orleans as I have already said, the younger married M. de Duc Bourbon. Both of these princesses had several daughters of a marriageable age and as the king was thinking of marrying M. le Duc Berri, his grandson, both of them desired that one of their daughters should be chosen. Madame the duchess had the favor of the dauphin, with whom she lived in very pleasant relations and indeed she was on good terms with the king, who admired her because she was both witty and entertaining; but she had committed a great indiscretion, for being very beautiful herself she had quarreled with the Duchess de Bourgogne having joked about that lady's large underlip and mouth. This offence, which women can never forgive one another, led her to espouse the cause of the Duchess of Orleans toward whom she turned for the purpose of mortifying her sister, and the time for the wedding of the Duc de Berri having come, she managed Mme. de Maintenon and the king so well, by her wit and skill, if not indeed, taking advantage of their blind complaisance, that the daughter of the Duke of Orleans was preferred to the other aspirant for his hand, who eventually married the Prince de Conti.

This marriage with the Duke de Berri seemed a favorable occasion for the enemies of the Duke of Orleans to persuade the public of the love of the Duke of Orleans for Mme. de Berri; the whole city and court spoke of nothing but this, especially when the Duke of Orleans had succeeded in winning the friendship of his son-in-law; they often ate together privately, served only by de Vienne, a confidant of his daughter, who was very entertaining; and as the Duke de Berri was only twenty-three years of age at that time, and as de Vienne was not wholly unprepossessing, the enemies of the Duke of Orleans openly said, that after having drunk a good deal, the four engaged in amusements which were unseemly in fathers and husbands. These rumors reached the ears of the king who was very displeased with them; his hatred of the Duke of Orleans was not diminished by what he heard, as we shall see later.

Mme. the Duchess de Berri on the eve of a great ball given at the court had endeavored to obtain from her mother some very valuable diamond earrings, which she seldom wore and which belonged to the queen-mother. The jewel which the king gave her the day of her marriage, completed her set; but Mme. of Orleans refused her daughter these jewels because the Duchess de Bourgogne, believing she also had some rights in them, made her promise that she would not give them to her daughter, who then would have more beautiful ornaments than she. Irritated by the refusal, Mme. de Berri, more loved by her father than by Mme. of Orleans, told him that if she did not obtain the diamonds of her mother through him she would break with him, and M. of Orleans asked his wife for them, under the pretext that he owed great sums in Spain, which he must pay. He asked Mme. of Orleans for the loan of them for six months and she sent him her casket full of jewels and precious stones. The prince only took the diamonds that his daughter desired, and he gave them to her.

Mme. de Berri triumphantly went to the ball with all these ornaments, as if to challenge Mme. de Bourgogne, with whom she had quarreled, and who was so annoyed at the turn of events, that she immediately made her complaints to the king, to Mme. de Maintenon, and Mme. of Orleans.

The king, having been for a long time displeased with Mme. de Berri especially on account of her unfaithfulness, called her to his private room, reproached her for her dissoluteness, for the nature and object of her loves and made her give up the diamonds to him and returned them to Mme. of Orleans. But the king died, the regency belonged to the Duke of Orleans and that prince no longer bridled his inclinations.

CHAPTER III.

Death of Louis XIV.—Various events.—Joys of the people.—Onions scattered along the route of the funeral procession.

As the death of Louis XIV. approached, Frenchmen foresaw, some with patience and resignation, the sad calamities of the empire; others seeing the king bowed with age awaited with joy a change in the policies of government; and all, as powerless as abject slaves, surrounded by objects of terror with which the military power had met their complaints, their sighs and their discontents, lived, schooling themselves to patiently bear the yoke.

It was in the silence of terror that such a reign inspired, in the midst of devotees, of arguing confessors, of bastards become princes, of a court, in short, which covered its crimes with ceremonies and with etiquette that death was to visit Louis the Great. Let Voltaire strive to prove him a great prince,—even in the story of his deathbed, let him endeavor to ignore the dreadful scenes which took place about the sick monarch. The time to paint him was come at last; on his deathbed—to show his true character and the character of his favorites, and of the princes—we can depict at last the duplicity and egotism which the courtiers were no longer interested in hiding from the eyes of the dying king, from whom they neither expected favors nor feared displeasure.

We shall not repeat here the discourse of the king, which is found to a large extent in his memoirs, but we shall preserve for posterity stories which have been passed by in silence, and the words of the king which one dared to report publicly at the time. The speech, addressed by the dying monarch to Louis XV., his successor, has been preserved; but he held another more laconic conversation with Mme. de Maintenon. It was not repeated at that time, because it seemed to the nobility to be too favorable to the people and because they themselves were sharers of the calamities of the state; but a king on his deathbed thinks but little of his subjects, of the nobility, or of the clergy.

"I have always heard it said," he remarked to Mme. de Maintenon, "that it was difficult to become reconciled to death; as for me, who am about to experience that moment so feared by men, I do not find that this ordeal is so painful." Mme. de Maintenon replied, " But this reconciliation with death is difficult when one has affection for friends, when one has hatred in the heart, or restitutions to make." The king interrupting her said, "Alas! as for restitutions to make I owe not a single soul a restitution as an individual; but may God have mercy on me for those that I owe to the kingdom."

That night he was very agitated. At intervals he rung his hands and prayed to God; he repeated prayers that he had always been accustomed to repeat, beating his breast and imploring pardon for having burdened his people.

After a confession of this sort we are surprised at the

Louis XIV. Blessing his Grandson

deception practised upon the Duke of Orleans. He called in this prince for the purpose of baffling him in his endeavors to secure the regency and for the purpose of destroying the effectiveness of any measures that he might take to secure this as of right; and for the purpose of leading him astray and drawing him into a fancied security as to the dispositions made in his will. "I have preserved to you all the rights that your birth gives you," said the king, whilst, as a matter of fact, he had given the principal prerogatives to the Duke du Maine, his legitimate son, whom he had made commander of his household troops, leaving the administration of the government to the majority of the Council of State. In spite of these provisions he caressed his nephew, recommended his successor to him, whom he had given over in his will to the declared enemy of the Duke of Orleans and Mme. de Maintenon. We cannot explain such duplicity unless we attribute it to the doctrine of Escobar, which his confessor, Le Tellier, had practised openly and with success; for the king was an upright man; prudence dominated him rather than duplicity and underhanded scheming, and historical truth compels us to add that most of his errors were only the common errors of the time in which he lived.

As to the Jesuit, Le Tellier, after having received the confession of the sick king and made vain efforts to persuade him to assign him a vacant office, he abandoned him for the purpose of intriguing about the regency. He had already by his secret plottings prevented the king from receiving a visit from the cardinal, de Noailles, who as his first pastor, had the right to be present with the dying king. And during the last days of the king's illness, he literally ran from place to place in Paris, in order to secure the execution of a will that would exclude the Duke of Orleans from the regency. Three times the king asked his domestic to send for him and each time he was deprived of the ministrations of the Jesuit, at a crisis, when a devout prince knows no other consolation than the presence of a confessor.

Mme. de Maintenon disappeared four days before the death of the king, that is, when she saw that he really was stricken with death. The king, who had implicit confidence in her, had taken her from obscurity and had made her his wife, yet this delicate person who had served her husband up to his last illness had not the courage to endure the agony of his death. She hastened to Saint-Cyr, to obtain a glimpse of the new court, and lift her hands to heaven.

As for M. du Maine, he had too much to do in preparing the *lit de justice* and could not contain himself for joy, anticipating his future power; the rest of the courtiers, excepting two friends of Louis XIV., abandoned the king to surround the Duke of Orleans, though the greater part returned to the dying king and left the future regent, whenever the king gave signs of improvement in his condition.

A lingering death permitted the monarch to realize all these perfidies. From time to time, he would gain sufficient strength to express himself more energetically than ever. Another time he called Mme. de Maintenon

Marriage of Madame de Maintenon and Louis XIV.

Engraved by A. B. Stracher after picture by Halle.

in an authoritative tone and she appeared a moment and immediately returned to Saint-Cyr. On his deathbed he was forced to recognize the fickleness of the homage of courtiers, the indifference of his son, the ingratitude of his favorite, her refusal to be present at his death, the falseness of his confessors, and the sincere devotion of a few servants only. "Let not kings therefore abandon themselves to all that surrounds them; let them beware of despoiling the people to enrich mistresses and courtiers. Louis' XIV. death and its effect upon his people serve as a great lesson.

The people, naturally demonstrative, took effective and bitter vengeance on the memory of the king; they went in crowds to Saint-Denis and engaged in scandalous jollifications; from the Faubourg Saint-Denis as far as the abbey, balls, fanfaranades and concerts were in full swing. People danced and sang in a boisterous manner; they poured forth imprecations on the head of the dead, whom they called the bad king; in short when the funeral passed, a band gathered in a marshy meadow, stole onions and distributed them; because they could not weep naturally, they said that they had to rub their eyes with onions in order to satisfactorily perform their last duties to the king. The people of Paris had acted very differently at the death of the good king, Henry. Tearing limb from limb and some even devouring the still palpitating flesh of the quartered Ravaillac, to take vengeance for the assassination of an adored monarch.

We know that courtiers accustomed to the calm peace of courts detest these obstreperous and violent public expressions so different from the silent proceedings of royal palaces; but princes never know the true state of an empire without observing the expressions of the people.

CHAPTER IV.

*The intrigues that marked the commencement of the regency.—
How the Duke of Orleans obtained it.*

FOR a long time, even before the death of the king, secret gatherings were held at the Chateau de Madrid, the home of Mlle. de Chausseraye, who had apartments there. Cardinal de Noailles, the Duke de Saint-Simon, the Duke de Noailles, the d'Alegres, the Maisons, the Marshalls d'Harcourt and d'Aguesseau, the Bishop de Montpellier and Father Bernard of Oratorio, who approached their meeting place by by-ways were accustomed to gather together. This council discussed the most important plans and it was sometimes reinforced by other interested persons, who dispersed themselves throughout the capitol in order to gauge public opinion, keep the Duke of Orleans before the public and make preparations for the revolution which was as yet only vaguely anticipated. De Noailles and Saint-Simon treated with the presidents of the parliament and Dubois with the councilors. The roués of the Duke of Orleans, who said that they were capable of a great *coup d'etat*, all those who were attached to this prince during his disgrace and who had given ample proof of their devotion, offered to negotiate, each one according to his opportunity. They acquainted the eminent men of the country with the fact that they would be needed in the affairs of the state. The Duke of Orleans promised Marshal de Villars that he would be president of the Council of War; a place in the ministry was the inducement offered De Noailles, who became responsible for the service of the troops which he commanded; his brothers-in-law also assured the revolutionists that the regiment of the guards would be devoted to him. Saint-Simon told some of the presidents of the parliament of Paris that he would secure for them the right to make remonstrance which the king had taken from them forty years before. They won over Abbot Pucelle, a chief amongst the councilors of the Jansenist party, and they promised him the repeal of the decree of banishment against the enemies of the constitution. Saint-Simon, who possessed the activity of a genius, negotiating matters in a discriminating way, as well as maintaining a proper respect for etiquette or ceremonial, treated with the Duke of Orleans only on condition that he should receive a promise that he would favor the peers in the contentions of the parliament. They wished to be saluted when they were asked for counsel, whilst the presidents did not wish to salute them unless covered with the *mortier*. This quarrel had up to the present time, served the ministry remarkably well in keeping the peers and the parliament divided; but the regent who had need of uniting them, promised Saint-Simon to serve him and did not carry out his promise. The Duke de Guiche was the most discreet of all the nobles; he was not satisfied with a vain hope; he wanted ready money, and the sum he demanded was paid him on the death of the king out of the royal treasury.

The Duke of Orleans also entered into negotiations, but very secretly, with M. le Duc, who jealous of the rank of M. du Maine, and of the Count de Toulouse and still more jealous of the great places with which the king had favored these natural born princes, burned with the desire to see them return to oblivion. He himself offered to aid the Duke of Orleans with his influence and his authority in recognizing and sustaining the regency, if he would annul all that the great king had done in favor of his natural children. The Duke of Orleans had similar desires, but he wished to temporize; he regarded this as too delicate and important an affair to treat of in the assembly of the parliament, or in the *lit de justice* which was to confirm him in the regency. He feared complicating his own affairs, by implicating those of the princes of the blood, and of the *legitimated* princes. He made M. le Duc promise to establish him in his regency first, and promised afterward to sustain him in his dignity, as well as sustain the interests of the royal princes, when his power should have been established and generally acknowledged.

There were also at this time quite a number of secret treaties. Blancmesnil, attorney general, his brother, his cousin Germaine, president of the court, the commissary of Languedoc, Basville, who had acquired great influence in Languedoc, through the fear that he inspired where he assumed the air and manners of a petty tyrant, all had hopes of being employed in the ministry. The seals were promised to the president, of Maisons, with a great show of probability, as it was known that the chancellor, Voisin, had had a good deal to do with the making of the will. But the premature death of the president gave the hope of this to d'Aguesseau, procurator-general, a zealous partisan of the prerogatives of his party, and already won over, by the promise which the duke had made him of giving the prerogative of remonstrance. What is still more surprising in this negotiation is the fact that its secrecy was its very life. It was guarded so scrupulously that the day after the death of the king, Cardinal de Noailles, who came to present his respects to the regent, surprised the throng of courtiers, who asked each other in a voice loud enough to be heard, "What is he going to do with us?"

The night preceding the death of the king a last meeting of the council was held, presided over by the Duke of Orleans, and attended by the attorney-general, Joly de Fleury, by d'Aguesseau, the procurator-general and several prominent members of parliament. The prince was instructed in the proper ceremony; and schooled in the address which he was to give. De Noailles had given orders to have the palace surrounded with French guards, and each soldier had been given powder and ball for six rounds. The body guards of the prince, some trusted and determined noblemen in civilian dress, and some of his profligate followers, had arms hidden beneath their doublets, besides their swords; so that in case of a refusal of parliament, the fear of violence, the sight of swords and glittering arms, and some concerted manœuvres would cause the assemblage to recognize him as regent.[1] Formerly France would have deliberated by free ballot on the question of the regency. But France had fallen under the military power, and scarcely remembered its rights of election, because monarchies in their decline forget those rights and only remember military rights and rights of birth.

All these preparations were as useless as they were ill-concerted. The parliament, already too much flattered at the thought of having annulled the will of a great king, who had trampled them under foot, and of having adjudicated the question of the regency, in spite of his testamentary dispositions, and of having regained the prerogative of remonstrance before enrollment, was all ready to break the will. It was to be feared lest the regent should himself decide upon something that the magistracy deemed it advantageous to accord him, and would grant it freely of his own accord. The regency was a prerogative which parliament had to give. If it did not give it to *him*, it would incur the risk of exciting the indignation of the prince, and putting itself in the position of favoring the literal execution of the will of Louis XIV. which would result in greater disorders. Parliament, on account of its situation, therefore, decided that the regency belonged to the Duke of Orleans. The Duke d'Bourbon, the Count de Charolais, the Prince de Conti, the Duke du Maine and Count

---

[1] Voltaire assures us that parliament was not surrounded by armed nobles. We can cite as against this opinion what the Duke of Berwick says about it. Marshal de Richelieu has left absolute proofs of it in his documents.

de Toulouse, twenty-nine peers, all the chambers, etc., were present at this session at which the regency was bestowed upon him, and the Duke of Orleans had scarcely taken his seat when the first president, opening the session, declared that "his company had ordered him to assure the prince that it would go to any length to prove the profound respect it had for him."

It was indeed the prelude of what the parliament was about to do. The prince, however, seemed embarrassed in this assembly and pronounced the address with some awkwardness, endeavoring to show his rights to the regency. He assured them that the late king, after having received the holy communion, had declared in his testament that all his rights of birth had been preserved to him, adding, that if he had not provided for everything, and if there remained some article subject to a contest, it would be changed. "I am therefore persuaded," said the Duke of Orleans, "that according to the laws of the realm, according to the will of the late king, the regency belongs to me; but I shall not be at all satisfied if you do not add to these good titles your votes and your approbation by which I shall not be less flattered than by the regency itself." The Duke of Orleans then asked them to consider his birthright first, and afterwards to decide upon the rights which the will vouchsafed him.

Flattery was then manifested in the most public manner. Joly de Fluery arose saying that not only did his birth entitle him to the regency but that nature also had destined him for this honor, having endowed him with eminent qualities, which alone rendered him worthy of being elevated by the suffrages of the assembly. He terminated the eulogy by requesting the opening of the will and of the codicils intrusted to the keeping of parliament, for the purpose of deliberating on the rights of the French and on the will of the late king.

The Duke of Orleans, still rather embarrassed, arose and seemed about to leave the assembly, not wishing to be present at a deliberation which concerned him, but flattery again prevailed: they said that the assembly would always be honored at having him in its midst. They were convinced that his presence would check the voices of all those capable of disputing the will of the late king.

All cast their votes with the exception of the Duke of Orleans who refused. The decree which intervened, in conformance to the decision of the royal household, ordered the reading of the testament, which they brought from the palace, where it had been deposited. The first president, the procurator-general, each with his key, met for the purpose of fetching it from the fortress where it had been hidden. The first president took it and it was observed that on his return to the great chamber, the spectators, who were awaiting the result of so great a deliberative body, paled on seeing pass before them, this last will of the late king, which contained the destinies of France. All the aisles of parliament were filled by the populace, attracted to the place by mingled fear and hope. The partisans of the Court of Louis XIV. fearing the great insult that was about to be done the memory of the monarch, and those of the Duke of Orleans, goaded on by their ambition, had already tried to further the success of the great event, by a *coup de main*.

The testament and the codicils passed through the astonished crowd, who never ceased to gaze on it, with craned-necks, and open mouths. The president placed the portfolio on his desk, and took from it the fateful packet, which was sealed seven times and presented it to the Duke of Orleans. The prince tremblingly and with difficulty opened it, for he knew well that it contained his exclusion from the regency and his own judgment. The unjust dispositions of the late king were read. They were contained in six sheets with the two codicils, and the Duke of Orleans, who showed great courage when he found himself in the midst of the greatest dangers, rising, said in a firm voice, that he was moved to see that the late king refused him the title due to his birth, by a document substantially contradictory to his last words, and he again asked that the court should decide on the rights of his birth.

The party of the king arose, and said that the rights of birth, and the last words of the late king, ought to make their votes unanimous; they added that if the testament only gave the right of *chef du conseil de regence*, under the title of regent, it was proven beyond question that the Duke of Orleans was rightfully regent of the kingdom, and that this title was confirmed by the last words of the king and by his right of birth. The matter was taken under consideration and passed unanimously in favor of the Duke of Orleans, who was nominated regent.

Thus ended this great day, which decided the fortunes of the Duke of Orleans and of France, which was to be governed so absolutely during seven or eight years by a prince, whom but a short time ago they had regarded with a feeling akin to horror. In a moment all hearts turned to him and conceived hopes of a wise government. The devotees of the old court alone were in consternation and openly said that it was the work of divine Providence, angered against France. Statesmen, however, attributed this change to the national and popular instability and especially to the secret negotiations of the principal men of parliament, to whom this prince had promised the restitution of the time-honored prerogative of making remonstrances.

The natural children of the late king united with the faction adhering to the party opposed to the Duke of Orleans, raised great murmurs against him, and the Duke du Maine, returning home, not only was subjected to insulting words from his wife, but was treated with the utmost scorn by her. That day also marked the beginning of the hatred that that princess cherished toward the regent, a hatred which increased day by day up to the time that the king deprived her husband of the rank of prince which he held from the late king. The Duke of Orleans, acknowledged regent by the court of parliament, by the peers of the realm, and by the princes of the blood, desired that his power be established officially; the king came for this purpose and held a *lit de justice* and confirmed all that had been done. The young monarch was but five years and seven months of age and the people of Paris who idolize their king, when there is no reason for discontent, greeted him with their hearty shouts of " Vive le roi." He was at that time in delicate health; and his pale and emaciated face made him still more interesting to the Parisians. They were confident that he would not live, yet his tranquil air and serious face rather improved his looks, and the love of the French for their king even in the cradle, manifested itself when he announced with the utmost grace, " that he declared the Duke of Orleans regent of the realm, to administer the affairs of his states, during his minority, in conformity with the decree of the parliament of the 2d. of September." These remarkable words had been dictated by the magistracy to which had been left the right of declaring the regency, and which had seized also the right of verifying even the money edicts of taxation.

CHAPTER V.

The Abbé de Saint-Pierre.—The pretext under which he was excluded from the French Academy.—His books poorly written; his morals not above reproach.

IF the regent and his government, composed of councils, each engaged in different branches of service, such as war, finance and the navy, had numerous partisans, the principles followed under the reign of Louis XIV. were, nevertheless, to others the object of great regrets. The ambitious ones, especially among those who aspired to the ministry, not daring to attack the administration of the regent openly, hurled their diatribes against the Abbé Saint-Pierre, a well-known writer of that time. The eulogy which his books pronounced on the councils of the regency was an indirect but incisive criticism of the administration of the late king. Cardinal Polignac who desired to enter the ministry, and Fleury, (consumed by the same passion, secretly cherished), were the first to attack the abbot. They belonged to the French Academy, as he did.

This society had been formed by Richelieu, who, in changing the form of the government, wished to make the most independent of the citizens subject to the ministry, and in this way hoped, according to his own expression, to influence their thoughts and opinions. He believed that a profound man of letters, capable of exciting the feeling of a nation still susceptible of change, might by his talents utterly destroy the plans of a ministry, and that he ought to be enrolled under the banners of the ministry. He did not wish to have this society engage in philosophical discussions; but feeling that the language was crude and that there was great chance for improvement, he desired that this academy should confine itself to vocabulary work only. He organized it with forty persons, declaring himself to be the patron of the academy, and in an article of the by-laws, he ordered that political discussion or papers, should be dealt with by the academicians in conformity with the state of the government, and with the approval of the academy, a quorum of which should consist of twelve members present, who should vouch for the opinions set forth. The object of the work of the academy was described in very expressive terms in the rough-draft of its charter, which was sent by the first academicians to the cardinal, prior to receiving letters of incorporation; they said that the functions of the academy would be to cleanse the language of the filthy slang contracted by the plebians, and by the court hangers-on, and the impurities contracted by habit of quibbling or by the bad grammar of ignorant courtiers, or by the abuse of those who corrupted it in writing. Thus the academy, according to its constitution, could engage in a discussion of the theory of phrases and in the mechanism of the language, but it was forbidden to discuss political economy, and in fact all matters pertaining to the government; or if its members did engage in discussions of this kind, they could only do it according to the by-laws with the approval of twelve associates and always in conformance to *l'etat du gouvernement*.

This corporation of men of letters was part of the plan of the cardinal, and its incorporation was necessary for the maintenance of the new ministerial constitution which Richelieu called *l'etat de gouvernement*. To support the absolute power of the ministry it was necessary that there should exist a band of panegyrists who would speak only in conformity to this state of affairs and who would eulogize or at least throw a gloss over the faults and errors of the public men, by its eloquence and praises. Such a company was to exclude capable writers, such as Mably, Rousseau, Raynal, to increase the dignity of the citizen, to maintain his rights and to guard against offending the government. Thus the Abbot Saint-Pierre, member of the academy and author of different works, well conceived but poorly written, ventured to praise the better form of government; he indirectly criticised that of Louis XIV.; he praised that of the regency and as a reward was excluded from the academy.

This ecclesiastic, of distinguished birth and cousin on the maternal side of Marshal de Belle Fonts, was born at Valogne, of which place his father was governor. He was the first almoner of madame, mother of the regent, and had gained a brilliant reputation by the talents displayed in his discourses on law which led Cardinal Polignac to take him to Holland to assist him in concluding a treaty of peace; but when it was discovered that he had given voice to new principles in the theory of government of people and the reform of monarchies, and when they saw that he was capable of causing a revolution, his fate was sealed. He wrote a magnificent work on the councils, for which he could not be punished by imprisonment nor by exile, for this work was an apology for the government of the regent, and because the regent himself had ordered him to write it; but the faction adhering to the ancient regime and the Jesuits resolved to exclude him from the academy. The Abbot Dengeau, its director, and Dacier, secretary, listened to Polignac and Fleury, who had sworn to ruin him. The academy called this work a tissue of calumnies against the great king, and said that the very glory of the society offended in the person of the monarch, its august patrons, could no longer tolerate the presence L'Abbé de Saint-Pierre in its midst.

The academy was soon possessed by a frenzy for persecution; the friends of the author, touched by his disgrace and acknowledging the enormity of his error, wished to ameliorate his punishment and proposed that he recant. "Let him be expelled; let him be expelled!" said the most embittered ones. "He has written on the subject of the government, that is forbidden us by custom and by our laws." And the most violent ones, among whom was the Cardinal de Polignac, declared that they would not enter the academy again if Saint-Pierre were not excluded.

After some debating they came to a vote and the Abbot de Saint-Pierre was almost unanimously excluded from the academy, on account of his book on the re-establishment of the monarchy. A single voice, that of Fontenay, was raised in his favor. Those who sold his book were imprisoned, the balance of the edition was interdicted and the first president and the Marshall d'Estrees were invited to join the academicians, who, already ashamed of their action, dared not inform the regent of their brutal and unpatriotic decision. That prince, without expressing disapproval, received them coldly, and was unwilling that they should proceed to a new election. The place was vacant, only during 1745; and although the academy had been reorganized and the judges of the dead abbot had passed away, it received Maupertuis, in his place only under the condition that he would not speak in his discourse of Saint-Pierre, and Maupertuis stultified himself by this silence. The great defect of the constitution of the academy was the perpetuity of the title of the academicians. The title should last for seven years only, and the officers of the association should be renewed from time to time, as the parliament in England is renewed. The perpetuity of a title renders its possessor indifferent and it often deprives the society of the works of writers who might contribute good work.

All those who aspired to the ministry, all the enemies of the regency, and of the Duke of Orleans, very readily approved of the expulsion of Saint-Pierre; for the councils, which had been applauded by the whole nation, had secret and powerful enemies. Monarchies, moreover, which have survived the ravages of time and the passions of ministers, always nourish in their bosom enemies more or less openly opposed to reform of any kind.

Saint-Pierre in his work had, nevertheless, not dared to penetrate to the root of our evils, nor to speak of the states' general, the very name of which caused every partisan of Louis XIV. who had suppressed that body during his reign of seventy years to shudder: he contented himself in his work with an apology for the large numbers of councils, for the eight large departments of the affairs of state. "The nation," said Saint-Pierre, "is not assured of having a sovereign sound in health, of noble mind and for whom the work of the cabinet is a pleasure. A Supreme Council would support him in infancy and in old age. This was the fundamental principle of the system of the author who, simple and honest, did not perceive that these weaknesses were the very qualities which the ministers desired in their kings." The councils, on the other hand, were their scourge and every aspirant to the ministry and every courtier secretly feared the system of the abbot de Saint-Pierre.

"This National Council," continued the abbot, "making amends for the weakness of the monarch, zealous for the state, industrious, often renewed but always existing, would give a uniform plan to the affairs of state, would prevent change in governmental policies, and fickleness in opinions. Every council would have an appointed president to obviate all pressure. Lastly," he said, "women are destined to ornament society and not to administer the affairs of state, and this rule would exclude mistresses." All these ideas brought about the ruin of L'Abbé Saint-Pierre; mistresses, in fact, were one of the tools of the ministry. Again the abbot desired that each minister should be the executive of the ancient rules discussed and adopted by the councils, a thing which aroused the wrath of those who wanted absolute ministers only and a thing which brought about his exclusion from the French Academy. Afterwards the abbot was attacked from a different standpoint. He pretended to respect marital vows in a time when, as far as morals went, there was utter laxness. Fleury, who had formerly been of loose moral character, unveiled the secret and inconsistent life of the abbot; a large family, the result of a more or less open libertinism on the part of the abbot was exposed and he never became bishop.

CHAPTER VI.

The general favor with which the administration of the regent was received at first.—The roués.—The quick repartee of a commissary of police to the brother of Louis XIV.—The society and entertainments frequented by the regent.—The Duchess of Orleans, his wife: the Duchess de Berri, his daughter.—An adventure at the Luxembourg.—The house of Condé.—Sojourn and fêtes at Sceaux.

THE first impression, which the new regency made on the minds of Frenchmen, was favorable to the Duke of Orleans; everywhere people told of his affability, of his humane character, of his determined, yet mild nature, but above all, of his candor and of his loyalty. His campaigns in Spain and Italy were recalled; the exploits he had accomplished in these campaigns were rehearsed, as well as the battles won and the places captured, all with a satisfaction, so natural to Frenchmen, who are always attached to princes who give proof of bravery.

His greatest fault, and one due to the influence of his instructor, was that he was devoid of every religious and moral principle.

Dubois had inspired him with such a poor opinion of mankind that he confounded the honest man with the rogue, saying that all were alike, even adding that those whom he had honored with his intimate friendship amounted to nothing. His highest compliment to his intimates was to say that witty people were able to divert and amuse him. He himself had dubbed the habitués of the palace and his favorites with the epithet roués a somewhat equivocal name for which the roués accounted by saying that they would have suffered being broken on the wheel for him, but which he explained, by saying that all they were good for was the wheel, not indeed as ordinary criminals, but as the courtiers of a prince, who applauded all sorts of actions that voluptuousness recommended to them. The principal roués was the Count de Noce, son of his instructor with whom he had been educated; the Duke of Orleans sometimes called him his brother-in-law, because he was loved by Mme. de Parabere, his titled mistress. Other roués were the Marquis de la Fare, captains of his guards, called *le bon enfant;* the Chevalier du Simiane who was a great rhymester and, moreover, a heavy drinker; Fargy, the most handsome young man of his time, ready with repartee and as gallant a man as it was possible to be, in such a depraved court. I cannot refrain from recalling the bonmot of the Commissary Renaut. Monsieur, the brother of the king, and father of the regent, a very popular prince, as was his son, being at Paris, the commissary of the quarter was present at his dinner and paid homage to him and, monsieur having seen him, said, " M. le Commissaire, how many bordeaux are there in our quarter at Paris ? " The commissary, without hesitation, replied, "Monsieur, the quarter is large, that is why there are so many of them, at least thirty-two, counting the Palais-Royal as one." This reply caused a hearty laugh.

The Duke de Brancas also had the title of roué of the regent, although he had not the reputation of being gallant toward women. The Marquis de Broglie was also a roué and one of the most amusing of them, on account of his wit. The Marquis de Canillac and the Duke de Saint-Simon, although intimate friends of the regent, were not exactly numbered among the roués, the ordinary title of his guests and the participants of his debauches, but they enjoyed his favor; they were his confidants, especially Canillac, whom the regent called his *Mentor*, because he did not drink heavily and disapproved of excesses of all kinds; a fact which gave him this title together with that of acting lieutenant of the night guards, which he sometimes exercised with authority, but which he exercised always with a view to the conduct of the regent, to whom he made known his displeasure by a profound silence. Whilst the genuine roués were on the other hand complaisant in everything. The ordinary life of the regent was to give a part of the day to business but in the evening he retired with his mistresses and roués to dine, to play, to drink, etc. All betook themselves to the Palais-Royal at nine o'clock with Mme. de Mouchy, Mme. de Sabran, the Duchess de Gesvres and often Mme. de Berri, daughter of the regent, who although still young had been admitted to all their nocturnal orgies.

To this strange company was added at times a bevy of opera girls for the purpose of amusing the company. Comedians and other persons were seen there, who without being distinguished by birth, might distinguish themselves by a light wit, by happy repartee, by their talent, or by their debaucheries. There both virtue and justice were discussed, they scathingly ridiculed everything pertaining to the maxims of the old court, which was referred to as the *antiquaille*. All lackies and cooks were excluded from this society; each guest had his or her duties to perform and when the accustomed hour arrived, the doors were closed; and had all Paris been burning there would have been no regent available, for there was absolutely no visible approach to the scene of these orgies. There were in this assembly no distinctions of birth, all stood upon an equal footing.

In these orgies the regent learned all the news of the day; he made his estimate, so he said, of the value of persons of distinction; and as there was absolutely no restriction on the conversation, he studied public opinion there; but he guarded his own secrets, permitting no one of the company to know what profit he might derive from this license; he himself even made use of the jokes often directed against himself and his mistresses, who were all there together and always in large numbers, the favorite one having no means whereby she could expel the others. All these debauchees dispersed in the early morning and several, who were the worse for wine, went to their own homes to recuperate from the fatigues of the preceding evening and gain new strength for the repetition of the orgies the next day.

No one was as amiable as the regent in these nocturnal gatherings; he was kindness and politeness itself; he refrained from offending any one personally; always affecting with a great deal of shrewdness the most kindly disposition; he usually contented himself with saying that it would be preferable to attack some other victim when one person was too continually selected as the butt of the railings of the company. It was thus that he dealt with those of his favorites who spoke evil of Law or other people unworthy of his favor. Amorous of all the pretty women whom he met he was jealous of none. Free in his conversation he knew how to dissimulate and although he knew people perfectly, he dealt with them as if he did not know them.

He gradually became so accustomed to these nightly gatherings that they were necessary to his happiness, and when he had not passed the night in this way, he at least passed it in the society of his companions in debauchery. His habit of making nightly sorties, with a small body guard and on foot, alarmed both his friends and his family; he often went as a simple citizen in companies known for their recklessness, and every company was pleasing to him if wit, fine arts, literature and libertinism were the order of the day.

Such was the character of the regent and of the lords of his private court. The princesses who had retained the tone of the former court, on the other hand, lived with the greatest reserve and propriety and Mme. of Orleans, daughter of Louis XIV., and Mme. de Montespan, never abandoned the proud reserve in conversation and conduct which she inherited from her father.

She regarded her descent from Louis XIV. (although a natural daughter) with such pride that she always insisted that she honored the Duke of Orleans by marrying him. She carried to such an excess all her claims, that the party faction opposed to the legitimated princes, gave her the name of *Mme. Lucifer*, an expression which her husband, the regent, sometimes made use of even publicly when dealing with the affairs of the natural sons of Louis XIV. From this fact resulted that coldness which she showed for her husband and the haughty manner which she always affected towards him, rarely showing the slightest feeling when he caressed her, nor jealousy when he avoided her, having no other fear than that she might fail in her respect for her father, Louis XIV.

The Duchess de Berri, daughter of the regent, was endowed with a great intellect, and with a brilliant though wild imagination which, like her father, caused her to consider the most daring enterprises the most praiseworthy. Her appearance was imposing, and her conversation full of charms, but she had a violent temper, and was a great pleasure seeker; traits in her character which spoiled all that was beautiful and noble in this princess, and which led her into the nightly orgies which this prince carried on with questionable or wanton women, his companions. The Duchess de Berri having become a widow felt no restraint in this society and apparently utterly disregarded all claims of propriety. Besides her actual love affairs, with which she was continually being reproached, she had numerous lovers toward whom she conducted herself in the most fickle manner. First she captivated the royal squire called

Salvert. La Haye, page of the Duke de Berri, succeeded him, assuming his title, a fact which won for him a disreputable name, (M. Tout-pret) on account of his living so near her whilst acting the rôle of a lover. In spite of this nickname, which was known to the whole city, the Marquis de la Rochefoucauld, deigned to succeed him. He was the captain of her guards and inherited the nickname of his predecessor. The Marquis de Bonivet, chamberlain of the Duke de Berri, was the next lover and after him came the Count Daidie, officer of the guards.

In spite of her loose and wanton behavior, Mme. de Berri was overwhelmed with remorse. Educated in the principles of the former court, as well as those of the new court, she was tormented in turn by the fears of religious libertines, and in turn by the fears of libertines without religion. When she was given over to repentance she renounced the world and returned to the Saviour of sinners with whom she became reconciled; at these times she buried herself in the dungeon of a convent of the Carmelites; she fasted and prayed, rising in the night to offer prayers with them, lamenting the waywardnesses of her past life and subjected herself to most rigid discipline. Again yielding to the desire for pleasure she returned as from another world, gave up her rosaries and her confessors and went back to Riom or to La Haye and held her court; so that her very short life was passed in alternative penances and pleasures; and as Louis XIV. and the great dauphin had established the custom of marrying their mistresses, Mme. de Berri wished to marry her lover. Maurepas, in his memoirs, says, that the Duchess de Berri was married to Riom in her chapel, adding that it was the Curé Saint-Sulpice who secretly performed the ceremony. Riom never cared to openly avow his marriage but he never denied it. He, at the time, acted with extreme harshness towards his princess, "having learned," says this insolent husband, "that one must treat amorous princesses of the blood harshly in order to make anything of them." He allowed his brutality to carry him even to the point of beating her. It is difficult to see what charms the princess saw in Riom; he was ill-favored, resembling a Chinaman. Nevertheless, having a seductive manner, he was much sought after by women. He caused Mme. de Berri to believe that the Kings of Spain had usurped the rights of his ancestors in his maternal estate in Aragon, and Mme. de Berri, haughty, and possessed with the desire for glory, conceived the hope of becoming herself reinstated in those rights by her father.

The last illness of this princess was frightful. After her confinement she left for Meudon where Lafosse, her physician, gave her permission to promenade in the garden; she took a chill, so dangerous to recently confined women, which eventually resulted in what is called *lait repandu*. She lingered about a month and died bravely, showing evidences of remorse for her sins. She received frequent visits from Father Honoré, a Carmelite friar, from Father de la Tour, a Jesuit, and from the Curé de Saint-Sulpice; she was mourned neither by her father nor by any one else, and all Paris repeated at that time a bonmot which was attributed to her, by the doctors who were trying to induce her to take some remedy to prolong her life. "Well," she replied to them, "my life will be short, but good."

Riom, her husband, was at the head of his regiment, with the army and a quasi exile, brought about by his insolence; for dining with Mme. de Berri and with the regent, this prince had reproached the latter in the presence of his daughter, with some scandalous episodes, which he had learned from the police. Riom, somewhat excited by wine, told the regent that he was not in the habit of seeking his amours from an inferior rank, as the prince did. The regent, annoyed, compelled Riom to leave Paris with the order not to return.

As soon as Mme. de Berri died M. de Mouchy who knew how cordially he was hated by the house and fearing that he might be insulted by those whom he had maltreated, took his sword and as secretly as possible, left by way of the Boulogne, and his wife soon after following, they both disappeared from the court and Paris and never returned.

As to the Count de Riom, who had always been the most obliging and the sweetest tempered of men, except toward his princess, he was mourned by every one. His fortune was so small that he could scarcely maintain himself honestly, and live in his accustomed luxury. He regretted the loss of a fortune less than the loss of a certain friend whom he had abused, and who, in spite of the abuse received at his hands, remained loyal to him. On his return to Paris a year later he rarely visited the court of the regent and was never willingly received by

The Royal Palace at Meudon

Engraved by Lepetit after picture by Alp. Testard

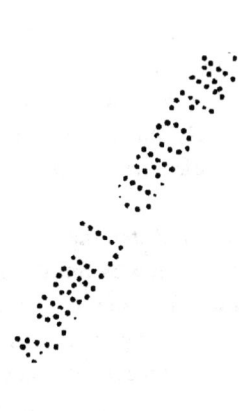

him. Before dying the duchess had commissioned a courier to carry several beautiful jewels of great value to Riom as a testimony of her love for him; but the regent, having been notified of this by La Vrilliere, secretary of state, asked him for these jewels, stating that he was her heir.

Mme. de Berri had imitated her father's habit of receiving every one and going to questionable places without the least compunction; she was very curious to know what was said of her in public and very frequently disappeared from the palace of Luxembourg, where she dwelt, to listen, incognito, to the conversations which were held there.

The discourse which she held one evening while promenading with Mme. de Muchy, Mme. de la Rochefoucauld, and d'Arjon provoked some attorney's clerks to insult them; these ladies, curious to know to what length this boldness would be carried, replied by bursting into shouts of laughter; but the clerks, impudently announcing their purpose, the women shouted for help and called the Swiss guards, who appeared at once and rescued them. Mme. de Berri felt obliged to close her garden, which caused a general complaint, as her motive for doing this was not known at the time. Nevertheless, in spite of her popularity with the common people, she was haughty towards those of her own rank, assuming the utmost scorn for the legitimate children of Louis XIV., whom she placed in a humiliating position whenever an opportunity presented itself, not even tolerating her mother because she was one of their number. One day she struck the house guard who had opened both doors for her; although she was submissive with those of her lovers who knew how to control her, whilst Riom or La Haye ruled her despotically and subjected her to their wishes, their tastes, and to their whims. Nothing could conquer her pride and neither her mother nor her husband ever succeeded in getting her to show them the least condescension.

The other children of the regent were still under age in 1715. The Duke de Chartres born in 1703 was educated by the Jansenists, in accordance with the intention of his father to affiliate himself with their faction. Louise-Adelaide who was nineteen years of age imbibed predilections for this party; Mlle. de Valois, afterwards the Duchess de Modena, was but sixteen years of age at that time; Mme. de Montpensier, afterwards Queen of Spain, and Mme. de Beaujolais still a child, were to reap the fruits of having imbibed the principles of a licentious court; but Charlotte-Elizabeth of Bavaria, Dowager Duchess of Orleans, widow of the only brother of the king and mother of the regent, still maintained her court at the Palais-Royal at the age of seventy-six, and maintained it with dignity. She had preserved all the privileges as well as the etiquette of the former court; she loved the ostentation, the pleasures, and the power of that court. Again she retained all that was brusque and almost savage in the moral atmosphere, in which she was brought up and which prevailed in her native land, being still German in her ideas and in her conversation. She was frank, without finesse, or false modesty, and always the open enemy of Mme. de Maintenon, whom she always called the sorceress, the bigot, the widow Scarron.

Madame wore men's wigs; she had a pack of hounds; she was an equestrienne, and could train the most unmanageable horses; she followed the chase; was an expert swordswoman; a good shot, and could handle every conceivable kind of weapon. She was passionately fond of the regent, her son, for she recognized in him many traits of character inherited from her, and her attachment was evident in her conduct toward the illegitimate children of the prince, whom she fostered. When she was alone at home she spent all her time writing to the German Courts, and she claimed to have addressed more than ten volumes of anecdotes of the French Court. She lived as unostentatiously as a peasant woman; possessing a constitution so robust as to be able to boast in her sixtieth year that she had never been sick.

The Prince de Condé, commonly called M. le Duc, had two brothers and six sisters; the eldest sister was hunch-back, and a nun in the Abbey Saint-Antoine; the second was Mme. the Princess de Conti; the third, Mlle. de Charolais, who had a marked affection for the Duke de Richelieu, was dowager; the fourth was Mlle. de Clermont; the fifth Mlle. de Sens, and the sixth, Mlle. de Vermandois. The Counts de Charolais and de Clermont were her brothers. The father of all these children, having died suddenly, the whole family came immediately to Versailles to seek maintenance from the late king. Mme. the Duchess, the Princess de Conti, first dowager, and his son, surprised the monarch at his morning levee, and monseigneur devoted himself to pleading for the young prince, fearing lest the king might give the greater part of these charges to the Duke du Maine, whom he hated, and who never forgot the injury monseigneur and the house of Condé had brought on his fortune which the king at that time was increasing day by day.

Thus M. le Duc was endowed, at the age of fourteen, with the pensions which his father had received, and found himself the head of his house. His father had always treated him with the utmost severity; but having become his own master, he gave up his studies and devoted himself to pleasures. Even in the army of Flanders he distinguished himself by his courage and by the kindness he showed to the soldiers. The life which he led there caused the king to issue a humiliating order against him, and have him watched, even in his tent, calling the attention of Marshal de Villars to his conduct. It was for these same reasons that the Princess de Conti, first dowager, determined to marry the youth to the daughter of the Prince de Condé, who was hated and persecuted by her own mother; but this marriage did not keep him from freely indulging his passions.

In 1713 the Duke de Berri wounded this prince while hunting and as the result he lost the sight of his left eye, having been struck by a small leaden bullet, which became lodged in the orbit of the eye. During his illness he visited the Marquis de Gesvres, his friend, who desired to serve him. Later, after his recovery, he became attached to Mme. de Nesle, because he was told that it was the distinguishing mark of *bon ton* to have a titled mistress, but Mme. de Prie, as we shall see hereafter, succeeded in undermining his affection for Mme. de Nesle.

The Duke du Maine was somewhat familiar with belles-lettres and the arts. He possessed the peculiar ability of pleasing every one in his conversation, and of appearing always amiable, but in his heart he loved no one but himself, living in a state of perfect apathy in regard to everything that did not concern him, and he was even entirely indifferent to his own interests, when they demanded actual mental or physical exertion. However, while it can truly be said that he had no great virtue, it is also true that he possessed no marked vices. Of a weak disposition, he permitted himself to be ruled by his wife, who held a superb court at Sceaux, and whose brilliancy and wit contributed much to its external grandeur. She gained such an ascendancy over the Duke du Maine, her husband, that this prince had no influence in his own home. Being an intriguer and an adept in chicanery, she was capable of concealing her dangerous talents and her schemes for the aggrandizement of her family under the guise of a life devoted entirely to pleasure, festivity, and to literary pursuits. It was part of her policy to attract to her home poets and talented persons of the period. She planned with them novelties in the way of nocturnal festivals, which she called *grandes nuits*, in opposition to those of the Duke of Orleans, whom she hated, and whose entertainments produced nothing but debauchery, whilst the nocturnal festivals of Mme. du Maine transpired with all the magnificence of party functions. On one occasion she determined to personify the divinities of night with all their attributes; but these farces being far from realistic appeared ridiculous in the eyes of the whole court, and were especially distasteful to the late king, who had exquisite taste in matters of this kind, and was a connoisseur of fêtes and pleasures. True artists disapproved the productions at Sceaux, of phantoms dressed in black crepe, which danced, sang and recited verses, referring to the princess. These entertainments were discontinued in due time, and were succeeded by the drama and the dance.

Mme. the Duchess du Maine conceived a new kind of amusement; she established the *Ordre des Abeilles* to which the greatest lords of the court eagerly sought admittance that they might enjoy the privilege of personal communication with Mme. du Maine. Ladies were not excluded from this order, and while these various entertainments at Sceaux seemed to have been invented for the temporary amusement which they afforded, the princess adroitly made use of them to attain her personal end, which was the aggrandizement of her house.

Among the talented persons who came to Sceaux was the Abbé de Chaulieu, a blind and mute octogenarian who still had the coquetry of a woman and the imagination of a young man of twenty-five. These peculiar qualities amused the court at Sceaux and made him an object of curiosity and interest. The Marquis de Lassay, a remarkably clever man, was another habitué · Le

Grange-Chancel, who had once acted as page and who had learned at Sceaux the anecdotes of the Philippiques, which he recounted several times, eliciting great applause; the Abbé Genest, a very respectable ecclesiastic, known for his brilliant wit; the first president and the Duke de Brancas, who contributed substantially to the entertainment and who invariably succeeded in amusing the Duke of Orleans and the Duke du Maine, were all received in this society.

But, however noisy and abounding in pleasures was the court at Sceaux, however modest and retiring the Count of Toulouse, he was loved and respected by every one, even by the regent, who disliked the legitimate children of Louis XIV. The Count de Toulouse led a most amiable life, cherishing ill-will towards none and devoting himself to the pleasures of others.

CHAPTER VII.

The regent and Mme. de Berri, his daughter, at the opera.—Masked balls given there.—Passion of Mlle. de Charolais for Richelieu.—Rendezvous that the princesses gave.—Nocturnal fêtes at the home of the Count de Gacé.—His duel with Richelieu, who is imprisoned in the Bastille for the second time.—Mlle. de Charolais visits him there.

VOLUPTUOUSNESS reigned supreme in all places frequented by the regent and Mme. de Berri. The opera was opened three times a week in summer and four times in winter; French and Italian comedians played there when there was no opera. The regent had a small private box in which he had a lounge and he went there oftener than to his regular box. Mme. de Berri had a similar one directly opposite, where she went with Riom and other favorites. The other princesses also had boxes but they were neither so large nor so luxuriant, although opening on the stage; there they took their lovers and friends. Father Sebastien, a Carmelite friar, honorary member of the Academy of Sciences, and a skillful engineer, had discovered a way to remove the floor from the pit between the ampitheatre and the theatre and to convert the hall into a regular saloon; masked balls were given there, and the greater number of ladies under the pretext of being affected by the heat, did not hesitate to expose themselves there, in reality wishing to be admired and to converse familiarly with the maskers. The regent

went into this room with some one of these mistresses
with whom he had amused himself during the ball.
These debaucheries were the more harmful to him in
that he was unable to attend to his affairs the next
day and ran the risk of entirely losing what little
insight he had in affairs. These indiscriminate debaucheries cost him the use of an eye in 1716. The festivals
and the amusements became still more frequent upon the
arrival of the Duke and Duchess de Lorraine, sister of
the regent, who had come to pay homage to the king for
their Duchy of Bar which they held in fief. His brother-
in-law entertained them at the Palais-Royal, as did the
mistress of the duke, without the duchess being able to
find any fault. On the other hand, she made her her
best friend, whilst the husband was the favorite of the
duke. Thus foreign courts, whose free fêtes were a continual play of ceremonial and etiquette, not at all in keeping with pleasures and amusements, were brought into
sympathy and gradually learned to imitate the laxness of
the court of the regent in France. Gradually the custom
was introduced in France for women to close their eyes
to the infidelity of their husbands, who in turn had to
give their wives the same consideration and very soon
it came to be considered at court among the great lords
an absolute folly to conduct oneself *bour geoisement*, as a
life of purity was termed. It was said that such a
life was adapted to the people of the former regime.
These principles gradually extended throughout France;
the princes were polluted and corruption was conta-
gious.

The princes of the blood after the example of the regent enjoyed the freedom of the times, and the king had scarcely passed away when Mlle. de Charolais, for example, conceived such a passion for the Duke de Richelieu, that in spite of his infidelity, she never ceased to love him passionately. Those about her were so touched by her sorrows, that they endeavored to ameliorate them by bringing about secret interviews, which were soon after divulged by the duke. The princess, her mother, furious on hearing of these amours, treated her harshly, not being able to endure the thought of having her daughter follow her own example; but the young noble went to the hotel during the night to carry on the liaisons; the apartment of the young princess being on the ground floor, and opening into a garden, to which he had the key, he habitually gained access to her apartment without being discovered.

Finally they were suspected, and at the very time when they were satisfied that they had nothing to fear, the servants continued to watch and to shadow the lovers, for it is a great satisfaction to those who surround persons of superior rank to hold them in their power in this way; therefore, they betrayed the two lovers for the purpose of compelling them to treat with them. This was a species of slavery to which the Duke de Richelieu did not care to have his princess subjected; he knew her to be capable of going to any length to preserve her relations with him; he, therefore, formed a treaty, so to speak, with the other princesses who also had lovers, thus strengthening their mutual position by mutual necessities. He treated with Mme. the Princess de Conti, sister of his mistress, to whom the Marquis de la Fare was deeply attached, in spite of the jealousy of her husband, and he also gained as an ally, of this amorous faction, Mme. de Berri, at that time beloved by Riom, his friend.

Mlle. de Charolais, Mme. de Conti, her sister, and Mme. de Berri, made appointments with La Fare, Riom, and with the Duke de Richelieu to meet first at the home of one princess, and then at that of another; so as to guard against the dangers to which the league might be exposed. Mlle. de Charolais wrote verses on the events of the time; she was intellectual, possessing much sound sense in spite of her libertinism. But soon the league was dissolved, for although the mother could not forbid her daughters from going to see each other, nor prevent Mme. de Berri from receiving them at her home, she soon suspected that the extremely interesting and questionable pleasure experienced in each other's company was the motive of their visits; they also knew that La Fare and Riom were accustomed to associate with the Duke de Richelieu. The enraged mother then severely reprimanded her daughter. Richelieu then took it into his head to leave his mistress alone with her ladies, and go to his own box. This imprudence on his part was noticed by many people; it passed from lip to lip as the news of the day; and it became generally known that the princess had deprived her daughter of the liberty hitherto enjoyed by her. Mothers of the princesses of the blood, having less freedom really than other parents, were forced to watch over the corruptors who gathered about their children from their earliest years. The mother of the princess reproached herself with having neglected her duty; Duchayla, a man of wit, skilled in repartee, and with his head filled with farcical anecdotes, was able to amuse and please her. The mother could not, at once, devote herself to her daughter and to Count Duchayla, and the obstacles which she placed in the way of these amours were unavailing, and only increased the passion of the young princess.

The court of the regent, whose members took pleasure in every scandalous amusement, set the pace for all princes and in fact for persons of less noble birth; everywhere people tried to imitate the orgies of Saint-Cloud and of the Palais-Royal.

It was said that some distinguished noblemen, indulging in these nocturnal festivities at the home of Count de Gacé had committed acts worthy of the time of Heliogabal; the names of Mme. de Nesle, the Prince de Soubise, the Count and Countess de Gacé were mentioned. Malicious gossips attacked the name of Mme. de Gacé with less consideration than that of any of the other ladies. They accused the Duke de Richelieu of having revealed the secret doings of these debaucheries; they attributed to him conversations he had never held, touching on the conduct of Mme. de Gacé. These rumors so irritated the count, her husband, (afterwards Count de Matignon) that he asked a certain writer of that period to compose a scathing poem about Richelieu. The first time that Gacé met him at the ball of the opera he sang this ballad to him, and whispered in the ear of a lady with whom Richelieu was talking: "Beautiful princess, do not listen to a masker so perfidious in love; he will reveal all." Richelieu rose in anger; the other followed him and they halted in the Rue Saint-Thomas of the Louvre, where a duel ensued! Richelieu wounded Gacé slightly, in the arm, and in two other places, while Gacé being both stronger and older had the longer reach and drew the sword across his body without injuring his vitals; they then separated. Gacé, scarcely wounded, returned to the ball-room. This incident took place the 17th of February, 1716, in the presence of a large assembly of people who had quickly gathered about them; it caused such a scandal in Paris that parliament, which then was engaging in endless quarrels with the peers, determined to take cognizance of the affair. We shall speak briefly of these differences between parliament and the peers.

The late king had scarcely closed his eyes in death when the presidents decreed the refusal of the prerogative of salutation to the peers and ordered that if the peers persisted in demanding it, and if the people continued to give their votes with covered head, their votes should be ignored. The peers, on the other hand, determined that they should be saluted and that in the ordinances of the lower courts, their rank and followers should not be interrupted by councilors, whom the court should always seat at the lower end of the bench. There were many other petty quarrels, but whatever concerns persons of rank is an affair of state in France, monarchical forms which are not well defined in public, demanding a definite determination.

The parliament and the peers, who formed a single legislative body, were therefore divided; but the regent who had promised to reconcile them, in regard to the article defining the salutation, a thing which seemed to be a great obstacle to their reconciliation, left them to pursue their quarrels and mutual animosities. He resembled in this respect the late king, who gladly saw perpetual antipathy between the lords of the court and the rest of parliament. The complete reconciliation of one body of the magistracy which thinks, and of the military body that executes the laws, would have been dangerous to the authority which this monarch had usurped, and he, like the Duke of Orleans, preserved only too well the principles of the old ministry on this delicate subject.

The regent knew that parliament was going to take action on the incident of the Rue Saint-Thomas of the Louvre. This court had, as a matter of fact, rendered a decision on the 27th of February, notifying the House of Richelieu of the following decree: that in two weeks, dating from the notification, the duke should betake himself to the prisons of the palace to justify himself for having dueled with the Count de Gacé. Richelieu presented a petition to the king in which he made remonstrance, saying that being endowed with two duchies, which he held as a vassal from his majesty, he could recognize no other judges than his majesty and the peers; he besought him therefore to preside over the trial, or to nominate a commission to try him, refusing to submit his case to the parliament, because of the pending trial between that body and the peers, and asked for a trial in conformity to the accustomed forms of the peers.

Two days later the Archbishop of Reims, the Bishops of Laon, and of Langres, the ecclesiastical peers, the Dukes de Sully, de La Force, de Charost, de Chaulnes, de Saint-Simon, de Luxembourg, de Tresmes, and d'Antin, charged with the power of attorney of the peers, presented a petition to the king against the proceedings of parliament which they pronounced as a usurpation. "It is no longer," said they to the king, "the external honors due the peerage, the propriety of a salutation, the order of sessions, nor the right of suffrage, to which the enterprises of parliament are limited; it even claims the right to judge the peers."

In order to sustain its jurisdiction, parliament cited to the king eight examples of trials of the peers, all without relevance to the present case; but the peers rejoined by mentioning fifty-six others which had established their independence, dating back six hundred years. Nevertheless, without awaiting the decision of the king, parliament had put its decree of the 27th of February into execution, with reference to the public incident of Rue Saint-Thomas of the Louvre. A simple *lettre-de cachet* stopped all technicalities and on the 5th of March, 1716, Richelieu as well as Gacé received an order to proceed to the Bastille.

Parliament not discontinuing its prosecution, the regent abandoned this trial to it on the 18th of May, by virtue of a royal decree, leaving the two adversaries however under the safe guard of the king. Parliament appointed Ferrant to examine them and both swore that they had never been engaged in a duel. No witnesses were presented, and on the 19th of June, the peers, summoned by the king, finding themselves assembled in parliament, published the proceedings which had come to light under a still more ample investigation of this affair.

The judges were up to this point well assured that they would be defeated but the investigations proved favorable to them. They notified Richelieu that he would be examined, which made the affair still more delicate. In order to forestall the possible results of this new kind of proof, Richelieu conceived the idea of concealing his wounds under thin tafetta and of making use of a tint to give the wounds a color resembling the natural skin; then all sorts of proofs were presented to show that he had never engaged in a duel.

He had passed but two months in the Bastille, during which time he was refused even a sight of his cherished princess when the gates of the prison were opened to him, the promise of great rewards, made by the royal princesses, having corrupted the guards and the gate-keepers and he was visited by his love. The law in vain threatens with death him who betrays the secret of the prisons of state. They were opened to the bribers, and the love-lorn Charolais, under less restraint by the old princess, her mother, making use of her liberty to exe-

The Duc de Richelieu Visited in Prison by the Princesses

Engraved by Le roy after picture by Le Clerc.

cute her plan of bribery, succeeded in effecting an escape for Richelieu from the Bastille. She persuaded Madame the Princess de Conti, her sister, to accompany her and, disguised as women of the lower class, they met him at twilight. They continued their dangerous visits without arousing the suspicions either of the court of the regent, or of the governor of the Bastille. It was perhaps the first instance of a like proof of love in a princess of the blood.

We may well imagine the result of this. Richelieu's wound reopened, although it had so often been dressed by tender hands. But the court, which the police had succeeded in informing of every detail, at last became cognizant of the whole affair, and the governor was ordered to ascertain the indentity of the charitable ladies who brought Richelieu salves and ointments. Having given their names to the regent, all communications were interrupted from that time on; as a result the cure was hastened and the wounds were healed again. It not having been proven that a duel had transpired the parliament declared them absolved from the alleged offence, and on the 21st of August, 1716, Richelieu left the Bastille, after having seen and embraced Gacé and having dined with him in the presence of the governor.

CHAPTER VIII.

Struggle of parliament against the nobility.—Memoirs of same.—Open war between the legitimate and legitimated princes.—Other differences between members of the high nobility and the peers.—The decree of the States-General pronounced.

THE regent not wishing to terminate, as he had promised, the differences between the peers and parliament, these two factions indulged in scandalous quarrels. The peers claimed that parliament belonged to the third estate; parliament replied that their chief chancellor of France was the peer of the constable and of the marshalls of France; and that the presidents of the Courts of Justice were the peers of the dukes and peers, and were beneath the chief of the magistracy in dignity. And as the peers had indulged in pleasantries regarding the descent of the presidents, the latter, to mortify the peers, addressed the famous Memoir to the regent, a manuscript in which they attacked almost all the titled families of the court, claiming that they were of ignoble origin and that their position and the favor of the kings had alone raised them to their present dignity.

At the end of this volume may be seen the memoir against the dukes and that of the dukes against the parliament.

The magistracy reproached the peerage with the fact that the Dukes de Crussol were descended from an apothecary, ennobled in 1304 by a bishop; the Bethunes from an adventurer; the Wignerots from a domestic, a lute player of Cardinal de Fleury; the Dukes de Saint-Simon, from the esquire of Mme. de Schomberg, and the Duke de la Rochefoucauld, from Jean le Vert, a butcher. They reproached the peerage with the fact that the Villerois were descendants of a fishwoman; the Noailles descendants of a valet of the Viscount de Turenne; it was claimed that the Dukes de Mazarin were descendants of an apothecary; that the d'Harcourts were the descendants of an illegitimate son of the Bishop de Bayeux, and the d'Epernons from another illegitimate son of the Canon de Leytour; and that, as a matter of fact, the Marshal de Villars was the great grandson of a registrar of Condrieux in 1486.

All the peerage assembled for the purpose of refuting this Memoir of Parliament, which was called an infamous libel. Those who were prejudiced in favor of birth were so aroused that these noblemen of the realm, could not otherwise characterize the Memoir of the magistrates, which took from them the consideration due to the antiquity of a nobility which they all forced themselves to believe dated back to the time of chivalry. All the peers, whose family trees were impugned, gathered together, nominated commissioners, brought their old parchments, to prove the nobility of their origin, and replied to the Memoir of Parliament. They would gladly have induced the ministry to take part in these quarrels of pride; but the Council of the Regency, composed of men who were desirous of having parliament interest itself concerning these trifles, and ignore the affairs of state, was very careful not to embroil itself in the dispute; and it granted a delay of proceedings until the king should become of age. The peers had raised questions of public law, which aroused the French nobility; they discussed the election of kings, to the prejudice of the princes of the blood, claiming that the great prerogatives of state were derived from them, that they were the chiefs of nobility, that they formed a separate order, and that they alone had the right to represent the ancient peers of the realm.

A second and still more delicate quarrel ensued, that of the legitimated princes against the princes of the blood. When the regency had wrought a change in public opinion, liberty demanded that they should repress all the abuses of power. M. le Prince had in his possession property subject to litigation between M. le Duc on one hand and the Duchess du Maine and her sisters on the other; there was some talk about a compromise between the relatives, and the Duke du Maine, having assumed the quality of prince of the blood, in the agreement that he signed, M. le Duc, in addition to his signature wrote a protest against this claim.

From that time on the legitimate and legitimated princes carried on open warfare against each other and their disputes were much more bitter, inasmuch as their wives were concerned in the quarrel. Mme. du Maine, haughty and proud of spirit and with an eye single to the glory of the house, employed every means in her power, fortune and rank, to maintain the dignity of the same.

She never forgot that the regent had despoiled the Duke du Maine, her husband, of the power that the late king had bequeathed him in his testament, and she bided her time for an occasion to avenge herself on the Duke of Orleans. She received his enemies at Sceaux; she caused satirical verses to be recited, and songs sung that were aimed against this prince. She criticised the doings of the regency and allied herself with the Court of Spain which was displeased with the regent.

The princes of the blood, if possible more bitter against the legitimated princes, presented their petition against the latter to the king, who, in turn, presented another petition. M. le Duc, the Count de Charolais, and the Prince de Conti, formed a very close protective league. The regent, pleased at seeing the Duke du Maine anxious, was nevertheless himself in great perplexity, as he did not dare to decide this great question, and he had reason to fear that the king having attained his majority would adopt the principles of his predecessor, and he was apprehensive he might acquire irreconcilable enemies thereby. He appointed commissioners to look into the great dispute. The city of Paris and the kingdom, as in all great questions, were divided. This division has flooded us with writings for and against the legitimated princes, among which are found the memoirs of the princes composed by Cardinal Polignac, Malezieu and Davisard, advocate-general of the parliament of Toulouse, who was the confidant of Mme. du Maine.

This princess, who united theory and practice in the great question, had sent to her thousands of volumes of writings, dealing with the history of France, and burrowed amongst the old chronicles and archives to unearth some prerogative of the illegitimate offspring of sovereigns. The Jesuits, who in order to flatter the king, Mme. de Maintenon, and her cherished followers, had ordered the history of France from their Pere Daniel, gave to Mme. du Maine a list containing three thousand, four hundred citations, some genuine and some false, founded on apocryphal monuments, all in favor of the natural offspring of kings. Mme. du Maine studied these citations and made use of them in every conceivable way in her conversation; and, as a matter of fact, the whole court became so well versed in the theory and facts of the case that little else was talked of but the legitimated princes, children of Louis XIV., and the bastards of Charlibert, of Clothaire, and of the most ancient kings of the French monarchy.

The princes of the blood, in their writings, strove to establish the fact that the kings of France were but the beneficial occupants of their throne, and that they could not dispose of it until after the extinction of the princes of the blood and that the finest title of the French nation was the prerogative of being governed by legitimate princes who had been elevated to the throne.

The legitimated princes based some of their rights on facts to which the princes had not at the time laid claim; they said that they could be judged only by the assembled chambers and that parliament which had registered an edict in their favor could not accept petitions contrary to the acts of the late king, which had been registered by it.

The princes of the blood replied that the absolute authority of the late king had imposed silence upon them; that the parliament itself could not register a decision without representations which had for a long time been forbidden.

These preliminary discussions brought in their train more important ones; the legitimated princes claimed that in the original house the natural sons had been kings.

All the legitimated offspring of Louis XIV. formed a sort of society or faction against the princes of the blood, and although Mme. of Orleans, wife of the regent, was allied with the house of the first prince of the blood, her quality as legitimated daughter of the late king was of more importance in her eyes than the title of wife of the regent and mother of the Duke de Chartres. She never considered herself as belonging to the party of her husband in the quarrels which the royal princes had during his regency against the legitimated princes; she even received the news that her husband had been declared regent by the court of parliament with extreme sorrow and was grieved by the fact that the Duke du Maine had been despoiled of the power that the late king had given to him in his will. Thus the court was divided into two great factions, so bitterly opposed to each other that they forgot the duties of kinship.

The quarrels of the peers and the princes against the legitimated children of Louis XIV. soon prepared the way for other quarrels between the peers. The nobility of the royal families considered itself insulted by the fact that the peers presumed to form a separate body and to judge the rest of the nobility; they even held assemblies in which petitions were drawn up, signed by the nobles, De Chatillon, Listenai, Conflans, Laval, Mailly, d'Estain, d'Hautefort, de Surville, Montmorency Fosseuse, and others. The Council of State, on the 14th of May, 1717, prohibited them from signing like petitions. They were dealing with subjects that concerned too vitally the existing nobility in the kingdom of France.

The council of the regency some days afterwards nominated commissioners to examine the form of judging the affair of the princes; but the nobility, always exacting in its desire to maintain its privileges which it believed were attacked by the edicts of King Louis XIV. in behalf of the legitimated princes, issued a protest to parliament claiming the invalidity of any judgment on the problem of the princes, which could not be discussed and judged, but by the states' general to which its petition was addressed. At this crisis the council of the regency became thoroughly alarmed. The assembly of the nation had determined to effect either the terror or the ruin of the ministry. All the councils, especially that of the regency, rose in revolt and Chatillon, Vieuxpont, Baufremont, Rieux, Polignac and Clairemont, were imprisoned, some in the Bastille and some in the Chateau de Vincent. The sergeant-at-arms who had *viséd* the act was suspended from his duties for six months, and the audacious noblemen who had been rash enough to pronounce the words *states-general* were guarded so closely that the Cardinal de Polignac could not even see his brother. The Duke de Chatres, who was then a student, having brought a volume which dealt with the laws of nations in the choice of a regent, demonstrated to his father that a regent came into power only by usurpation, parliament having no right to determine the matter, and birth not being a right to be contested. This young prince, suing for the deliverance of the imprisoned lords, obtained this concession from his father within a month.

Finally the day, fatal to the princes of the blood, came; in the month of July, 1717, the king revoked the edict of Louis XIV. in favor of the legitimated children, whom he deprived of the quality of princes of the blood; he left to Count de Toulouse the honors that he had enjoyed up to that time, but he despoiled the Duke du Maine against whom the vengeance of the regent was particularly bitter, because it was to him that he justly attributed his loss of influence with Louis XIV. He justly thought him equally culpable with Mme. de Maintenon, in having deprived him of the absolute authority of the regency, and he was displeased with him because he had some secret knowledge of certain Spanish intrigues, which, if brought to light, might seriously incriminate him.

CHAPTER IX.

Jansenism at the court of the regent.—Mlle. of Orleans, Abbess de Chelles.—Her life as an artist at Savant and as a woman of the world under the veil.—Her interview in the guise of a convert with the Cardinal Bissy.—The princesses, daughters of the regent.—Morals of the court.—Rivalries between the prince and the Duke de Richelieu.—Two women fight a duel on account of him.

WHO would believe that Jansenism, that terror of the late king, would receive, perhaps, for this very reason, favor during the regency and that it would make such progress in Paris and throughout France that it was introduced even amongst the princes and the princesses of the blood. The Duke de Chartres studied its doctrines and accepted the belief of the Jansenists so thoroughly that for the rest of his life he was greatly occupied with it, writing from early youth treatises on grace, and whole volumes of dissertations on subjects of this nature. His father was greatly averse to it and his mistresses tried to interest him in the affairs of court. At the age of eighteen years youthful debauchees were called *pour lui donner du sentiment;* but the prince, always bashful, reserved and of a religious temperament, did not yield to their temptations.

About this time Mlle. of Orleans, angered against her father and jealous of her sister, Mlle. de Valois, notwithstanding her love of worldly pleasures, suddenly retired to a convent, where she became an extreme Jansenist.

She brought with her, into the Abbey de Chelles, love of the fine arts, which she inherited from her father and she attracted bands of musicians to the convent for the purpose of giving concerts. She went about in the vicinity in her own carriages, accompanied by several nuns, with whom she was very intimate. She was especially fond of Mme. de Fretteville, who had at once won her friendship. The abbess, Mme. de Villars, not being able to quell this love of worldly pleasure in Mlle. of Orleans, offered to resign her position as abbess to Mlle. of Orleans when she should become a nun. The regent consented to it and his daughter became abbess; then she caused a part of the monastery to be demolished and remodeled. The inclosures were changed; a brilliant company of men and women were then enabled to listen to the music, and often partook of dainty suppers. All Paris was amused by the news which daily came from the Abbey de Chelles; the regent, desirous of having these rumors cease, endeavored to influence his daughter to change her conduct. She had been, up to that time, a zealous Molinist, having been instructed by Pere Trevoux, a Jesuit, who had induced her to join his society and faction. At Chelles, she took as her confessor, a benedictine monk, called Le Doux, who converted her to Jansenism and condemned her to gloomy meditations, and thoughts of death. Her progress in spiritual life was such that one morning, in an excess of religious devotion, she shattered all her musical instruments and made a bon-fire of them, kindling the fire with rolls of music. She gave no more suppers, except to the nuns, and meditated constantly on the subject of death as the benedictine friar had instructed her, until one evening at ten o'clock, rising from the table, she announced her intention of visiting the place destined for her in the tomb. Each nun, with a torch in her hand, went with her into the church; the tomb was opened; they descended into it by means of a ladder; she took her place in the sepulchre and seemed content with her resting place.

Having become a devotee to Jansenism, as the result of the fatherly cares of her benedictine director, she expressed a wish to study the Scripture carefully and collate the passages which seemed favorable to her creed. Two secretaries selected these passages, and she commented upon them. She also wrote to Cardinal de Noailles upholding everything she had done. When her conduct had become notorious, the regent, who had certain matters to transact at the Court of Rome, which had refused Bulls for several nominative bishops, besought his daughter not to show so much zeal, and sent her her former director, Pere Travoux, for the purpose of dissuading her. She neither wished to recognize him nor to receive him, and forbade him to appear in her presence. This caused the Duke of Orleans to send into exile the Jansenist confessor, who had thus succeeded in gaining an ascendancy over his daughter's mind. The Jesuits never ceased persecuting her; they won over Mme. de Fretteville, the most intimate of her favorites, who did all in her power to convert the abbess, but she became more determined in her course as she encountered opposition, and demanded the return of her confessor; her father yielded, and he came to see her every Tuesday at Chelles, and annoyed Mme. Fretteville to such an extent that her former favorite was obliged to leave the convent. Furious at the leaders of the Jesuit faction, who had brought about the exile of her confessor, she avenged herself on them one day in the following manner.

Mme. de Rohan, Abbess d'Hières, visited Mme. de Chelles frequently, and she, in turn, returned those visits. One day Cardinal de Bissy, chief of the Molinist party, going to see Mme. de Rohan, asked her the attitude of her relatives towards the Bull, to which the latter replied that she had but one sister, a convert, who did not care to obey the Bull. Bissy ordered her to appear before him, and Mme. de Rohan sent Mme. of Orleans to him, who escaped recognition as she had assumed the costume of a lay-sister.

Bissy contended for submission, and the Abbess de Chelles parried by talking of appeal and reappeal. The cardinal, becoming angry, threatened to have her do penance, and the sister in a very calm manner recounted her history, assuring him that she played her rôle for ambition alone. Fury seized the astonished cardinal, who said to the lay-sister that she was ignorant of the fact that he was a prince of the church, but the sister, who was a shrewd conversationalist succeeded in disconcerting him. Mme. de Rohan, who listened to all this conversation, burst out laughing, and Bissy, thereupon carefully examining the face of the lay-sister, recognized Mme. of Orleans. Then, rising from his chair, he most humbly apologized to her. The princess turned from him and said, "Profit by the lesson." The cardinal, full of wrath, did not wish to dine with Mme. de Rohan, who had invited him, together with Mme. de Chelles; he left the convent muttering angrily to himself. The most laudable and humane action that the Abbess de Chelles did, was to declare herself the protectress of every one persecuted by the Jesuit faction. The Abbey de Chelles was the refuge of all who were exiled when Jesuitism triumphed under Cardinal de Fluery. Bissy, who still grieved over the adventure of the Abbess d'Hières, entered complaints against the cordial reception which she gave those whom he had punished. The princess, always courageous, answered the king that she did not know those whom his majesty exiled; that she only knew that those whom she received had been unfortunate enough to displease him, and if she had succored some unfortunate persecuted one, she could not repent of it, having taken the vow of hospitality, especially to those in affliction. Madame, the abbess, confident from the fact that she was concealed in convent, and that she could fear no greater punishment from the Jesuit faction, ignored his complaints. The Jesuits conspired in league with her mother, Mme. of Orleans, who made plain to her the indecency of her conduct. The abbess, still more determined, quarreled with her, and Mme. of Orleans had to visit her in order to bring about a reconciliation.

The Jesuits, whom she outraged, avenged themselves by attacking this princess. A rumor was spread abroad that she had accepted the constitution, and all Paris believed it. She replied by means of a sort of manifesto, the principal expressions of which we present here because they give an excellent idea of the spirit of the times, as well as of the character of this princess. "The acceptation of the constitution which has been attributed to me," she said, "could have but one of these three causes; political views, or attachment to a course of action which I have taken and left without examination, or the conviction that will oblige me to join a new party.

"To all this, I make reply as follows: First, that I have had no need to deal with politics as long as M. of Orleans is alive to obtain what I desire.

"Second, if it is imagined that I declared myself without knowledge of the cause, people are mistaken, and those who believe me fickle do not know me. When the Bull was published, I was young: in fact, but fifteen years of age. The excitement which it created throughout the realm made me curious; it seemed to contradict all that I had learned. The persecution which the constitutionalists instituted displeased me; I was convinced that violence and justice were incompatible. Prelates and distinguished persons who had been persecuted sought my aid; pity caused me to sympathize with them, and at that time I became a Jansenist. The reproach heaped upon me for this act had never caused me to regret it, and I am more worthy than people believe. The first years of my seclusion were employed in study, during which time I became convinced that the

Gospel, St. Paul, St. Augustine, St. Prosper, St. Fulgence and St. Thomas, are condemned by the Bull."

The Abbess de Chelles did not confine herself to the study of Jansenist and Molinist literature alone, but busied herself with many other things in the abbey. She knew how to make all kinds of coiffures, and work machines of various kinds, and superb embroideries. She amused herself making fireworks; she had a pair of pistols which caused terror throughout the house.

Having inherited a very active disposition from her father, her mind was continually engaged in some enterprise. Like him she was ambitious to learn and was interested in the most abstract sciences. Her fondness for physics led her into an investigation of chemistry; and the knowledge which she acquired of chemistry led her in turn into the science of simples and she devoted herself to pharmacy; finally from the science of pathology she engaged in surgery, which science she desired to practice. It was said after her death that she was a musician, artist, embroiderer, skillful in fashions, in the art of head-dressing, and in the art of joinery. She was a physician, chemist, apothecary, surgeon, theologian, a thorough adept in all the vagaries of the subtle heresy of Jansenism which engaged the attention of the most profound men of the seventeenth and part of the eighteenth century. She made a profession of faith, thereby claiming a thorough knowledge of the cunning of this school. She was also a skillful turner. As she moved her foot to start the lever when manipulating her machine, all the humors of the body became conjested in her right hip, to such an extent that gangrene was feared. This, however, did not deter her from continuing to indulge in this amusement.

As to Mlle. de Valois, the third daughter of the regent, she had the pallor of an invalid; she possessed a beautiful figure, however, and like her sisters inherited from her father a penchant for pleasures. She became, at length, passionately fond of the Duke de Richelieu. While seated side by side at the gaming table they exchanged signals by nudging each other with their feet, and since this amused them both, a mutual attachment was the result of these pleasantries. Mlle. de Charolais, the first love of the duke, observing this, forestalled them and putting her own foot forward, the duke sometimes mistook it for that of the other princess. Mlle. de Charolais consumed with jealously had the patience to continue this long enough to ascertain that Mlle. de Valois was the object of his passions and learned by the aid of this method of communication how far they had progressed in their love affair. At the end of a game she would rise like a fury with fiery eyes and under the pretext of indisposition, would go home, wild with anger, and thoroughly aroused against Mlle. de Valois, leaving the duke embarrassed on account of his mistake and little inclined for the time being, to continue his communications with Mlle. de Valois, who was more furious than her rival, at perceiving the mistake. Neither manifested resentment against the duke, who deceived them both, but toward each other they swore eternal enmity.

The regent, displeased with these quarrels that were being introduced in his court, some days after, gave the Duke de Richelieu a singular bit of advice, relative to the friendship that the princess, his daughter, showed for him. There lodged in his hotel, Montconseil, a young man charming in deportment and possessing an admirable character, readily welcomed in society, and even agreeable to the regent, who one evening wore a cloak to the ball which was similar to one which Richelieu was accustomed to wear. He talked so earnestly with Mlle. de Valois, that the regent who already suspected the intrigues of his daughter, approached Montconseil who was seated by her side, and thinking that he recognized Richelieu in his cloak, said to him, " Masquer, be careful, if you do not wish to go to the Bastille for the third time." Montconseil, in order to undeceive the regent, removed his mask and made himself known; and the prince, in an angry tone, added: "Tell you friend Richelieu what I just told you," and turning his back, disappeared.

It was soon known in Paris which princess loved him, and what the obstacles were in the way of their love. The princes and princesses of the blood gave to all France a scandalous illustration of the improprieties of court. The dowager duchess lived publicly with Law; the Duchess de Bourbon, despised by her husband, consoled herself with Duchaila; the Princess de Conti, daughter of the king, often agitated by religious scruples and remorse, and always criticising the princess, because of the latter's love affairs, was courted by her nephew, la Vallière. The young Princess de Conti, in spite of the jealousy of her husband, loved La Fare and Claremont, the handsomest nobleman of her house. We have already recounted the love affair of the beautiful Charolais; her youngest sister was in love with the Duke, de Melon. Mme. de Berri lived with Riom and others, and the Abbess de Chelles had "pensioners" in her convent. Marton idolized Mlle. de la Roche-sur-Yon and Cardinal Polignac was by no means spurned by Mme. du Maine, in spite of the jealousy of her husband who wished to preserve the external ceremonies of the Court of Louis XIV., at Sceaux. Thus the princesses and princes of that period avenged themselves publicly for having been subjected to surveillance by the late king. The disposition of the people resembled the impetuosity of a student, who upon leaving college where he has been restrained and constantly watched, enters the world and utterly casts aside every restraint. We shall omit the details; a mere hint is sufficient to warn sovereigns and princes that the courtiers who surround them apparently in fear and trembling, and who lavish flattering expressions upon them, secretly write the truth, transmitting it to posterity. A public man is apt to think that his faults are unobserved but when the history of the time is written, they seem to spring into prominence.

As for the regent, he concealed neither his amours, his fickle character, nor his dissoluteness; introducing into the orgies of Saint-Cloud and of the Palais-Royal some new sensual and obscene feature every day. Having assumed the regency he returned to Desmerre, exiling Baron, whom she secretly preferred. Weary of her, he devoted himself to Fillon for a short time and in turn abandoned her for a comedienne, named Emelie, a woman both virtuous and dignified; he then turned to Souris, another actress, so named on account of her pleasing and delicate form. As to women of quality, the regent loved all those who submitted to his attentions. Mme. de Parabère, daughter of Mme. de la Vieuville, and lady-in-waiting of Mme. de Berri, who was still loved by Béringhen, whom the regent exiled, also loved the prince; Mme. d'Averne and the famous sister of Cardinal de Tencin, also, were in love with the Duke of Orleans. Although indulging himself in all pleasures indiscriminately, he opposed the attachment of his daughter for the Duke de Richelieu, and the latter, to avenge himself, determined to kidnap Souris, with whom the prince lived publicly.

In order to execute this wild project, Richelieu took a celebrated actor of the opera, a favorite of Souris, named Thévenard, into his confidence, and gave him two hundred louis to defray the expenses of a festival which was to be held in a house that the actor owned at Auteuil. Throngs of people were invited to the ball to witness the fireworks and illuminations, and La Souris was to be the queen of the affair. Richelieu arrived there in the afternoon in one of his carriages which at that time was called a phaeton; two men informed Souris that a gentleman wished to speak with her. She was lifted into the carriage and driven at full speed to Paris. The regent was neither angered nor did he resent the insult. Emelie then succeeded Souris in his affections.

However licentious, unfaithful, inconstant and capricious Souris was, she was kind and good natured and among all his mistresses, she lived for the longest time with the regent who was utterly incapable of centering his affections upon one woman for any length of time. Souris, even when she was loved by the regent, never ceased to have other liaisons. Regardless of her own fortune she gave the subject of acquiring wealth for herself never a thought, bestowing whatever wealth she acquired upon a young page of the Duke de Luxembourg, who lavished his easily acquired income on another woman. Emelie who would not accept from the regent more than a simple livelihood did not wish to relinquish her position and awaiting the time when she would lose the good wishes of the prince, as the other mistresses whom she succeeded had done, determined to renounce all pleasures and lovers. Fimarçon was Emelie's first lover. Charmed by her modesty, he left the army of the Duke de Melon and formed a liaison with her and it was he whom the prince succeeded in her affections.

Wishing one day to present her with a set of earrings worth fifteen thousand francs, Emelie, who had already received some jewels, modestly replied, that these diamonds were not made for her, that they were too beautiful. She refused them, begging the prince to keep them and give her ten thousand pounds in money instead with which to buy a house at Pantin, to which she wished to retire when she was no longer loved by him, adding, that after having enjoyed the kindness of so great a prince, no one would be worthy of succeeding him. The regent promised fidelity, embraced her tenderly and sent her twenty-five thousand pounds, instead of ten.

Emelie always very reserved, took five thousand and returned the rest saying that His Royal Majesty had made a mistake; but the regent assuring her that it was his intention to give her the whole sum, insisted that she keep it, assuring her that he felt towards her a respect far more profound than towards any other woman.

The Abbé Dubois, on his return from England, having important despatches to communicate to the regent, relative to foreign affairs which demanded an immediate reply, entered the chamber of the regent at seven o'clock in the morning, and found him with Emelie. Dubois wished to retire and await his rising; but the regent stopped him, and asked why he came so early that morning. "Emelie is discreet," added the regent; "she has an excellent intellect; she will give us good counsel." Dubois obeyed and transacted his business with the regent, who asked Emelie her opinion of what she had heard. Emelie answered so shrewdly that the regent adopting her advice, exclaimed, "Did I not tell you, Abbé, that Emelie would give us good counsel? Therefore, execute what she has decreed." Dubois, displeased at seeing state secrets confided to a mistress, forgot that his own principles and conduct were much more reprehensible than those of this courtesan.

The attachment of the regent for Emelie lasted more than six months, but Fimarçon, returning from the army at the end of 1719, sought his Emelie, and upon finding her, ill-treated her, and cruelly threatened that if she returned to the regent, he would kill her. Emelie was so terrified by his conduct, that she voluntarily went to a convent at Charenton, where he visited her. His passion and jealousy were so violent that he had the convent watched by spies so that none could approach without his knowing whom the venturous parties were, and he told the nuns who attended the turning boxes that he would have them, together with the whole house, burned, if they allowed any other than himself to speak to Emelie. He spent, to maintain this system of espionage, two hundred thousand pounds that he had won in stock-gambling. Richelieu, in league with Fimarçon, did not know which to admire most, the bounty of the regent, who for the second time allowed a mistress to be kidnapped by Fimarçon, or that of Fimarçon. He was surprised at the magnanimity of the man who had exiled Baron and other young men in love with his mistresses. The regent, however, had him arrested the next year and condemned him to one year's imprisonment at Fort L'Evêque. But the gate-keeper was bribed to allow him to go out every night to dine with his friends. He visited Richelieu and amused the company with a detailed recital of his adventures.

The best known nobles and ladies modeled their conduct on the examples of the court of the regent. Richelieu courted a large number of ladies at the same time and often times Rafe, his confidential lackey, gave him a dozen letters requesting a rendezvous for the same evening. The duke never stopped to read all these love notes, for the greater part of them, especially those from princesses, were in cipher, and took a great deal of time. He read the letter of the person whom he wished to visit and locked the others unopened in a box, leaving the task of reading them to the historians of his time, who had access to his papers. Richelieu amused himself greatly by deceiving women, and would send as if by mistake, a letter addressed to their rivals. Bitter quarrels between women resulted from this; for they were all deeply attached to this courtier. He had a way of engendering jealousy between rivals for his affection. He aroused enmity between them, purposely giving them reason to suspect his fidelity. After their quarrels, however, they still remained his friends.

It was as a result of circumstances of this nature that a duel occurred between two well known women. This was a thing unprecedented, and it absorbed the attention of the capital and especially the court of the regent. It was stated that Mme. de Polignac and Mme. de Nesle had fought a duel with pistols in the Bois de Boulogne, their place of rendezvous, that they might determine which one should have Richelieu, if indeed both were not killed. In vain he tried to dismiss Mme. de Polignac, for she was insanely devoted to him and his infidelities did not wound her; she was only disturbed by the jokes leveled at her by the duke on the occasion of her periodical returns to him as he had avoided her since 1715. Jealous of all the ladies who had succeeded her, she at length attacked Mme. de Nesle and called her into Bois de Boulogne, challenging her to come armed.

The Marchioness de Nesle determined to kill her rival. At the first meeting on the place of their rendezvous and after a preliminary salutation, these ladies, clad as Amazons, fired at each other; Mme. de Nesle fell, wounded in the breast.

Mme. de Polignac, proud of her victory, returning to her carriage, said, "Go, I will teach you to live and follow in the wake of a woman like myself. If I had the false one, I would eat her heart out after having blown her brains out." "You are avenged," replied one of Mme. de Nesle's witnesses, "and it is not fitting for you to insult the misfortune of your enemy, whom you have wounded; her valor should cause you to esteem her." "Silence, fool," she replied, " it is still less fitting for you to advice me."

Curious persons, whom this novel spectacle had attracted to the spot, approached Mme. de Nesle, who had fallen to the earth, and found her weltering in blood. They thought that she had received a mortal wound, but on a closer examination it was seen that the blood flowed from a mere scratch on her shoulder, the ball having but slightly grazed Mme. de Nesle. Recovering her senses, she thanked Heaven, saying that she had triumphed over her rival. These words gave the bystanders to understand that the affair was the result of an amorous rivalry, and they asked Mme. de Nesle if this lover were worth the trouble. "Yes, yes," said the wounded lady, "and he is worthy of having better blood than mine shed for him." They staunched the flow of blood with nettles, ground between stones and dressed the wound. They bore her from the field of battle to her carriage and when they asked who the happy person was for whom she had shed her blood she said, "He is the most amiable noble of the court; I am ready to shed my last drop of blood for him. All the ladies are laying their traps for him; but I hope that the proof which I have just given of my love will win him completely. I am under too great obligations to you," she added, "to conceal his name. It is the Duke de Richelieu; yes, the Duke de Richelieu, the eldest son of Venus and of Mars."

The next day a page of the regent, who witnessed the incident, called on him during his morning lévee to tell him the news; but the court was already aware of it; the Count de Saint-Pierre and Noie were joking about it, and asked the page to tell them all the circumstances, knowing that he had been a spectator. The company instead of sympathizing with poor De Nesle roared with laughter, when the page said that he had visited her, and dressed her wound himself and rehearsed the expressions of Mme. de Nesle, who said she would shed her blood for Richelieu. The regent at these words, replied, "*Tu veux briller, mouton de Champagne.*" The page replied that he was telling the exact truth without exaggeration. These anecdotes are causing us to unconsciously digress from the thread of our story; let us resume the same relating its incidents in chronological order.

CHAPTER X.

The man with the iron mask.—Different conjectures.—What Richelieu knew of him.

THERE was a time during the reign of the late king, when the question was asked, in every rank of society, "Who is the famous personage answering to the name of *Masque de fer?*"; but curiosity increased when Cinq-Mars, having conducted him to the Bastille, it was given out, that if this prisoner made his indentity known, he would be killed. Cinq-Mars also announced that he who should have the misfortune to discover his identity would suffer the same fate. This threat to assassinate the prisoner, as well as those anxious to fathom the secret, made such an impression that tongues were everywhere hushed so long as the late king lived. The anonymous auther of *Mémoires secrets de la cour de Perse*, published fifteen years after the death of Louis XIV., was the first one who dared to speak of the prisoner and publish any anecdote concerning him.

From that time on, greater freedom of expression manifested itself in France from day to day, both in society and in literature, and the memory of Louis XIV. gradually losing its influence, people began to discuss the mystery of this prisoner more freely; still the question is asked to-day, seventeen years after the death of Louis XIV., "Who was this prisoner with the iron mask?"

This was the question that the Duke de Richelieu in 1719 asked of the lovely princess, whom the regent loved, but by whom he was detested. He thought that he might be able to corrupt her as she did not love the regent. However, as it was thoroughly believed at that time that the regent knew the name, the history, and the causes of the imprisonment of the masked man, Richelieu, more inquisitive and bolder than any one else endeavored to extract the secret from the regent, through this princess. She was wont to rebuff the Duke of Orleans, and to show him the greatest aversion; but as he remained deeply in love with her, and at the slightest encouragement from her, granted whatever she demanded, the duke aroused the interest of this charming princess naturally curious to know the secret and induced her to assure the regent that he should be well repaid if he would permit the reading of the memoirs of the man with the iron mask.

The Duke of Orleans had never revealed any state secret; he was remarkably circumspect in this respect, for Dubois, his preceptor, had trained him to keep them inviolate.

The Duke of Orleans, whose conduct had usually been very free with his companions in pleasure, had upon certain subjects maintained the greatest reserve towards them; he had a keen sense of honor, and it was not to be supposed that he would disclose this memoir which might reveal the identity of the masked prisoner. It was known, indeed, that the young King Louis XV., during his minority, continually annoyed the regent by

The Man with the Iron Mask

trying to learn the circumstances connected with the life of this mysterious man, and that his curiosity became greater as the reserve of the Duke of Orleans increased, and that he had remarked to the king, that the duties of his office required him to maintain the most profound silence, until his majority. In like manner the attempt of the princess to ascertain the secret of the regent proved unsuccessful at first but finally as an especial favor the regent gave her the manuscript, which she sent to the Duke de Richelieu, together with a note written in cipher. We owe it to history to give here in full the contents of those papers. They are, moreover, valuable in that they prove the authenticity of our story. Whenever the princess wrote of love, she employed cipher, and she told in this note what promise she made in order to get possession of the memoir, and, on the other hand, the conditions under which the regent had submitted it. We shall not here record the details, but borrowing the modest language of the patriarchs, we may say that if Jacob was obliged to buy the daughter of Laban, whom he loved most, twice to obtain her in marriage, the regent, demanded of the princess still more than the patriarch did. Here is the note in cipher:— the historical memoir will follow.

L e u o i l a l e g r a n
2. 1. 17. 12. 9. 2. 20. 2. 1. 7. 14. 20. 10.
d s e c r e t p o u r
3. 21. 1. 11. 14. 1. 15. 16. 12. 17. 14.
l e s c a u o i r i l m a f
2. 1. 21. 11. 20. 17. 12. 9. 14. 9. 2. 8. 20. 5.

a l l u m e l   a i s s e
20. 2. 2. 17. 8. 1. 2. 20. 9. 2. 21. 1. 5.

t   r   o   i   s   f   c   i
12. 17. 15. 14 1. 15. 14. 12. 9. 21. 5. 12 9.

s   p   a   r   m   d.
21. 16. 20. 14. 8. 3.

Story of the birth and education of the unfortunate prince withdrawn from society by Cardinals Richelieu and Mazerian, and imprisoned by the order of Louis XIV.

(Written by the governor of that prince, on his death-bed).

"The unfortunate prince, whom I have taught and whose interest I have striven to protect, throughout my whole life, was born Sept. 5, 1638, at 8.30 o'clock in the evening, while the king was at supper. His brother, now reigning, was born in the morning at twelve o'clock, while the king was eating dinner; but while the birth of the king was welcomed and gaily celebrated, his brother's advent was carefully concealed; for the king being told by the midwife that the queen would bear a second child, had caused the chancellor of France, the midwife, the first almoner, the confessor of the queen, and myself to remain in her chamber, to be witnesses of what should happen and of his action in case of the birth of a second child.

"For a long time the king had been warned by sooth-sayers that his wife would bear twins; for there had come to Paris, a few days since, some shepherds who said that they had been divinely informed of this fact, and it was also said in Paris, that if the queen should bear two dauphins, as was predicted, it would be the greatest misfortune that could happen the state. The archbishop of Paris, who caused these seers to come, had them both imprisoned in Saint-Laxare when he saw that the people were excited by these predictions. This caused the king great anxiety for he feared lest disorders should arise in the state. The thing having transpired as predicted by the sooth-sayers, the cardinal to whom the king had made known this prophecy, by courier, had replied that he should take the matter under advisement; that the birth of two dauphins was not an impossible thing and that in such an event, the second should be carefully hidden, because he might in the future desire to become king, wage war on his brother, and conspire against the state.

"The king was in fearful suspense until the queen, uttering cries of pain, gave birth to a second son. We inquired for the king, who was almost overcome. Fearing that he was to be father of two dauphins, he said to M. Bishop de Meaux, whom he had asked to relieve the queen: 'Do not leave my wife until she is delivered. I have a fearful presentiment.' Thereupon he called together the Bishop de Meaux, the chancellor, M. Honorat, Perronette, the midwife and myself, and said to us in the presence of the queen, that should she bear a second child and this fact should become known we could be answerable for it with our lives, and that he willed that his birth should be a secret of state to prevent evils that might arise inasmuch as the Salic law made no statement as to the heritage of the realm in case of the birth of two elder sons of the king.

"What had been predicted happened and the queen gave birth to a second son while the king was eating his supper. The second dauphin was more delicate and more beautiful than the first and he never ceased to moan and cry, as if he already experienced regret at having entered this world wherein he was destined to endure so much suffering. The chancellor made an official report of this wonderful birth, so unique an affair in the history of France. His majesty was dissatisfied with the first report, however, and ordered it burned in our presence, whereupon he commanded the chancellor to make several reports until his majesty found one satisfactory to him, although the almoner remonstrated, claiming that the birth of the prince should not be concealed. The king replied to the remonstrance that there was a state reason for it.

"Straightway the king ordered us to sign a written pledge of secrecy; the chancellor signed first; then monsieur the almoner; then the confessor of the queen, and last of all, I signed the document. The oath was subscribed to by the surgeon and by the midwife who attended the queen, and the king attached this document to the official report, which he took away and which has never, to my knowledge, been seen since. I remember that his majesty conversed with the chancellor in regard to the formula of the oath and that he spoke for a long time about monsigneur the cardinal. After that, the midwife was charged with the care of the child last born, and although it was feared that she might say too much about this birth, she seemed to realize that if she ever spoke of it the penalty would be death; even we who were witnesses of this birth were forbidden to mention the child.

"None of us have violated the oath; for his majesty feared nothing so much as the possibility of a civil war brought about by the rival claims of these two children born at the same time. The cardinal always augmented his fear and finally was permitted to oversee the education of the child. The king also ordered us to examine the child very carefully and it was found that he had a wart above the left elbow, a yellowish spot on the right side of his neck and a smaller wart on the fleshy part of his right hip. This precaution was taken by his majesty, and rightly so, that in the event of the decease of the first born he might put the royal child, whom he was to give into our charge, in the place of the deceased. For this reason he required our signature to the official report which he caused to be sealed by a small royal seal in our presence and we signed it according to the order of his majesty. Notwithstanding the fact that shepherds had prophesied his birth, I have never heard it mentioned since. The cardinal, who took charge of this mysterious child, succeeded in concealing the fact of his existence.

"As to the childhood of this second prince, the woman, Perronnette, cared for him as her own child, while he passed as the illegitimate son of some great noble of the time, people surmising by the care which she tendered him and the money expended that he was a rich and cherished son, in spite of the fact that he was disavowed.

"When the prince grew older, monsieur, the cardinal, Mazarin, who had charge of his education, as successor to Cardinal de Richelieu, submitted him to my care and bade me instruct him as the child of a king, but in absolute secrecy. The woman, Perronnette, continued in her duties until her death and there existed between them an affection as between mother and son. The prince was educated in a house in Bourgogne with all the care due the son and brother of a king.

"I have had frequent conversations with the queen-mother during the troubles of France and her majesty seemed to fear that if the birth of this child became known, while his brother still lived, the young king, together with malcontents might make it a pretext for an insurrection, for many doctors believe that the last born of two twin children is the first to be conceived, and consequently that he is the rightful heir; though this opinion is not generally held.

"This fear, however, never went so far as to determine the queen to destroy the written proofs of his birth, for in case of the death of the young king, she was resolved to have his brother recognized. She told me often that she preserved these written proofs in her casket with great care.

"I saw to it that the unfortunate prince received as good an education as I could wish to receive myself, and the sons of avowed princes could not have received a more thorough one; all that I reproached myself for, is for having, against my desire, caused the misfortune of the prince, for when he was nineteen years of age he was possessed of a strange desire to know who his parents were, and as he saw that I was firmly resolved to preserve silence on the subject, resisting the more stubbornly when he overwhelmed me with prayers, he determined from that time on to conceal his curiosity from me and he affected to believe that he was my son, born of an illegitimate love. I often told him when we were alone and he called me 'father,' that he was mistaken; but soon I ceased to dispute this belief on his part, which he affected for the purpose of making me talk, and permitted him to believe that he was my son. In this way I checked his efforts to ascertain his own identity. Two years had passed when an unfortunate imprudence on my part, for which I shall never cease to reproach myself, revealed his identity to him. He knew that the king had recently sent messengers to me, and having carelessly left these letters from the queen and from the cardinals in my casket, he read a part and guessed the rest, afterwards confessing to me that he had taken the letter which revealed the particulars of his birth.

"I remember that a peevish and unseemly contempt took the place of his former respect and friendship for me, but I could not at first recognize the cause of this change for I had not as yet ascertained how he could have rummaged in my casket, without my knowledge. If he had accomplices whom he did not care to expose, or if he employed some other means to accomplish his purpose, he maintained absolute silence.

"One day he had the imprudence to ask me for the portraits of the late King Louis XIII. and of the reigning king. I replied that I had some very poor ones and that I was waiting for an artist to make better ones.

"This reply did not satisfy him, and was followed by a request to go to Dijon. I learned afterwards that it was to see a portrait of the king, at that place, and to visit the court, which was at Saint Jean-de-Luz and to witness the marriage of the infanta, where he might compare himself with his brother and see wherein he resembled him. I became aware of his intentions and did not leave him.

"At that time the young prince was as beautiful as Apollo. For some months a young governess of the house had greatly attracted him and by his caresses he pleased her so well that in spite of the commands enjoined on all the domestics, to give him nothing without my permission, she gave him a portrait of the king. The unfortunate prince recognized his own features in the picture as well he might, for it was a perfect likeness of himself. This discovery threw him into such a fury that he came to me and showing me a letter from Cardinal Mazarin, exclaimed, 'This is my brother and who am I! What has he stolen from me?' There ensued a scene.

"Fearing lest the prince might escape and go to the marriage of the king, I became greatly alarmed and despatched a messenger to the king informing him of the opening of my casket and asking for new instructions.

"The king sent an order by the cardinal to have us both imprisoned until further orders, and to inform him that the prisoner's presumption was the cause of our common misfortune. Together we suffered in our prison until the moment when the decree of parting from this world was pronounced by my Heavenly Judge and I cannot refrain from insuring my soul's peace nor that of my scholar by making a declaration which will designate a means of escape from the ignominous position in which he now lives, in case the king should die without children. Can even a compulsory oath force one to maintain silence concerning incredible stories that are to be transmitted to posterity?"

This is the historical memoir which the prince gave to the princess and it cannot fail to give rise to numerous interesting questions. It will be asked, in fact, "Who was this instructor of the prince? Was it Bourguignon, or simply the proprietor of a house or castle in Bourgogne? How far from Dijon was this estate? He was certainly a remarkable man, since he was at the Court of Louis XIII., enjoying the confidence of the king, of the queen, and of Cardinal de Richelieu. In fact, he was at court in the character of a favorite. Will the book of peerages of Bourgogne give us an inkling as to the identity of the person in that province who disappeared from society with an unknown lad about twenty years of age? Why was this memoir, that appeared after a century's concealment, anonymous? Was it dictated by the dying man, without being signed by him, and moreover how did it reach the outside world?" These are the questions that this memoir calls forth. It does not certify that this young prince was the same as he, who was known as the prisoner with the mask, but all these facts tallied so well with this mysterious personage, concerning whom we have recorded several anecdotes, that it seems very probable that they were identical.

Indeed the *Memoires de la cour de Perse* had scarcely been published when many men of letters began a discussion as to the probable solution of the mystery. Voltaire states many facts and yet does not reveal the secret, although he was supposed to know more of it than any one else ; Saint-Foix, Père Griffet, La Rivière, Linguet, La Grange-Chancel, the Abbè Papon, Palteau, M. Delaborde, and several other writers in different journals and especially in the *Journal de Paris*, have published anecdotes concerning him ; we shall relate those which we have reason to suppose authentic, italicizing the expressions which seem to indicate in this prisoner a great personage, and give some insight into his character.

The first author who spoke of this personage was the anonymous writer of the *Memoires de la cour de Perse;* he cites a number of definite incidents and statements, which have always been regarded as facts, but he is mistaken in believing that the masked prisoner was the Count de Vermandois. "This prisoner," said he, " was given in charge of the commandant of the Isle of Sainte-Marguerite, who had in advance received orders from Louis XIV. to let no one see him. The commandant of the Isle Sainte-Marguerite treated his prisoner with the most profound respect and served him himself, taking his meals to the door of his apartments, and taking them from the hands of the cook, none of whom ever saw the face of the prisoner. This prince took a notion one day of engraving his name on the bottom of the plate with the point of his knife. A slave, into whose hands it fell, thought that he would gain favor by carrying it to the commandant, and flattered himself that he would be rewarded; but the wretched man was deceived. He was put out of the way at once, that this secret of such great importance might be buried with him. The man with the iron mask remained several years in the castle of the Isle Sainte-Marguerite, and he was removed from there only to be transferred to the Bastille, when Louis XIV., in recognition of the fidelity of this commandant, gave him the governorship of that prison. It was indeed a matter of policy to invest him, to whom his fate had been intrusted, with supreme control over the prisoner, and it would have been contrary to all rules of prudence to give him a new confidant, who might have been less faithful and less painstaking. The precaution was taken, both at the Isle of Sainte-Marguerite and at the Bastille, to have a mask made for the prince, that he might not be exposed to the view of any one from any cause whatsoever. Several reliable persons have declared that they saw this masked prisoner, *and they all declare that he spoke to the governor as an inferior, while the latter, on the other hand, showed him the most profound respect!*

"Some days after the death of Cardinal Mazarin (says Voltaire, in *Siècle de Louis XIV.*, which is the second work in which he mentions the prisoner) an event occurred which has no precedent in history, and what is still more strange, is the fact that all historians have ignored it. An unknown prisoner, somewhat above the medium height, was sent in the greatest secrecy to the chateau of the Isle Sainte-Marguerite, in the sea of Provence. He was a young man of most noble and commanding figure. This prisoner en route wore a mask, the chin piece of which had steel hinges, thereby enabling him to eat without removing the mask. His keepers had orders to kill the prisoner if he revealed his identity. He remained on the island until a confidential officer named Cinq-Mars, governor of Pignerol, who, on receiving the governorship of the Bastille in 1690, went to the Island of Sainte-Marguerite to conduct the prisoner thither. He remained masked throughout this journey. The Marquis de Louvois visited him on the island before his transfer. This unknown man was taken to the Bastille and lodged as comfortably as possible in that castle. No wish of his was denied. He had a great fondness for linen and for laces of the finest texture. He played upon his guitar, and partook of the finest viands, while the governor rarely remained seated in his presence. An old doctor of the Bastille who had often visited this singular man, when his services were needed, said that he never had seen his face, but had often examined his tongue and other parts of his body, and could testify to the fact that the prisoner possessed a remarkable constitution, and that his skin was very dark. The sound of his voice was enough to interest one. He never complained of his condition, nor permitted any one to discover his identity. A famous surgeon, son-in-law of the doctor above mentioned, and who was in the service of Marshal de Richelieu is a witness of what I assert, and M. de Bernaville, successor of Cinq-Mars, has often confirmed it. This unknown man died in 1704, and was buried at night in the parish of St. Paul. It is a most astonishing fact that when he was sent to the Isle of Sainte-Marguerite his disappearance was not noticed in Europe. M. de Chamillard was the last minister to learn this mysterious secret. The second Marshal de la Feuillade, his son-in-law, told me that while his father-in-law lay dying, he besought him on his knees to reveal the identity of this unknown man, who was known only as 'the man with the iron mask.' Chamillard replied that it was a secret of state and that he had taken oath never to reveal it.

"The governor, himself, guarded him while he was on the Isle, and retired only after he had securely locked the door. One day the prisoner scratched his name with a knife on a silver plate and threw the plate out of the window, toward a boat moored at the foot of the tower. A fisherman, to whom the boat belonged, picked up the plate and carried it to the governor. The latter, astonished, said to the fisherman, 'Have you read what is written on this plate and has any one seen it in your hands?' 'I cannot read,' replied the fisherman, 'I have just found it; no one has seen it.' The peasant was detained until the governor assured himself that he could not read and that no one had seen the plate when he said, 'Go, you are very fortunate in not knowing how to read.' One of the witnesses of this incident, whose word is to be relied upon, still lives. (The author noted above said that the fisherman, peasant, or slave, was put to death. Can it be that this is the same tale with variations, or can it be that the masked man wrote his name on several different silver plates?)

"The author of *Siècle de Louis XIV.* (says M. de Voltaire in his book entitled *Mélanges,*) is the first reliable historian who has referred to the man with the iron mask. He was, however, mistaken as to the date of his death, fixing it in the year 1704 instead of 1703.

"He was imprisoned at Pignerol before being imprisoned in the Isle of Sainte-Marguerite and afterwards in the Bastille, always in charge of this same man, this Cinq-Mars, who witnessed his death. Père Griffet, a Jesuit, exposed the Journal of the Bastille to the public, wherein these dates are confirmed. He had ready access to this journal, for his was the delicate duty of confessing the prisoners in the Bastille. Some have said that 'the man with the iron mask' was the Duke de Beaufort; but the Duke de Beaufort was killed by the Turks in the defence of Candia in 1669, while this man was at Pignerol in 1672. Moreover, could the Duke de Beaufort be arrested while in charge of his army? How could he have been transferred to France in absolute secrecy, and why would he have been imprisoned and why forced to wear this mask?

"Others have thought that he was the Count de Vermandois, natural son of Louis XIV., who died of smallpox in 1683 while in the army, and was buried in the little city of Aire, not in Arris, a slight though unimportant error made by Père de Griffet.

"Again it has been conjectured that the Duke of Monmouth whom King James publicly executed in London in 1675 was the man with the iron mask.

"These suppositions being inconsistent, it remains for us to discover who this prisoner was, at what age he died, and under what name he was buried. *It is evident that if he were not permitted to enter the court of the Bastille, and was prohibited from speaking to his doctor except when covered with a mask, this was from fear lest his features might reveal a dangerous resemblance to some public man.* He was permitted to show his tongue but *never* his face. As to his age, he himself said to the apothecary of the Bastille, some days before his death, that *he believed that he was sixty years of age;* and Marsoban, surgeon of Marshal de Richelieu and afterwards of the Duke of Orleans, the son-in-law of this apothecary has often referred to this statement. Again, why give him an Italian name? He was always called Marchiali. He who wrote this article may know the reason for this better than Père Griffet. He says no more."

La Grange-Chancel is the third historian who has referred to the prisoner. Himself imprisoned in the Isle of Sainte-Marguerite some time after the transfer of the masked man to the Bastille, he succeeded in ascertaining some facts.

"My sojourn in the Isle of Sainte-Marguerite," said La Grange-Chancel, "where, when I arrived, the detention of the *Masque de fer* was no longer a secret of state, furnished me with many details which a historian more careful in his researches than M. de Voltaire could have learned had he taken the pains to investigate. This extraordinary event which he places in 1661, some months after the death of Cardinal Mazarin, did not transpire until 1669, eight years after the death of His Eminence. M. de la Mothe-Guerin, who was commandant in these Islands when I was detained there, assured me that the prisoner was the Duke de Beaufort, who was said to have been killed at the siege of Candia, and whose body, according to the report, could not be found. He also told me that the Cinq-Mars, who obtained the governorship of these Islands after leaving Pignerol, felt a great respect for this prisoner; that he always served him himself, using silver plates, and that he often brought him very expensive garments. He told me, moreover, that when obliged to procure the services of doctors or surgeons the prisoner was forced on pain of death to appear in their presence, masked, and that when alone, he amused himself by pulling hairs from his beard, with a very delicate pair of pincers. I saw the pair which he was in the habit of using and which are in the possession of M. de Beaumauier, nephew of Cinq-Mars and lieutenant of an independent company enlisted to guard prisoners. Several persons told me that when Cinq-Mars assumed his duties at the Bastille, to which place he had brought his prisoner, the latter, wearing his iron mask, was heard to say to his conductor: 'Has the king designs against my life?' 'No, my prince,' replied

Cinq-Mars, 'your life is safe. Simply permit me to lead you.'

"I have learned, moreover, from a man by the name of Dubuisson, cashier of the famous Samuel Bernard, who, after having passed some years in the Bastille, was taken to the Isle of Sainte-Marguerite, that while in a certain cell with some other prisoners, the unknown prisoner occupied a cell exactly beneath him and by means of the tiling of the chimney they could communicate with one another, but as they had repeatedly asked him why he kept his name and his adventures secret, he at last declared that if he gave information about himself it would cost him his life, as well as the life of those to whom he revealed his secret.

"However that may be, to-day the name and rightful claims of this political victim are no longer secrets in which the state is interested, and I thought by informing the public of all that came under my observation in regard to him, to stop the fallacious ideas that many persons have formed, basing their belief upon the statement of an author who has gained for himself a great reputation, dealing with the mysterious, giving an air of genuineness to the efforts of his imagination. We see this even in his 'Life of Charles XII.'"

The Abbé Papon, in his *Voyage en Provence*, thus speaks of the man of the iron mask:—

"The famous prisoner with the iron mask, whose true name doubtless will never be known, was transferred to the Isle of Sainte-Marguerite towards the end of the last century. There were but a few persons in his service who had the privilege of speaking with him. One day M. de Cinq-Mars was holding a conversation with him just outside of his cell in a sort of corridor, from whence he could see people that might approach. The son of one of his friends came and walked towards the place where he heard talking; the governor hearing his approach suddenly closed the cell door, hastily ran to meet the young man and anxiously asked him if he had heard anything of the conversation. After satisfying himself that he had not, he bade him leave the prison; that very day wrote to his friend that the adventure had come very near costing his son dearly and that he had sent him away to avoid a repetition of the imprudence.

"Lead by curiosity I entered the cell of this unfortunate prisoner Feb. 2, 1788; it was lighted by a single window facing the north, and cut in a thick wall; which was guarded by three iron bars placed at equal distances from each other.

"This window faced the sea. I found in the citadel an officer of an independent company, about seventy-nine years old, who told me that his father, who served in the same company, had often told him that a barber of his acquaintance had seen something white floating on the water under the prisoner's window. He straightway procured and carried to M. de Cinq-Mars what proved to be a very fine shirt, carelessly folded, all over which the prisoner had written.

"M. de Cinq-Mars, after having unfolded it and read a few lines, anxiously asked the barber if he had not had the curiosity to read it. The latter protested several times that he had read nothing; he was found dead in his bed, however, two days afterwards. This incident related by the officer to his father and the almoner of the court at that time, he regarded as incontestable. The following incident seems equally authentic and is vouched for by witnesses whom I found on the scene, and in the monastery of Lerins, where tradition has preserved it.

"It was thought desirous to procure a female companion for the prisoner; a woman from the village of Mongin presented herself, believing that this would be a means of gaining a livelihood for herself and children; but when she was told that she would have to give up for all time her relations to them and have no dealing with any other men thereafter, she refused to be imprisoned with one whose friendship would cost her so dearly. Another interesting detail in connection with this mysterious affair is that two sentinels had been placed at the extreme ends of the fort on the seaward side and that they had orders to fire upon any boat approaching beyond a certain point.

"The woman who served the prisoner died on the Island of Sainte-Marguerite. A brother of the officer of whom I have just spoken, and who was to a certain extent the confidant of M. de Cinq-Mars, often told his son how at midnight he went for the body in the prison; and how he bore it on his shoulders to a place of burial, thinking it to be the prisoner himself who had died, but discovering afterwards that it was the body of the women who served him. It was at this time that another was sought to take her place."

It is well known that Cinq-Mars transferred the prisoner to the Bastille in 1698 stopping over at his country place in Palteau. Freron, for the purpose of contradicting the statements made by Voltaire who had written so voluminously on this subject, asked the master of Palteau for anecdotes and he kindly replied in the following letter, which was inserted in the *l'Annee littéraire* in the month of June, 1768.

"Since it is apparent by the letter of M. de Saint-Foix, an extract from which has just been printed, that the man with the iron mask still continues to exercise the imagination of our writers, I am going to impart to you all that I know concerning this prisoner. He was known in the Isle of Sainte-Marguerite and the Bastille only by the name of La Tour. The governor and the other officers had great respect for him, and he was in the habit of receiving every attention from them. He often walked out, always wearing the mask on his face. Only since the *Siècle de Louis XIV.*, written by M. de Voltaire made its appearance, have I heard it said that this mask was of iron and had springs. Perhaps this circumstance had been forgotten by my informants; but he never wore this mask except when taking exercise out of doors or when obliged to appear in the presence of some stranger.

"M. de Blainvilliers, an infantry officer, who enjoyed the privilege of visiting M. de Cinq-Mars, governor of the Isle of Sainte-Marguerite and later of the Bastille, told me several times that the fate of this La Tour had greatly excited his curiosity and to satisfy it he had assumed the uniform and arms of a soldier, who was to stand guard over him in a hall under the windows of the cell occupied by this prisoner at Sainte-Marguerite. He told me that he obtained a good view of him; that he wore no mask; was of a pale complexion, tall and well-knit and that he had gray hairs although he was in the prime of life. He had passed the greater part of that night walking back and forth in his room; Blainvilliers added that he always dressed in brown and that he was given fine linen and many books to read. He also informed me that the governor and officers remained standing and uncovered in his presence, unless he beckoned them to cover themselves and be seated; that they frequently went to while away the time with him and eat with him.

"In 1698 M. de Cinq-Mars passed from the governorship of the Isle of Sainte-Marguerite to that of the Bastille. On coming to take possession he passed several days with his prisoner at his country residence of Palteau; the man with the iron mask arrived in a litter which preceded that of M. de Cinq-Mars; he was escorted by several cavalrymen. The peasants went to pay homage to their master. M. de Cinq-Mars ate with his prisoner whose back was turned toward the window of the dining room opening into the court. The peasants whom I questioned could not see whether he ate with his mask or not, but they very readily saw that M. de Cinq-Mars who sat opposite him at the table had two pistols beside his plate. They were served by a single valet, who went for the dishes that were brought into the antechamber, alway closing, carefully, the door of the dining room. When the prisoner crossed the court he wore a black mask on his face. The peasants remarked that they saw his teeth and his lips; that he was tall and his hair gray. M. de Cinq-Mars occupied a bed which had been prepared for him near that of the man of the iron mask. M. de Blainvilliers told me that after his death in 1704 he was secretly buried at Saint Paul and that certain chemicals had been put into his coffin to consume the body."

Having arrived at the Bastille, Du Jonca, lieutenant of the king, registered the arrival of the masked man as follows, in the books of the prison, and it was Père Griffet, a Jesuit, that first published the two scraps of information taken from the archives of the castle, whence no paper ever came to light; but he was confessor of the Bastille and the Jesuits and governor doubtless had good reasons for publishing these anecdotes. "Tuesday, September 8, 1698," says De Jonca, "at three o'clock in the afternoon, M. de Cinq-Mars, the governor of the Bastille, made his first appearance here, coming from the Isle of Sainte-Marguerite and Saint-Honorat, and bringing with him in his litter an old prisoner from Pignerol. The name of this prisoner is not given and he was compelled to remain masked and placed in the tower of Basiniere, awaiting nightfall, and I, myself, about nine o'clock in the evening, led him to the third cell of the tower of Bertaudière which cell I had been ordered by M. de Cinq-Mars, to furnish completely before his arrival. Accompanying him to the aforesaid room, I was attended by M. Rosarges, whom M. de Cinq-Mars had brought for the purpose of serving and caring for the prisoner."

Other anecdotes, dealing with this interesting character were published by M. Linguet, who, long detained at the Bastille, had succeeded in obtaining some information from the older attendants of the castle; he gave his notes to M. de la Borde, which were published as follows in a small work devoted to the known facts concerning the man with the mask.

"Firstly, the prisoner wore a velvet, and not an iron mask, at least, during the time he remained at the Bastille.

"Secondly the governor himself always served him.

"When he went to mass, he was expressly forbidden to speak or to show his face; the order had been given to the veterans to fire upon him if he disclosed his identity; their guns were loaded; and as a matter of fact, he was very careful to remain apart and maintain absolute silence.

"When he died they burned all the furniture he had used. They tore up the flooring of his room, they ripped off the ceiling and carefully examined every nook and corner that might conceal a bit of paper or a piece of linen; in short, they took every precaution to destroy whatever might lead to an exposure of his identity. M. Linguet assured me that there were yet at the Bastille, men who had learned these facts from their fathers who had been eye witnesses."

This unfortunate prisoner after a long martyrdom finally died in 1703 at the Bastille, after being confined there five years and two months: and the same person who registered his arrival, recorded his death in the prisoners' books as follows:—

"Monday, Nov. 19, 1703. The unknown prisoner, always wearing a velvet mask, whom M. de Cinq-Mars brought with him from the Island of Sainte-Marguerite, and whom he had been guarding for a long time, took ill last evening when returning from mass. To-day he died, after a short illness. M. Guitaut, our almoner confessed him last night when suddenly overtaken by death he could not receive Extreme Unction and our almoner exhorted him a moment before he died. He was buried the 20th of Nov. at four o'clock in the afternoon in the cemetery of Saint Paul. The expense of his burial was an amount of forty pounds."

His name and age were concealed from the priests of the parish and the archives describing the events of that day speak of his burial in these terms, which we take from the registers:—

"In the year 1703, Nov. 19th, Marchialy, some forty-five years of age died in the Bastille. His body was buried in the cemetery of Saint Paul, the 20th, inst., in the presence of M. Rosarges, major and of M. Reilh, surgeon-major, of the Bastille, who have signed 'ROSARGES, REILH.'"

It is well known that after his death orders were given to burn everything that he had touched, such as linen, coats, mattresses, bed-clothing, covers and even the doors of his prison, the bed-steads and his chairs. His silver-service was melted, his room scraped, and the walls of the cell in which he lodged were whitened. They took the extreme precautions of taking up the tiling for fear lest he might have hidden some note that might betray his identity.

All these papers and notes, having been subjected to careful examination and criticism, lead us to suppose that he was a man of great importance; that the habitual care exercised to prevent him from showing his face under pain of death demonstrate the danger that might have ensued in such an event; that one look at his features would reveal the identity; that he himself was desirous of making himself known rather than auxious to escape detection; that no prince having disappeared from France at the time of Mazarin's death the masked man must be an important personage, yet unknown at that time, and that the royal house must have had great interest at stake, in keeping his name, adventures, and condition concealed, for the order had been given to kill him if he revealed himself.

Another fact to be observed from the examination of all this literature is that wherever this unfortunate man was, whether in the Isle de Provence, or traveling, or at Paris, he was always ordered to conceal his face.

Therefore, it is reasonable to presume that the sight of his face in any place in France would have revealed some secret of the court.

Moreover, we must consider that his face was concealed from the time of the death of Mazarin up to the time of his own death, which occurred at the beginning of this century, and that the government carried their precautions so far as to have his head cut off before interment.

His face, therefore, would have been, if exposed, recognizable from one end of France to the other during a period of fifty years.

There must have been for a half century a face well known in every department of France that resembled that of the prisoner.

Now, whose face was this if it were not that of Louis XIV., his twin-brother? Is it not possible that the resemblance between these faces made the revelation of this secret of state so much to be dreaded? If there is, henceforth, any doubt on the subject it surely cannot be based upon the cruel orders given to the governors of the prisons of state to assassinate in cold blood such a prince if he should reveal the secret. This ferociousness is not at all compatible with what we know of the character of Louis XIV., who was a good man. All those who know anything of the prisoner, however, assure us that this order was given.

Louis XV. proved himself much more humane than Louis XIV. On attaining his majority he would have freed the masked prince had he been alive at that time. He often questioned the regent for the purpose of ascertaining the history of the prisoner. *Yet the regent always replied that his majesty could not be acquainted with the facts until he attained his majority.* The day before he was to be crowned, the king again asking if the secret was to remain a secret of state, the regent replied in the presence of a great number of noblemen, "Yes, sire, should I reveal the secret to-day I would fail in my duty, but to-morrow I shall be obliged to answer the questions that it pleases your majesty to put to me."

The next day the king, in the presence of the lords of the court taking the prince aside for the purpose of ascertaining the secret, saw the Duke of Orleans arouse the feelings of the young monarch. The courtiers could hear nothing of the conversation, but the king said in an audible tone on leaving the Duke of Orleans, "Well, if he were alive to-day I would give him his liberty."

Louis XV. was more faithful in keeping the secret than the Duke of Orleans; yet when Père Griffet, the Jesuit, and Saint-Foix discussed in their well known writings the circumstances of the secret, Louis XV. said in the presence of several courtiers, "*Let them dispute; no one has yet told the truth concerning the iron mask.*" The king had in his possession at that time the book written by Père Griffet.

It is well known that the dauphin, father of Louis XVI., often asked the late king to tell him who this famous prisoner was. "It is well for you not to know," answered the king, his father, "it would cause you too much pain."

It is also well known that M. de Laborde, first chamberlain of Louis XV., with whom that prince often discussed different historical and literary subjects, one day mentioned some new anecdote concerning the man with the iron mask. "You would gladly have me tell you something in regard to him," said that prince, "you shall know no more than the rest, but you may rest assured that the imprisonment of this unfortunate man has never wronged any one of the court, and he never had wife nor children."

Louis XV. had maintained the same reserve toward Mme. de Pompadour and his other mistresses, all equally anxious to ascertain from him the true facts concerning this mysterious person; they sought in vain to extract the secret from him, and he finally gave orders forbidding every one to mention it to him.

It is evident that the prisoner's taste for fine linen, which the wife of the governor of the fort of the Isle of Sainte-Marguerite was ordered to procure for him, was the necessary result of his sedentary life. The hours passed in the open air, the ordinary activities of his body, the exercise of all his faculties, had not obviated that excessive sensitiveness that is common to monks, to young men brought up in luxury, or to over-delicate women. The blood, in action, circulates to the very extremities of the body, and the skin which incloses it is vivified thereby. On the other hand, persons accustomed to travel, or to violent exercise, men engaged in campaigns, or in exacting toil, are less sensitive to contact with external objects. We need not, therefore, be surprised, too, that this prince, imprisoned since early youth, and knowing hardly the use of his feet, and unacquainted with violent exercise of any sort, had an extremely delicate skin.

These are the only facts known concerning this mysterious man; the author of this work is desirous of having every possible investigation made to discover his name and of having every place containing the archives of the official records of the birth of Louis XIV. examined. It would be well to examine the royal library and the chamber of records; for it is certain that these anecdotes, which have lately come to light, well deserve the attention of learned men and historians. If their discoveries confirm the fact that this prisoner was really a twin brother of Louis XIV., they will render the memory of this interesting prisoner, so long the object of general curiosity, more dear to every Frenchman and will dishonor more than ever the arbitrary orders of ministers and tyrants.

As long as Marshal de Richelieu lived he was very reserved as to the secret of "the man of the iron mask," whose imprisonment also dishonored the memory of Cardinal de Richelieu, his great uncle. The Abbot Soulavie one day asked him for a few moments' conversation concerning the prisoner and said to him, "You had the kindness, marshall, to send me some very curious papers relative to the history of your times and you have told me things so secret that I must ask you the favor of a more confidential statement as to the real truth concerning the *Masque de Fer*. It would be very interesting to leave to posterity the knowledge of this great secret in your Memoirs. Louis XIV. passed away long ago; Louis XV. has been dead ten years. Our king is so kind, so tolerant and so merciful that under his reign, we are enjoying full freedom of the press. The generations of the princes, who were interested in maintaining the secret, have passed and what has the government to-day to fear in revelation of events that happened a century ago? Your familiarity with the favorites of the late king, always very anxious to know every secret and with all the old court, which was extremely eager to ascertain the truth in regard to this mysterious prisoner, must have revealed the truth to you. You, yourself, told Voltaire about it, yet imposed secrecy upon him. Is it not true, marshall, that this prisoner was the elder brother of Louis XIV., born without the knowledge of Louis XIII?" The marshal appeared very much embarrassed at these questions; he did not wish to explain himself, neither did he wish to deny me a reply. He acknowledged that this great person was neither the elder brother of Louis XIV. nor the Duke of Montmouth, nor the Count de Vermandois, nor the Duke de Beaufort, as many of those writers have claimed. Like Louis XV., he called all writings idle fancies; but he added that the authors had, for the most part, reported anecdotes that were quite authentic; he said that it was true that an order had been given to despatch the prisoner if he made himself known. Lastly, the marshal concluded this short interview by confessing that he knew the secret of state and these were his words: "All that I can tell you in regard to this subject, M. L'Abbé, is that the prisoner was not so interesting at his death, nor at the beginning of the century when he was very old, as he was at the beginning of the reign of Louis XIV., by whom he was imprisoned for important state reasons."

This was the reply of Marshal de Richelieu; the anecdote was immediately written by Abbé Soulavie in his presence and given to Richelieu for his perusal. Richelieu asked him to correct some expressions and as the

Abbé Soulavie entreated him to add further observations which without actually disclosing the secret, yet would satisfy the curiosity of all France, the marshal replied : " Read what M. de Voltaire published last, concerning the ' man with the iron mask,' especially the last words, and reflect upon them."

CHAPTER XI.

The conspiracy of Cellamare.—Richelieu imprisoned in the Bastille for the third time.—The price of his freedom.

THE Duke of Orleans having ruined the house of the legitimated princes, Mme. du Maine, full of resentment, determined upon revenge, and allied herself with his enemies. The Jesuits were embittered against this prince; she leagued herself with their chiefs; Count de Laval a young lord full of activity, genius and ambition, was discontented; she associated herself with him.

The Court of Spain, for a long time jealous of the absolute power of the regent and always secretly agitated because of the former ambition of this prince, who had formerly cast eager glances on the crown of Phillip V., was furious on receipt of the news of the quadruple alliance, which deprived the Spanish branch of the French crown in case of the death of Louis XV. Mme. du Maine laid a plot and interested all the legitimated children of Louis XIV., of both sexes, with the exception of the Count of Toulouse, who did not care to interfere in the intrigue. As to Mme. of Orleans she abandoned the interest of her husband in a most cowardly manner, to ally herself with the faction of the legitimated princes, and this powerful confederacy, reinforced by all the malcontents that could be enlisted, began to hold secret nightly meetings at Sceaux, the home of the Duchess du Maine.

First they were embarrassed at the suggestion of plotting against the prince. They formed plans and conspiracies which they resolved to conceal, under the veil of pretended public weal. They discussed the advisability of kidnapping him, of convoking the states-general, of reforming the state, of extinguishing the debt of the late king, and of electing a new regent in the national assembly. Thus the Duchess du Maine, full of resentment and anger, formed plots and conspiracies with the Cardinal Polignac against the Duke of Orleans and the despotic power of his regency.

On account of his youth, his spirit of adventure and restless character the Duke de Richelieu inspired Cardinal Alberoni with a desire to inveigle him into the conspiracy against the regent. The conspiracy at that time was poorly managed by Spain and the Duchess du Maine. It is certain that the duke received letters which compromised him. As the result he was imprisoned in the Bastille for the third time.

Alberoni, at that time the all powerful minister in Spain, was filled with sublime ideas and plans and if they could not be executed it was only by reason of their magnitude and extent. He had, moreover, great genius, great erudition and the observers of his operations and of his policy were astonished that while occupying the position of a simple country curate without apparent means for acquiring knowledge, he had, nevertheless, come into the possession of profound knowledge and learning. He knew perfectly every detail of the administration of the late King Louis XIV. and of the old constitution of the monarchy. He said that no good deed had been performed in Europe for thirty years, nor in France for a century. Our National Assembly presided over by the sovereign, discussing with them subjects of finance and legislature, seemed to him preferable to the privy councils of the king with his ministers. He knew that Louis XIV. had established imposts in his realm in an illegal and arbitrary manner and in violation of the laws of the nation and he saw in the clergy of France and in the departments, the remnants of our ancient privileges fallen into disuse. Full of these ideas, he stated that the taxes could never pay the national debt and that the states-general had the sole right of providing for their security and for their payment. It was said that the king alone had the right to name a regent in France, as well as in Spain, and that this power was shared by the king and the national assembly; he claimed that parliament not having maintained the will of the king, could not, in consequence, give the regency to the Duke of Orleans and that the national assembly alone could grant it and recognize it, when a prince, such as the king of Spain, called by the laws of the state to that dignity, had made no provision for the same; and he concluded that the regency belonged to the King of Spain in view of his status as next of kin to the king.

Moreover, Alberoni saw, in the triple and quadruple alliance, treaties very burdensome to Spain and he desired to have the states-general of France annul them, and put the maxims of the ancient court into operation.

Again by the same right and in case of the death of Louis XV., which was at any moment to be expected on account of his ill-health, he wished them to assure his succession to one of the sons of King Phillip thereby depriving the Duke of Orleans of it. But in order to succeed in this plan it would be necessary to kidnap this prince, establish him in a place of safety, not in France, but in Madrid under the power of the King of Spain. It would be necessary to convoke the states-general in France and treat with it concerning the succession and the government of state and even make use of the discontent of the partisans, if that were possible, in order to forward this great plan.

"You will be the benefactor of your country," said Alberoni to the Duke de Richelieu, in a letter which he wrote on this subject, "you will be the benefactor of your country if you devote your energies to this great revolution; you will restore to your country her ancient glory and splendor. Crushed by taxes, overburdened with an enormous debt, it cannot but succumb to such a burden; the assembled nation alone can deliberate and choose the means to pay this debt." Afterwards Alberoni asked the Duke de Richelieu in the name of the King of Spain to facilitate the capture of the city of Bayonne, promising him the special protection of the king and of the queen and a very great promotion.

Alberoni gave this letter into the keeping of an officer who was to deliver it together with several others in France, but they were intercepted, given to Dubois, and the officer was arrested. In order to expose the intrigues of Richelieu, d'Argenson, the former lieutenant of police, and a man skillful in the artifices of espionage sent him a Neapolitan by the name of Marin, who spoke Spanish fluently and who moreover resembled a foreigner. He gave him the original letters intercepted from Alberoni, Dubois having first taken the precaution of carefully resealing them. This Marin first made him secret offers; he spoke to him of Spain and of the schemes that were to be carried out; he besought him on behalf of King Phillip, to aid the foreign troops to gain possession of Bayonne, the frontier city occupied by his regiment. He told him that he was popular with the soldiers; that all his officers were devoted to him and that it would be an easy matter for him to win over his intimate friend Du Saillant, the colonel of another regiment that was in garrison at Bayonne. He added that he knew his attachment for this Corydon and their tender feelings. He renewed the promise of a prospective promotion which had already been made; this was waiting in the regiment of the French guards in command of Grammond: finally he ended his insidious interview by rehearsing the contents of the letter which had been given to him, knowing well that the seal was intact. Marin disappeared and left Richelieu to reflect on these propositions.

The regent, being informed of these efforts, was not slow in speaking of them at the Palais-Royal. Mlle. de Valois sent him at once Mme. Pichet, her chambermaid, who gave him the following letter. We give it here in cipher as a historical monument of that time.

Some people erroneously believe that Mlle. de Valois had intrigued with Richelieu against her father. This is her explanation; half was written in cipher, the rest has been deciphered.

Comme vous m'avez assuré qu'il ne pouvait
y a v o i r e p r e u v e
9 20 17 12 9 14

In a subsequent note Mlle. de Valois again warned Richelieu that M. le Duc of Orleans was saying quite publicly that he had in his possession original documents, which would soon prove to him that a number of conspiracies had been planned against him. This information from Mlle. de Valois gave him to understand that he had been deceived by Marin, and he was awaiting imprisonment in the Bastille when a young lady, who saw the regent and who was intimate with Richelieu, warned him of what was in store for him.

Richelieu meditated on his destiny which for the third time condemned him to re-enter that infernal dwelling, when on the 29th of March, Dubois sent Duchevron, lieutenant of police, at ten o'clock in the morning to his home. Duchevron was followed by twelve archers. This meant that he was to be arrested as a common felon; it also gave the same impression to the whole peerage, who complained of it to the regent that the Abbé Dubois, in charge of his expedition, was not capable of acting with the respect due to the dignity of a peer of France. Rafé, the confidential lackey of the duke, and a charming young man of his age, was permitted to follow him to the Bastille and (as the Bastille was full of prisoners, or perhaps as the regent was full of jealousy and anger towards Richelieu, whom he had deprived of all his mistresses and at that very time boasted of one whom the prince loved desperately), the prisoners were thrown into a sort of octagonal dungeon, without light, cut off from all communication with the outside air, except through a narrow and longitudinal hole which is frequently seen in prisons.

This terrible cell was so damp, that on entering it a musty, almost unbearable odor was noticeable. Not even the stones of the prison could keep out this dampness and their garments, after a few hours, were permeated with the exhalations from the walls and the air of the pent up place. Moreover they found neither table, nor bed, nor books, nor furniture and when they asked for them they were informed that the Bastille, being full of prisoners, they could not get any more furniture. This inhuman treatment, worthy of a barbarian, became known to the public; and the regent, in order to exculpate himself, claimed that he had letters from Alberoni addressed to Richelieu, three of which were signed by that cardinal. It was customary at the epoch in which these Memoirs appeared to exaggerate the picture of the horrors of the Bastille. Neither Mlle. de Louney, nor Marmontel, nor Demouriez ever depicted it in such sombre colors.

This imprisonment of Richelieu threw Mlle. Charolais into the greatest consternation. She, as well as the other princess, the daughter of the regent, was still in love with him. They were madly jealous of one another and had become enemies, but when they learned that he was a prisoner in the Bastille, they joined hands in their endeavors to save him, the object of their love. The regent was very much annoyed and let it be known that Richelieu was to be condemned as a traitor against the state, that the probability of inflicting capital punishment on him was already under consideration, though doubtless he did not intend to go so far. It was rather his intention to mollify his mistresses by according them his pardon, after a conviction of a capital crime.

As the regent's threats were of a most alarming character the two princesses determined upon a united effort to save Richelieu, and Mlle. de Charolais promised her cousin that she would see him no more if she obtained his deliverance from the regent, her father. By this means she endeavored to incite her cousin to activity in his behalf.

The princess then commenced to fall out with the regent who was imprisoning her friend so cruelly, asking him haughtily for his freedom, publicly and in a tone of despair. She even threatened to commit a desperate act of folly, if he were not soon delivered from prison. The regent, seeing the princess in despair and fearing sensational scenes, recalled to her mind all the kindnesses he had shown the duke, all his favors to him and the duke's ingratitude; he told her that instead of having made a grateful friend he had found a cruel enemy, who had determined on his ruin, and who desired to rob him of not only his liberty but also of the regency, for the purpose of calling his enemy the King of Spain to France. He reproached the princess with conspiring with such a man and with betraying her father, adding that the treason of Richelieu was worthy of death, and insisted that he should be tried. The princess, terrified, from that time on held herself in the greatest reserve toward the regent that she might obtain pardon for her lover, if he should indeed be condemned to death.

However, Mlle. de Valois was allowed to visit him in his dungeon; she went there to weep with Richelieu, to show her tenderness for him, and to promise him that she would never consent to marry the Duke de Modena and that she would never leave for Italy until she had obtained his freedom. She knew that Mlle. de Charolais had bribed the officers of the Bastille during the duke's imprisonment of 1716 and had thereby gained access to his cell. Like her cousin, Mlle. de Valois sacrificed two hundred thousand pounds to corrupt the guards and she plotted with Mlle. de Charolais to that end, using methods with which the latter was familiar through her previous attempts at bribery. These two princesses came in the evening silently, brought candles, a tinder-box, bon-bons, and money to be prepared for emergency. Richelieu rehearsed with them what reply he should make to the insidious examinations of Le Blanc and of d'Argenson. Love, ingenuity and shrewdness came to his aid and enabled him to evade the insidious questions of d'Argenson and to combat his false arguments.

The regent did not yield to the prayers of his daughter, nor to the demands of the cardinal, archbishop of Paris, until a lapse of six months, when he was told that Richelieu would probably die of dysentery if kept in the Bastille. This event would merely bring accusations against the regent, charging him with cruelty, since he had nothing but indifferent circumstantial evidence against Richeleiu, and no strong proofs of his guilt. The regent yielded and allowed Richelieu to come out of the prison on condition that the Cardinal and Duchess de Richelieu, his mother-in-law, should take him from the prison and watch over him and that they should care for him at Conflans until he was in a condition that would justify his removal to Richelieu, where he should remain until further orders. The style of *lettres de cachet* may interest the curious; we present a sample to the reader.

" My cousin, having judged it fitting, according to the advice of my uncle, Duke of Orleans, permits you to leave my castle of the Bastille, where you are detained according to my orders. I am giving the necessary orders to the governor of the aforesaid castle, and I am at the same time writing you this letter to inform you that on leaving my aforesaid castle of the Bastille, you are to betake yourself at once without delay to that of Conflans near Charenton, in which it is my intention that you shall remain thenceforth without leaving it under any pretext whatever, until the receipt of new orders from me, and not doubting that you will conform to my will in this matter, I shall not prolong this letter, but pray God that He may preserve you in His holy and worthy keeping." Signed LOUIS, and lower down, LEBLANC.

This was consummated on the 30th of August, 1719, and as the illness was feigned, Richelieu passed the fifteen days at Conflans receiving his friends by day and going to thank them at night, scaling the walls of the garden of Conflans, both going and returning; this fact impelled the regent, ten days later, to send him four leagues further away, giving the order in another *lettre de cachet* which was sent and was couched in as kindly and polite terms as the first one. He had, however, some good reasons for couching these documents in courteous language for Richelieu had already obtained some of them from his mistresses.

" My cousin having judged it proper for private reasons that you betake yourself immediately to my Villa of Saint-Germain in Laye, I write you this letter on the advice of my uncle, the Duke of Orleans, regent, to inform you that immediately on receipt of it, you are to leave the place in which you shall have received it and betake yourself by the shortest and most direct road to the aforesaid Villa of Saint-Germain in Laye, where it is my will that you shall remain without leaving, until new orders from me, finding it well, however, that you may see during the time you remain there such ladies as you may deem proper, and that you may hunt and sally forth in the surrounding country without, however, remaining away over night from the aforesaid Villa, under any pretext whatsoever. Moreover have charged Dulibois, lieutenant colonel of dragoons, to accompany you and to remain with you until I recall him, and not doubting that you will conform to my will, I shall not continue this letter but pray God that He may preserve you, my cousin, in His holy and worthy keeping. Given at Paris, September 10, 1719." Signed LOUIS, and further down, LEBLANC.

This Dulibois was the very person to allow Richelieu to continue his excursions and nightly promenades freely. This good military man, sixty years of age, retired early; the duke dined him well and had him drink freely and when he began to snore, or seemed to, Richelieu jumped out of bed where he had pretended to retire. Horses were ready and with light and fleet phaetons he went, as usual, to show his gratitude to his two benefactresses, but especially to the daughter of the regent.

He learned what had been done to deliver him from prison, he learned of the complaisance of Mlle. de Valois, who to obtain his liberation had consented to pass her life at Modena in a little corner of Italy and to exile herself, so to speak, that the duke might not be exiled. And all this she was willing to endure notwithstanding her love for the pleasures of the court of the regent.

She kept her word, married the Duke of Modena, lived happily with him without, however, forgetting Richelieu. Nor indeed did he ever forget her. We shall see in the succeeding chapter how they met again at Modena.

CHAPTER XII.

Richelieu at Modena, under the disguise of a book-colporteur.—His interviews with the duchess.—He is surprised by the duke, but throws him off the scent.—His return to Paris.—Reception and dress at the French Academy.—Details of gallantry.

HE received several letters from Modena full of love and pledges that would never be forgotten; in them she informed him that her husband knew all about their former relation and that therefore he must be most circumspect. She begged him to come to see her, but only in disguise. Richelieu, who was fond of overcoming difficulties and for whom every kind of obstacle was but a new goad to activity, immediately determined to go to Modena. He left with a retinue, assumed an alias and reached Italy. The man who accompanied him was provided with pamphlets and books of that epoch.

He put up at an inn in Modena under the name of Gasparini, and passed for a book-seller, as did his confidant, La Fosse, who had changed his name to that of Romano. The first day they wandered about the city and gave the impression in the tavern that they were merchants who made their living by dealing in second-hand books.

They did not delay their visit to the palace of the princess, who had been informed of the arrival of the duke. He was to station himself in her path as she was going to mass. Romano and Gasparini exposed their books for sale; the curious public gathered around them. Gasparina watches for the moment when the princess comes from her palace. She appears, he exposes his merchandise to view and takes care that the importunate ones, who might prevent the princess from seeing him are kept away. She stops a moment near the pseudo merchants, examines their books, and continues her journey to the chapel.

Richelieu thought that he had not been recognized; he had presented some books to the princess, however, and had spoken to her and was now in despair because she had not paid any attention to him. This farce only pleased him in so far as he thought that it might procure him an interview. He had undertaken this voyage he said to bless the Duke of Modena with an heir. He hoped that he would be more happy on the return of the princess and he continued to retail his merchandise, which Romano took great pleasure in seeing sold.

Mme. de Modena returned to the merchants, examined their books with great attention, fixed her eyes on the duke, spoke to Romano, asked him what nationality he was, if he had a good supply of books, then addressing Richelieu asked him to procure a certain book for her. Richelieu assured her that it was at his tavern and that she should have it in a moment. The princess seemed satisfied and gave orders for the admission of this bookdealer to her apartment in an hour.

The duke, enchanted at the rendezvous given, promptly left his itinerant shop and went to his tavern to await the moment of happiness. It was eight months since he had seen Mme. de Modena and long absence made his pleasure of seeing her more keen. Moreover the pleasure in deceiving a jealous prince was a source of great enjoyment to him.

He betook himself to the palace of the princess, was introduced, and found himself alone with the woman who adored him. Nothing can depict the joy which she had in seeing him. The rôle that he assumed in order that he might meet her was greatly amusing to her and her pleasure amply requitted him for the little annoyances that it had caused him to bear. She found her dear duke more charming, under the name of Gasparini. His disguise was not at all satisfactory, but it portrayed his love and that gave satisfaction.

Although very lively, this first interview was disturbed by the fear of being surprised. Prudence, that virtue so littled listened to by clandestine lovers, warned them that a long conversation might be suspicious. The princess had not dared to prohibit entrance to the room where she was, for fear of arousing suspicion; they had to separate at once with the promise of an early meeting. The prince was to go to the chase two days later. That was the day chosen for greater security as the day for their enjoyment of new transports. The day came, although the intervening days dragged slowly by. The Duke of Modena left for the chase to make war on timid animals and Richelieu came to occupy his place beside his wife. He had agreed to bring her new books and Mme. de Modena, having become less cautious on account of the absence of her husband, had given orders not to be disturbed.

The duchess had arranged the night before a very cosey little apartment which was to be used, so she informed the household, as a reading room. Allegorical emblems, that Richelieu and she alone could explain, recalled to them their first pleasure, the memory of which is always enchanting. A tress of hair that she had taken from her lover rested on a little altar, surmounted by a crown, where two interlaced hearts were seen. She showed him this treasure, telling him that it had been her only consolation since her marriage, that not a day passed without her visiting it, without covering it with kisses and often wetting it with her tears. Then she threw herself into the arms of the duke, who hastened to make her forget her pain and her sorrows.

Several meetings followed and were not disturbed by intruders. Our lovers free and fearless endeavored to make good the time they had lost. The princess desired to have a living picture of her lover; she was impatient to possess a pledge of his tenderness and did not wish to separate from him until she possessed it. What pleasure she promised herself in caring and raising this scion of the man whom she preferred above all.

The Duke of Modena returned from the hunt, that day, the fervor of the two lovers was greater than ever and the time had passed as if on wings. Richelieu must leave immediately. The duchess could not decide to leave him; she continued to have messages to impart to him, and the hour passed without their knowing it. A noise was heard, there was no time to lose; it was the Duke of Modena, who was returning from the hunt earlier than usual; it had been a most lucky hunt and he was coming to inform his wife of his success. The lovers promptly gave over their mutual pleasure, and hastily prepared to meet the rising storm. Richelieu, who had great presence of mind, reassured the princess, begging her not to be afraid and to trust all to him.

The prince entered the room, and Richelieu, who had heard him coming, held the books which he had brought under his arm. He assured the princess in bidding her good-day that he would procure for her the next day those books that she had done him the honor of asking for. The Duke of Modena examined this colporteur narrowly as he was about to leave, asked him to wait, and questioned him about his business. Richelieu made bold replies; he spoke a poor French dialect, mixed with Italian, and questioned anew as to the place of his birth, he said that he was Piedmontese.

After several questions the prince asked him if he had ever been to Paris. The merchant replied yes, and said that it was in that city that he had carried on his best trade; that the satires against the systems of law, and the pamphlets treating of the love affairs of the Abbé Dubois, as well as the manner in which he had been consecrated Archbishop of Cambrai, having received on the same day the orders of priesthood, the diaconate and the subdiaconate, and the four minor orders, the tonsure, all of which caused the celebrant to exclaim: "Ought he not to receive baptism also?" to which some complaisant bystanders replied that it was at least the day of his first communion; and that all of these pamphlets would have made his fortune, if the new archbishop had not given very stringent orders to imprison in Bicêtre all those who sold that book; that he threatened him with the rest, and that he had come to Italy to continue his trade in books. And thereupon he entreated his highness to accord him his protection.

The Duchess of Modena was not entirely at ease; however the assurance with which her lover spoke, and the tone of credibility that he made use of in uttering his falsehoods, soon calmed her uneasiness. The duke, her husband, who was very much amused in listening to this pretended book-seller, continued to interrogate him on different subjects, and asked him if he had ever sold his pamphlets to many of the gentlemen who were enemies of the regency and of the archbishop, who gave rise to these pamphlets. The Duke de Richelieu, who knew the intrigues of this court thoroughly, amused the prince by the recital that he made of doings there, and by the anecdotes that he recounted. In the conversation, which became interesting, the prince asked him if he had had occasion to sell his books to the Duke de Richelieu. The latter assured him that he was one of his best customers; that no new book ever appeared that he did not sell him, and that he had spoken more than once with him, just as he was now speaking to his highness.

The Duke of Modena was very much charmed at the fact that this colporteur knew the man of whom he was so jealous, and whom he had often heard spoken of. "I am very sorry," he said to him, "that I did not have the opportunity of seeing him during my sojourn at Paris. However, I often dined where he was, but he was never near me, and I did not pay much attention to him. Have you ever heard his adventures spoken of? Are they as true and numerous as report would have it?" "Sir," replied Richelieu, "I have heard it said everywhere that he had liaisons with the first ladies of the court, that he had been adored by different princesses, and that he had a very marked talent in the seduction of women. The one subject of conversation in Paris while I was there was his good fortune, and the tricks that he played on husbands and mothers." "He is, therefore, very adroit and seductive," replied the prince. "So much so, sir, that if he had wagered that he would come into your palace without your knowledge for the purpose of attempting some extraordinary adventures, I should willingly take half the wager." "Oh, as for that, that would be very clever, but I should challenge him, in spite of all his skill, to play me such a trick."

The colporteur returned after having received an order from the prince to bring him different books when he delivered the books ordered by the princess. Richelieu enjoyed the whole scene that had just passed, and could not refrain from blessing the influence of his star which enabled him at the same time to possess so charming a princess and to so pleasantly deceive her husband.

He filled the orders of the prince, and again had a somewhat similar conversation with him. One can easily imagine how the two lovers, who met some days afterward, amused themselves by recalling all that had passed. They took new pledges of love, and determined that at last they must separate. The princess did not leave his arms without shedding tears; she told him that she would use every pretext to journey to France, and that this hope would sustain her courage.

Richelieu, with new triumphs awaiting him at Paris, gladly left Modena. He commenced to grow weary of the rôle he was playing; it was complaisance on his part that had prolonged its duration. He had written women who were interested in him that he was obliged to make a journey to Richelieu; and he had sent all his letters from Modena to a man who had readdressed them from that city whence they went to Paris. With this precaution he had averted suspicion from his journey, and had caused all his mistresses to share the ennui in which he said he was plunged. On returning to Paris, literary cares, together with the intrigues of gallantry, occupied his attention.

The Marquis de Dangeau died, and the Duke de Richelieu was unanimously chosen his successor. At once several men of intellect were charged with the duty of composing his reception address. Fontenelle, who never allowed an opportunity to slip by of doing homage to the great, took up the pen for the duke; Destouches Campistron imitated him, and he was embarrassed in making a selection. He himself corrected all that was defective in these works, and guided by a natural tact he was more concise though less eloquent than these authors;

grasping facts alone he never said anything but that which was absolutely necessary. Thus his address became the work of his own intellect, and it honored him. We do not find, however, in the materials which he left anything more than a few ideas, little logic and poor spelling.

In this discourse he eagerly seized the opportunity of praising Louis XIV. Some phrases will enable us to see that he regarded him as the greatest of all kings.

"We have not risen," said he, "to the glory of the academy nor to the perfection of the happy designs of Monsieur the Cardinal de Richelieu that is justified by the fact that the greatest king on earth has honored us with his protection. It is indeed fitting that a prince under whose reign the arts and belle-lettres have had so much glory should be the chief of a body that ought and deserves to be its judge. Louis the Great wished to be chief everywhere and to cause mind and taste to triumph throughout his realm as he caused his arms to triumph abroad. He had lighted the torch of war and spread terror amongst his enemies; but at the same time he did not wish to have his conquests disturb order and tranquillity at home."

Again he adds still speaking of this same prince, "I shall only say that I saw him exhibit in himself a pride most redoubtable to his enemies while possessing a kind and loving heart. His court has always been an asylum for unfortunate princes. Never did a king ascend a throne in greater majesty nor has a king ever been more approachable, ready at all hours of the day to listen to the least of his subjects and ready to do him justice, and always charmed when he could grant them a favor. Ready to do a kindness on every hand he knew how to accompany them with kindly grace, that doubled their worth. Respected by his subjects, feared by his enemies, adored by his servants, he died with heroic and Christian courage, mourned by his whole realm and admired by entire Europe."

What more would you say of a sovereign who had continually wrought for the welfare of his people. Richelieu believed what he said; Louis XIV. was, according to his estimate, the first of kings.

All the women who were interested in him, and the number was quite large, wished to be present at the academical reception. His discourse, which was affirmed to be his own work, was in their eyes a new proof of his intellect; everything is beautiful in the one we love. Very prone to admire, these ladies enjoyed the praises accorded to their favorite, who for that very reason seemed to be an acquaintance who was worthy of being cultivated.

Sometimes too much merit is burdensome; the Duke de Richelieu learned that very evening the truth of this. Covered with literary laurels, love also destined him to wear a triple crown. He received three notes indicating as many rendezvous given by Mlle. de Charolais, Mmes. de Duras and de Villeroy. Other letters which we will not mention definitely announced the desire the authors had to see him. Richelieu at once decided that he would make none unhappy.

The Duchess de Villeroy, as his latest mistress, was reserved for the last. She would have the apple; he found that it would be prudent to change the hours of the rendezvous and to fix them to suit himself. Mlle. de Charolais was the first to compliment him on his success. She was elated. The academician had to temper the excess of her pleasure. Richelieu always ready to oblige beauty brought calmness to this agitated soul. He hastened that very day to receive the felicitations of the Marchioness of Duras and ended by replying very eloquently to the compliments of Mme. de Villeroy.

After all these academical labors, he passed some days quietly at home seeking repose. However, he sent his carriage about in Paris stopping at doors that he designated in order to make it appear that he was always busily engaged and that he was never idle.

CHAPTER XIII.

D'Argenson was made keeper of the seals through the influence of Dubois and of the roués.—His birth.—He was at first lieutenant of police.—Indispensable to Mme. de Maintenon he is feared in Paris.—Leads from that time on the Duke of Orleans.—His tastes for convent life.—Relations between him and Richelieu who, in the guise of a nun, enters the Abbey of Tresnel.—The pleasant existence that D'Argenson enjoys there.

D'ARGENSON came of a very ancient though somewhat unfortunate family, whose name was Le Voyer. He was at first simply a lieutenant-general in Angoulême, his native land. Louis XIV., having sent people out into his realm, the Abbé Pelletier, Counsellor of State, one of his commissaries, appreciating the intellect of this young man asked him to come to France and accorded him his protection, which was very powerful at that time, his brother being comptroller-general. He made him a member of his household, cared for him, gave him a home and in spite of some obstacles, caused him to be chosen procurer-general of the Chamber of Redemption, a ministerial commission of the times for financial affairs. Fermet, receiver-general of Angoulême aided in sustaining him in the capital by money which enabled D'Argenson to purchase the office of master-of-petitions, and by his intellect and through his protection he was made lieutenant of police in Paris. This place prior to his time had been only a commission of Châtelet. D'Argenson, who knew both the necessity of Mme. de Maintenon in the way of a spy, and the curiosity of the late king, who always wished to be informed of the secret news of this capital, changed this commission into a ministerial office, both important and lucrative, corresponding directly with the king when he desired it. Two armies were maintained by him subject to his orders. The first was a veritable military power for the execution of arbitrary decrees in a ministerial way; the second was a secret army of spies of all conditions and sexes who were scattered throughout society, making themselves known. They penetrated all houses; they mingled in all bodies, even in parliament, to pursue their hidden intrigues and their secret plots and penetrated the very beginnings of every event. By these unique measures d'Argenson knew everything that was passing. He knew thoroughly the interior of homes, receiving information from unfaithful valets and from the loyal police.

He attached himself to Mme. de Maintenon and became indispensable. He informed her of everything that she desired to know and punished every one that did not pay her due respect. Having introduced into the ministry the custom of *lettres de cachet* this new institution was the terror of the capital. Formerly, when the lieutenant ordered the arrest of some citizen an appeal to parliament at once gave him over to justice; but by this new method he was punished ministerially whenever the lieutenant of police judged it necessary; this rendered Paris more dangerous to public liberty, provoked the parliament in spite of their profound respect for all the institutions of Louis XIV. and it angered the people who for a long time never called this magistrate anything but *le damné*. D'Argenson had the face and make-up of the accursed one; a frightful countenance, a wig, black and frowning eyebrows, averted the glances of every one. He frightened children who saw him for the first time and his only way for pleasing women was a free use of money. His external appearance and his skillfulness soon made him so feared in all Paris that he was more feared than the king. Nature created him to be a lieutenant of police or to use a more exact term *the inquisitor* of the kingdom of France.

Jansenism was another spectre that rendered him still more terrible to many people. Le Tellier, the confessor of the old monarch, attributed this heresy to those whom he wished to ruin; d'Argenson was his " commander-in-chief " and he carried on war against the Jansenists skillfully indeed; he punished them with exile and with imprisonment, to teach Frenchman, that under a Christian king, under a pious favorite, under a Jesuit and orthodox confessor no systems of religion were permitted, if they had been condemned by a papal Bull. D'Argenson, nevertheless, so terrible when he executed the desires or orders of the king, knew how to be of service to the nobles, to parliament and even to the Jansenists by hiding their faults, their stubbornness and by revealing to the king only their well-known and sensational actions, which were already known to every one. Persecution for him was only the effect of a character devoted to every wish of the king for the purpose of maintaining his place and putting no obstacle in the way of his aggrandizement; his frightful face became less terrible in the society of his intimates; he had pleasures which these alone could know, for he received with a kind of humor those who were first presented to him. It was he who had taught the ministers and the official class that scornful grimace, known for so long a time to always accost one coldly. Harsh menacing, cruel and sullen words coming from his lips, hesitatingly, a physiognomy à *Callot*, even hideous, preceded the business he was negotiating; but as d'Argenson proceeded with a matter in hand or granted a favor his frightful face became human; so to speak, his brow became serene, his countenance assumed more tranquil lines and he dismissed people with mild and agreeable expressions and with kindly and flattering remarks. It is thus that he always dealt with the Duke de Richelieu in the various visits that he made him when he was taken to the Bastille, whither he went to interrogate him, to terrify him and to inspire him with fear and terror, pointing out to him the place where Baron had been executed. D'Argenson, a shrewd man, had foreseen, even during the reign of Louis XIV., that the Duke of Orleans would one day govern the realm of France; he concealed from the late king all the adventures of this prince, he hid from him his nocturnal excursions and all the scandalous details of his debauchery. His devotion in having him guarded when he traversed the byways at night and sometimes on foot was so assiduous that on one occasion he handed the Duke of Orleans, at the end of the year, the diary of his nocturnal debauches and the disgusting stories of his doings during the year. It must be said here in his praise that in spite of the hatred that the legitimated princes and Mme. de Maintenon had sworn against the Duke of Orleans, he never ceased to assert and to persuade the king, Louis XIV., that his nephew was not guilty of the crimes imputed to him; but the secret conspiracy (cabale) tried its best to destroy the reputation that d'Argenson endeavored to build up for him and never appreciated the fact that this magistrate had a shrewder eye and saw further into the subject than it, by doing homage to the prince, whom he sought to destroy. Thus the lieutenant of police was only redoubtable to the people, who feared him and those whom the court wished to ruin or annoy; he was even so implacable to these latter that he influenced courts of justice and even ignored all the established legal forms in order to execute the well known wishes of the king, of the favorite, or of the confessor. However, in spite of this fear that the people felt for d'Argenson, his enemies, during a famine, having caused the rumor to be spread abroad that the monopolies were causing it, the people of Paris justly feared when hungry or when sorely oppressed, were incensed against him. D'Argenson wishing to leave his home, people gathered about him shouting: "There is d'Argenson the demon," and he was followed by a hail of stones, which he only escaped by a hasty retreat. Another time the women of the place Maubert gathered together near the church of Saint-Nicolas of Chardonnet, seized him as he alighted from his carriage, placed him under a spout, which was still flooded by a heavy rain, and washed his villainous face, never ceasing their cries of "negro," "demon." "You are a sorcerer," said the most intelligent woman of the Halle; "you are an enchanter, for I do not know what invisible power prevents us from strangling you." The magistrate without attendants (for they had been dispersed) pleaded for mercy; when the people had accorded it, he coolly entered a church, and joked about the incident. Some years after, about the time of his death these same women of the Halle indulged in similar facetious acts, when he was to be interred in this church, for they dispersed the funeral procession at this same place.

Such was the official character of M. d'Argenson; the private life of this man was also curious, for his private character was bound up in that of the magistrate. As a matter of fact this grave personage made lewdness his only pleasure. He became attached first to Mme. de Tencin, who had escaped from a convent some years goaded by poverty, who was naturally witty, shrewd, insinuating, active and reasonable when she wished to be, and who served this magistrate in many ways. This lady, through the influence of the Abbé de Louvios, her lover, succeeded in obtaining from Rome the annulment of her vows, or perhaps it may be more simply expressed by calling it the closing of her career as a nun, and retired to an apartment outside of the Convent of the Conception; it was there that d'Argenson acquired the taste for convent pleasures; but he soon became satiated with the woman, Tencin, having fallen in love with a novice of the Faubourg Saint-Marceau.

He had so thoroughly seduced this young woman that he had promised her to aid her in escaping from the convent and she had accepted. The mother superior, warned of the plan, prevented its execution, a thing which angered d'Argenson so much, that he suspended the construction of a building begun for this convent.

D'Argenson had, as a matter of fact, in his official capacity of lieutenant of police, the commission and the prerogative of inspecting convents; he inspected them so well that he very often visited them to seek out the most beautiful virgins devoted to a heavenly career; under the pretext of examining the walls of the house and devoting his attention to their preservation. The king had promised him the disposal of an annual sum, taken in lotteries, to be devoted to the rebuilding of delapidated monasteries, that could not, from there own revenues, undertake either remodeling or reconstruction. The mother superior of the Convent of Conception begged him to have an interview with her and what she told him was of such an alluring nature, that the lieutenant of police permitted the reconstruction of the building to be begun.

D'Argenson, soon wearying of this superior, became attached to another abbess, to whom he accorded fifteen per cent. of the lottery revenues. Tinted toweling and other stuff coming from India, which were at that time contraband goods, not costing him anything, were misappropriated for the decoration of the cells of the good women. Finally from pleasure to pleasure he came to La Madeleine de Traisnel where his fickle heart became fixed. This is how the secret conduct of the magistrate in this convent became known.

Fermet, mentioned before who had lent forty thousand francs to d'Argenson, when he became master of petitions, had a pretty daughter, whom Richelieu courted; but as Père Fermet detested his own wife, by whom he was adored, and idolized his daughter by whom he was detested because she loved Richelieu, Fermet consoled himself with a niece of his wife and a friend of his daughter called Mlle. Husson. D'Argenson amorous of the latter placed her in the convent of Traisnel.

Through the aid of this young woman Richelieu succeeded in seeing Mlle. Fermet in the convent. They were lodged in the interior and only accessible to d'Argenson, but as Richelieu was still young, of a youthful figure, and of a fine and delicate build it was easy for him to assume the disguise of a woman and profit by the permission given to another whose name he assumed, in order to enter the convent. Husson pointed out the mother superior in the choir calling attention to her beautiful complexion and beautiful eyes, making a picture as beautiful as cupid. D'Argenson, coming to visit Mlle. Husson, had become so wildly in love with this mother superior that he sought a pretext to commence building operations there that he might visit her the oftener. The revenue from the lotteries enabled him to begin a house adjacent to the convent where he could retire at the end of his days. The cells were carpeted with the colored stuffs from India and the piety of d'Argenson even led him to build a chapel dedicated to Saint-Mark, his patron. It was his wish to be buried here. The court of the late king had taught the whole world the possibility of reconciling all pleasures with religious devotion, provided it was done secretly. It was in this solitude that the chief of the magistracy hid his pleasures secret from the rest of mankind just as the sultan in this seraglio. He was jealous of the whole world. He did not have an excellent opinion of woman's fidelity and it was because he was constantly tormented by the demon of jealousy that Richelieu had all the more pleasure in violating the secrecy of these respectable asylums to fathom to the very depths the mysterious secrets of d'Argenson. Mlle. Husson kept Richelieu informed on all transpirings within the walls. Here is the life of this official in the convent.

Sa Grandeur (for this was the title that the late king had tacitly allowed to be given his ministers) retired most every evening to his apartment, which was in communication with that of the superior. Arriving there he retired to his bed and remained there. He was attired in the superb *robe de chambre* which these ladies assisted him in donning, and he was as one lost in a wilderness of downy pillows which these kind girls themselves placed beneath his head, shoulders and arms. A still more pleasant ceremony was repeated every time he visited the convent and however disgusting and disagreeable it may have been, the mother superior accustomed several of the nuns to this service; this was to rub the feet of monsieur with *eau-de-vie*, and he also asked them to scratch them very softly. The youngest and prettiest nuns attended in service about his couch; the most beautiful emptied his pockets and his portfolio, the most beautiful eyes read his letters and his documents and the heart and feelings of these girls more than once became softened at the recital of punishments, meted out to victims of the court. They often changed that which was cruel and austere in the decision of this officer. Unfortunate ones often, and always successfully, addressed the mother superior, who very soon saw herself the recipient of all sorts of presents, which she gladly accepted.

After work came the pleasures of conversation and relaxing readings. After these amusements supper was served. The gallant conversation gave zest to the meal and continued long after supper. At eleven o'clock the seraglio retired. They embraced d'Argenson and fondled him. The most delicate hands caressed his chin and face and d'Argenson gradually fell asleep. Such was the retreat of the magistrate in the days of his old age; death was to meet him in the midst of his nuns, and his ghost haunted them for the rest of their days. (Marshall de Richelieu has impressed the author of these memoirs not to pass by in silence this article concerning d'Argenson. He replied that it was difficult to speak with decency of the pleasures of the convent. Richelieu told him that history could only be written by a citizen who was absolutely impartial. He was told that history prohibited scandalous details and Richelieu said that he would assume the blame for it all. "Will you come from the other world," he added, "to take me from the Bastille? for the Marquis de Paulmy, who is d'Argenson, is going to purchase the ministry; he already asks the royal library and offers to unite his with it." "Yes, if he sends you there I promise to deliver you therefrom," replied Richelieu, "for in the Bastille I did just as remarkable things as returning from the other world and you will never know them." "Well," replied the historian, "if I do not know it I shall not report the history of the seraglio of d'Argenson." Thus passed this interesting interview when the third wife of Richelieu, who never ceased to watch over his old days, came and interrupted this colloquy. The author of these memoirs is not the only person who has been curious to know the relations between Richelieu and d'Argenson. The Marquis de Paulmy never ceased to pay homage to him, often asking for his papers and memoirs relative to his former adventures, but his writings and his compilations were so varied, they were so tainted with the ministry, that the duke, judging that he would not tell the truth, charged the author of these memoirs with them, being well assured that the truth would not be changed.)

Let us resume this story. When parliament learned that d'Aguesseau was exiled to Frênes and that d'Argenson, the old enemy of the magistracy occupied his place and that of Noailles, it determined to oppose his operations by every means in its power. Parliament had determined, on the death of the king, to try him and did not cease in unearthing his doings until his secretaries and clerks had been examined to surprise him in some sort of fraud and they had imprisoned the Commissary Cailly, his chief confidant, and five other rogues that he employed for the most important and most dangerous undertakings of his office. They accused them of monopoly and of various exactions against the merchants subject to his jurisdiction. But the regent smothered all these investigations and d'Argenson, full of resentment against parliament, assumed his position, resolved to dominate parliament, to deliver the regent from the annoyance he experienced from that body, and to subject the magistracy to the absolute authority of the king as it had been under Louis XIV. He busied himself at once with financial affairs, showing zeal and application, working with the under ministers, all very skillful, whom he had retained in office and settling the affairs with them up to the very hours when the others retired, when he went to the convent of Traisnel, though not to retire. In order to have a clear head he never dined; he supped late; he arose early and was an indefatigable worker.

The fall of Noailles soon brought another in its train; for it is usual that the downfall of the great of the court is followed by a series of smaller ones. Rouillé, a man of honesty, was assailed by the contractors and the farmers of the revenue, and without awaiting his downfall, he himself sought it of the regent and thanked him for the favor he honored him with; but Desforts resolutely kept his position as commissary or finance counsellor although he had an aversion for d'Argenson.

The Abbé Dubois triumphed over Noailles and d'Aguesseau at London; he had counseled the regent to remove these gentlemen *à formules et à rubriques,* in order to establish the state on a new plan, and he nourished in his heart a plan to humiliate parliament, to induce it to register laws relative to a plan of finance, which Law had communicated to him, without these "prerogatives of representation which stopped the march of power," as he said. Dubois from a distance prepared the abolition of the council which also presented the same annoyances as this court of parliament; moreover after the signing of the treaty that he had planned and negotiated at London, he had exacted the promise of the regent to be made minister of foreign affairs. He was already a counselor of state and when he obtained this distinction from the regent, he was so despised throughout the realm, that madame, mother of the regent, showed her surprise at the appointment, when he, presuming to believe that she had interested herself in his behalf, went to thank her for it. This princess, who was truth personified, in her conversation told him that she knew nothing at all of what he was speaking, and assured him she had no part in it. "I speak, madame," said he to her, "of the favor which monseigneur, the regent, has accorded to me in appointing me counselor of State." "You, counselor of State!" replied madame, "ah, a fine counselor indeed! my son doubtless was joking!" Then she turned her back on him.

In spite of these insults and the scorn that pursued the Abbé Dubois everywhere, he was consumed by a boundless ambition which never ceased goading him on, since he had been in the service of the Duke of Orleans.

We remember what words escaped his lips in the presence of the late king from whom he asked a cardinalship. This eagerness to become a cardinal followed him to London and unfortunately foreign princes who had need of his services skillfully made use of his ambition to obtain what they wished. It is well known that Austria, Spain and France never presented any candidate for the cardinal's cap without the mutual approval of the three powers; thus Dubois, in order to secure this dignity betrayed the interests of France to foreigners and his deplorable and dangerous example has been but too frequently imitated since. One day, on receiving despatches from Paris, he read a letter that acquainted him with the fact that he had been made fun of at the Palais-Royal; they had described him as a fool who vainly aspired to overthrow Europe, adding that he would never succeed. Dubois, who feared the nocturnal orgies and the select court of the regent, replied that if it were true that he was somewhat foolish at times, it was also true that Cardinal de Richelieu, even, had had fits of folly but having the talents and the means to elevate himself to the cardinalship, he would one day govern the realm of France with as great brilliancy as did that cardinal.

But what a difference between the genius of these cardinals. The first appeared in France with new principles; he wished to create another monarchy and cause it to rise triumphant above civil wars; on the other hand, Dubois made his appearance in times of peace and public tranquillity. The former had had the talent to subject all minds to his plan and to royal authority, even though they still remembered their former liberty, and there is not the shadow of a doubt that this great genius, after having conquered the whole nation to the royal will, would have recognized, as did Henry IV., the necessity of making this people happy, in spite of the principles of that period. Dubois, on the other hand, had but to enjoy authority already concentrated and solidified, contenting himself with confounding his own personal enemies and increasing his own power, without any great plan, nor public benefit, as an objective. Richelieu worked for the power of the ministry. Dubois worked still harder for his own power. The former had laid the plans for the humiliation of the house of Austria, so much feared under Charles V.; he wished to free France from this dreaded enemy and to fortify the position of the house of Bourbon; the latter estranged the two branches of this house, attached himself to Austria, which flattered his ridiculous ambition there, and he carried his foolish plans to the point of making war on Spain, against the grandson of King Louis XIV., who had shed so much French blood for the purpose of elevating that young prince to that throne. Finally the memory Cardinal d' Richelieu, in spite of his *coups d'etat*, for which neither history nor the French people will ever pardon him, still presents elements of power that excite the respect of posterity, while the memory of Dubois has left in the mind of posterity only scorn for his baseness, his follies and his mediocrity.

1919em: Naming Cardinal Dubois Prime Minister

Engraved by Lehmaletto, picture by Chasselat.

was capable of. The Duke de Saint-Simon, who hated the Abbé Dubois, Law and Tencin, the Prince de Conti, who experienced a keen pleasure in humiliating this triumvirate, and all the factions opposed to Dubois and Law, were notified of the day on which the decision would be handed down; the court-room was full of society people and the court was brilliant with peers.

Tencin was disputing a priory with La Vaissière, his compatriot on account of the union of a benefit to the Abbey of Vézelay, which Tencin possessed. It was said that in order to preserve this priory, Tencin had expended a good deal of money and had pocketed half the sum. Aubry, a famous lawyer, led Tencin into a trap and asserted that he would win his case against Vaissière, if he would swear that he had never given money. The Abbé Tencin, who was present, replied haughtily, "If I would swear? I am ready to raise my hand and protest that I have never negotiated for the priory, if it pleases the court to receive my oath." This was just what Aubry wished to come to. "Let us avoid, let us avoid, the double scandal," said the advocate to him, "this is the truth," showing to the whole assembly the original bill of sale of the benefit, signed Tencin.

The court and the whole assembly, owing to the intense suspense which they felt, were thrown into a frenzy of indignation against Tencin; the peers hooted him; he wished to escape; but his adversary, who awaited this dramatic event, compelled him to reappear and be a witness at his trial. It was won.

Tencin was the very ambassador that Dubois needed;

he left for the conclave in which Innocent XIII. was elected; he was charged with a secret mission from the Court of France and Laffiteau was dismissed.

The Cardinal Conti, scion of one of the four principal families of Rome, was favored in the conclave by the French faction, and as he had had a brother killed in the armies of the emperor, and had been papal nuncio in Portugal, he rallied about him the suffrages of the principal factions of the conclave. Cardinal de Rohan was disposed to exact a promise from him that he would make Dubois cardinal before declaring himself in his favor, and Conti promised this to Tencin, a fellow conclavist of Rohan, who had charge of all the details; but the abbot did not content himself with the simple promise; he wished before election that Cardinal Conti should promise and sign an agreement that he would make Dubois cardinal. Conti, who was weak enough to sign, was sanguine; but the pope, naturally weak, yet virtuous, lamenting over the fact that he had allowed himself to give this unfortunate evidence of guilt, declared to Tencin that when he was seated in the Chair of St. Peter he would die of sorrow for having purchased the sovereign pontifice by a sort of simony, and curtly declared that his peace of mind would not permit him to aggravate this fault of his by raising Dubois to the cardinalate. Tencin, angry, petulent, and threatening, and strong in the knowledge of having the written evidence, told the pope that he did not at all understand the meaning of this action on his part and demanded the red hat for Dubois. The pope, stammering, uttered the word *conscience* and Tencin simply said *obligation;* this dispute lasted for a long time, while Dubois at Versailles was enraged at the many difficulties, and regarded the delay and obstacles as tantamount to a refusal.

Tencin, to wind up the affair, went one fine morning and declared to the pope, that if he did not make Dubois a cardinal, he would publish the whole story and the note. "Let it be published," replied the poor old man, in terror.

But Dubois was made cardinal and Tencin, wishing to profit still more by the terror of the pope, determined to frighten him, and exact from him still another cardinalate.

He told him that he was the mainspring of the whole affair, that he had had only cares and sorrows as his reward whilst Conti had been created sovereign pontiff, and Dubois cardinal. The rogue added that as the price of returning the note which he asked from him, he, also, desired a cardinal's hat.

The pope this time replied to Tencin that he would wash away his sin by death and sorrow. His remorse and the threats of the infamous Tencin threw him into such a melancholy state that he died a few months afterwards. Tencin's conduct was known at Paris; it is written in the Memoirs of Maurepas and Duclos and a part of it is in the ministerial correspondence in the department of foreign affairs; it recalls that of Laffitteau who was recalled because instead of using money sent by Dubois to secure his cardinalate, Laffitteau used it to obtain one for himself.

If there is any work painful, even repulsive, for a historian, it is to follow the trail of the ambition of Dubois in his endeavors to become a cardinal. Let us remember that he asked Louis XIV. for the cardinal's hat; that while in London he determined to obtain it some day; that he treated with the emperor, and that he sacrificed our policy towards the house of Austria, in following his ambition.

In France he filled the Bastille with Jansenists, whom he had formerly protected; he had parliament exiled under the pretext that it had caused popular sedition and we have seen the indignity he caused it to endure even up to the enrollment of this Bull. He had already changed the Council of Conscience by appointing Molinists councilors, removed Noailles and threatened that prelate with extreme punishment, if he did not give an order of acceptance.

In Rome he corrupted cardinals and prelates. The ill-gotten plunder, from the ruin of a thousand families by the bank, was used to satiate his cupidity; he also negotiated with Cardinal Rohan to obtain the cardinal's hat; he negotiated in Spain with d'Aubenton and sold the confession of the king to the Jesuits in return for a protection that would bring him the cardinalate.

When the Duke of Orleans thoroughly understood all the intrigues of Dubois he could not avoid showing him his displeasure. He was Archbishop of Cambrai, nevertheless he treated him as a menial, and spoke to him in tones of the utmost scorn; several times he even struck him. Some days after his installation it is known that he kicked him. Dubois was the only person whom the regent ever maltreated, for he was naturally very kind-hearted, indulgent and given to jesting.

Another time, the archbishop was impertinent enough to look brazen and to attempt to show the irritated regent his archepiscopal dignity; the latter shoved him into the corner of the room, gave him one kick for his former quality of minister, a second one for being a hypocrite, a third one for being a rascal, a fourth one for being a priest and a fifth one for being the archbishop of Cambrai. "I pardon you for it," answered the prelate, "for I expect to get a sixth one when I become a cardinal."

The emperor indeed plotted secretly at the Court of Rome in his behalf, that he might be created cardinal, and Phillip V., who was at first opposed to this, declared to the pope that he would place no obstacles in the way of any favor that it would please His Holiness to accord him. Thus the hat came; and the regent who presented the new dignitary to the young Louis XV. said to him in the presence of courtiers that it was to M. Dubois that his majesty owed the tranquillity of the state and the peace of the church of France, which without him would have been torn to pieces by a cruel system, and as a reward the pope had created him cardinal.

The elevation of Dubois to the purple did not content the Molinists, who had made him cardinal, for long. Having obtained what he wished of them, Jansenism and Molinism were alike indifferent to him. The fanatics of the two factions therefore declared against him and blamed his spirit of conciliation and indifference;

for their interesting relations ended in quarrels. The nobles, jealous of his dignity, parliament that he had humiliated, the former court that he had estranged, the party of the legitimated princes that he had proscribed, the scandalized religionists, the honest people whom he laughed at, fell upon him in emulation of each other. A thousand satirical verses, filthy songs, and cartoons followed him everywhere, so that if he had had any shame he would have suffered dearly for his elevation. For six months he was called *Cardinal Cartouche* and yet as he still lacked the cross of the order, before being clothed in all the dignities due him as a cardinal in France, he requested Clairenbeau, the genealogist of the order, to obtain it for him. This genealogist replied that there were none; that he could only be of the order by an expense the nature of which would be incompatible with this dignity as cardinal and that he knew of no precedent which showed that any one had been received as a chevalier or commander without having given the customary proofs. Dubois was sorrowful when he thought of the new expense necessary for his decoration with this cordon, and only thought of presiding over the council of state. In order to succeed in that without any obstacle he first tried to have himself named Chancellor of France and had the proposition made to d'Aguesseau to yield his dignity in return for an indemnity of one hundred thousand francs which he offered to remit to him. On the refusal of the magistrate, with the remark that gold had never attracted or seduced him, Dubois tried another plan, that of persecution; it was determined to persecute all the councilors, firm and honest enough to oppose the presidency of Dubois and unfortunately he was sustained in this by the regent.

The Cardinal de Rohan, arriving in Rome after the election of Innocent XIII., had to be introduced in the council of state as a recompense for his services and to subject the councilors to his presidency and he had to take precedence of the others in rank. His noble birth forced them to silence and it was this very silence of the council that Dubois wished to secure in order to impose it on them thereafter when his case came up; Cardinal de Rohan from that time on was called the *Cardinal le Planche* for he had been presented there only as a means to an end. Cardinal de Rohan therefore took his seat in the council next to the princes of the blood and in precedence of the marshals of France. Some days afterward Cardinal Dubois arrived in the council and placed himself immediately next to Rohan, which caused the dukes, chancellors, peers and marshals of France to remain away from the council. The Duke de Noailles even went so far as to say to Dubois that history would not fail to say that his entry in the council had driven away the great men of the realm. Dubois, who knew that they would speak to him of the great men of state and who knew the value of these expressions, replied: "Since I know whom they called *Les Grands* I find them *si petits*, that I shall never place this day among the number of my triumphs." The regent who could not mollify Noailles exiled him; the marshalls of

France retired from the council. The ministers alone, whose fate and fortune depended upon Dubois, remained there. Villeroy, who had great influence on account of his age and his position next to the king, whose governor he was, protested and drew upon himself the resentment of Dubois, who never pardoned him for it. He determined that d'Aguesseau, as inflexible as the others, should be exiled and that a more complaisant man, d'Armenonville, should be Keeper of the Seals of France, and he was installed in this position under the cardinal without difficulty.

There remained in official position, therefore, none of the dangerous and discontented spirits who had endeavored to disturb the views of the ministry or the projects of the regency. The faction of the legitimated princes had been dispersed; the Duke du Maine and the chiefs of the confederation had vanished; Spain, that had armed the malcontents, had made a treaty of peace with France. Alberoni who had wandered from village to village in Italy was not only too glad to preserve his life and his liberty; lastly a double marriage seemed about to make an intimate union between the two branches of the same family reigning in France and in Spain.

But there still remained a very great lord in a place of responsibility and, in fact, in the very bosom of the court, who was the cynosure of all eyes. He was a surly old man and always grumbling, a remnant of the old court, (using an expression of that period) who, after having thwarted Dubois on various occasions, after having surmounted all sorts of dangers of losing his place, maintained himself in position with haughtiness, defied the ministry, refused to receive any favors or pensions from the regency, heaped criticisms and sarcasms on its every operation, had already captivated the good will of the young Louis XV., and was struggling to gain his confidence. Such was Marshal de Villeroy, governor of the king.

Villeroy, appointed by the very will of Louis XIV., governor of Louis XV., thought that he had been left in position because he was an indispensable man; he bore a name distinguished under Henry IV., and under Louis XIV., whose governor was his father, and for this reason he was intrusted with the education of Louis XV. Villeroy had been made prisoner in 1702; he had lost the battle of Ramillies and for that reason had not presented himself at the Court of Louis XIV. so often; then Mme. de Maintenon, who knew him thoroughly and who was in need of a confidential person, such as he, to perform a thousand details, asked the king to recall him; and his gratitude to the favorite never failed; he maintained friendly relations with her until his last breath. He never acted contrary to her principles, and her wish was law to him. He bitterly expressed his extreme displeasure at the elevation of Dubois to the cardinalate, never letting an occasion slip by to show how out of place he was in the ministry and how unworthy he was of holding the place he occupied in the church.

Villeroy had one of those indomitable characters that always weary indolent and frivolous characters, such as that of the regent and Dubois. A great firmness in moral and religious principles, a great indifference as to the details of etiquette, disregard of common and ordinary pleasures, caused all the friends of the regency to detest him, whilst Villeroy, outside of the immovability of his soul, was known for the uncouthness, so to speak, of his character, not being able to constrain himself in anything, nor to hide his feelings about the extraordinary events that the facile regent had brought on. Villeroy moreover believed that the regency was a veritable usurpation by the Duke of Orleans; that the will of the late king was the only legitimate law that compelled the allegiance of every good Frenchman devoted to his monarch. The exile and imprisonment of the Duke du Maine and of his partisans was nothing but an intolerable tyranny; the cardinal was no more than a monstrous criminal and perhaps Villeroy, who was credulous and not an adept in the study of human nature, lightly put faith in the atrocious calumny that the old Court of Louis XIV. gave credence to, in so falsely accusing Phillip of Orleans of having poisoned the rest of the royal family to get possession of the throne, after he had committed all the preceding crimes that were necessary in order to attain this end.

Whatever may have been his sentiments as to this or whatever he may have inspired in the young monarch, it is certain that he comported himself with his young pupil, as if he were afraid that he would be poisoned. He never lost him from view, he never permitted a single interview with the regent; he was always present with the king when working; a course of action displeasing for a prince such as Phillip of Orleans.

This prince and the Abbé Dubois therefore suffered from Villeroy all sorts of annoyances from the old man, who believed himself all powerful and impregnable; they listened to the perpetual complaints he made of every new action and they endured his railings and his sarcasms.

But when the king was nearing manhood, when he might receive from a governor moral principles and rules of action, the regent and Dubois, for fear that they might be one day sacrificed to the hate of a person, whom they had vainly tempted to win over by favors, determined to ruin him without awaiting the attack from Villeroy and they sought an occasion suitable to bring this about. The marshal, by one of those acute perceptions that a man however dull always has with regard to his dearest interests, discovered this plan and perhaps Villeroy was informed of it in advance; but whether his self love made him believe that he could not lose his authority, since its source was the will of the late king, and had been acknowledged by decrees of parliament when the regency was accorded to the Duke of Orleans, or whether he was stricken with the blindness that prevents ministers and officials to see the hidden rocks that surround them, Villeroy failed to take warning from his own forebodings.

Dubois, in order to ruin him more quickly in the mind of the regent, planned out a stratagem that would hasten this end. He caused letters to be written in

Brittany and addressed to Villeroy in which new plots were discussed. In this province there was always a state of irritation against the regent, there remained a faction of malcontents and if the accusation was a calumny, it was at least not rash. The first president of the parliament of Paris also received a letter similar to that received by Villeroy, in which it was said that a similar letter was being written to the marshall. The president, a man of the court, did not fail to carry his letter to court; but the marshal did not send his and Dubois took occasion to accuse him, like a criminal, in the presence of the regent. From that time on the prince and Dubois held the marshall under a constant espionage and especially were they careful as to the nature of the sentiments he inculcated in the mind of the young monarch.

The marshal, on the other hand, firm as a rock and never weary in opposing the regency dragged the name of the new cardinal minister in the mud. The latter tried to pacify this redoubtable old man, who was the chief of those who complained so loudly of the honors that were being heaped on him. The cardinal even sent him several messages to show him that he still was kindly disposed toward him, in spite of all his adverse comment and he attributed, so he said, his fault findings to a laudable desire to see the state governed in a still more perfect manner.

Villeroy, always in ill-humor when his resentment caused him to rail at the new court, and who was in the habit of lauding the doings and the persons of the time of Louis XIV. to the skies, was pleased with Dubois' kindness. They visited each other, but we shall see what the marshal was thinking of and what hatred he felt toward Dubois.

One day in one of these visits that the cardinal and the marshall had lately begun to pay each other, the latter, having chosen the occasion of a public audience that Dubois was giving, brought with him, in his carriage, two other cardinals to be witnesses of what he intended to do and to say to Dubois.

Villeroy, having come to the audience, threaded his way through the crowd present in this illustrious assembly; he spoke with a few individuals, he made known his presence to all and that it was Marshal de Villeroy who was going to speak to the minister.

He accosted him in a room on the side of the assembly and there he began his usual compliments. He spoke very tranquilly about the affairs of the administration and of the education of the king for some moments, but gradually gave way to the discontent of his soul and began to shower reckless criticisms on the operations of Dubois. He began a bitter invective against his personal character and ended with a review of his scandalous life. He told him publicly that he was married and at the same time a cardinal. He mentioned the name of Bretueil, commissary at Limoges, who it was said had stolen the proofs of his marriage and publicly made known that he would be rewarded. He recalled his lowly origin and how he had risen from serving as a domestic of an old priest, who had enabled him to study.

He raised his voice so that all might hear him say that he had perverted the childhood of the Duke of Orleans, whose natural abilities would have made him an accomplished and devout prince if he had not changed him by his lessons and examples and spoiled a naturally kind, pliable and gentle character. He told him that he had sacrificed the whole court or the late king to his passion, that he had exiled the great men of the state, that he had ruined fortunes, the kingdom and the department of finances. He added, that the extravagance of his house was the result of scandalous robberies made with impunity during his regime. He said that in order to elevate the Duke of Orleans to the regency he had destroyed the royal authority, having leagued himself with parliament, and that in order to get a cardinal's hat he had exiled and persecuted this parliament when he could no longer use it as his tool. "You are a criminal," he said to him on leaving him; "you are the abomination of France and of all those who curry favor with you and yet detest you. In a short time France will take vengeance for the venom which circulates in your blood and for the evils which you are bringing on her. While awaiting that time, revenge yourself on me, if you can, and have me arrested, exiled or imprisoned, if you dare."

Such a scene caused the courtiers, who had come to see Dubois on business or to solicit favors, the greatest consternation; they dared neither speak to each other, nor breathe, nor look each other in the face. Dubois, naturally brutal and feared by every one on account of his irascibility, was himself frightened. He listened, it is said, to the review of his personal history attentively and with downcast eyes without daring to interrupt Villeroy. Finally he contented himself by saying to the assembly that this old man had been for a long time somewhat insane, and deserved to end his days in Petites-Maisons, but that he wished to prove by his moderation and his supplications to the regent, that if Cardinal Dubois were guilty of such great crimes he knew at least how to pardon offences and that he would go at once to tell the story to the regent and to his council, and entreat them to forget this act of folly, this act of perfect insanity.

Several days passed during which the regent and Dubois laughed about the occurrence, when they met those whom they knew had heard the recital of the history of Dubois. Therefore it was believed for some weeks that the cardinal was capable of some kindly act at least and could forget vengeance either through scorn or through the fear of attacking such a powerful personage; but the most shrewd knew well that such sacrifices are not at all known to ministers, therefore they awaited the dismissal of the cardinal or the marshal. It was much more probable that Villeroy would be punished for the pleasure he had taken in humiliating Dubois, than that the latter should suffer. And sure enough, Villeroy was the sufferer.

Indeed the regent, wishing to work with the king on some secret matters, or perhaps simply wishing to talk with him on ordinary subjects and to seek a pretext for the dismissal of the marshall, begged the young monarch whom the governor never left when he was with the regent, to kindly arrange for a talk on state affairs which he alone should hear. Villeroy, offended by his exclusion, replied that he would not allow the king to go out of his sight; that the keeping of his person had been intrusted to him by the will of Louis XIV., verified and acknowledged by a decree of parliament and by national law; that he was responsible for the life of the king and that he was determined to be present in person at all functions and secret conferences, that the regent asked to have with him.

To these words the Duke of Orleans replied that the person of the king was in just as great security in his presence, as in that of Villeroy; he told him curtly that he forgot himself and that he should be aware that he was talking to the regent of the realm and to the first prince of the blood. He left without further adieu leaving Villeroy to his own reflections and to the duties of his charge; but he at once summoned an extraordinary council and showed how the pretentions of Villeroy had become dangerous to the peace of the ministry and of the state. The prince received the necessary approval for the punishment of Villeroy; the carrying out of the plan was postponed until the next day.

On that day Villeroy, tranquil and reassured, in spite of the two scenes that had taken place in the presence of the king and at the home of the cardinal, presented himself to the young monarch to fulfil the duties of his warship. He was at once surrounded in the antechamber of the king, by a band of young nobles, the companions in pleasure of the Duke of Orleans, who were to seek diversion by kidnapping the old governor. Villeroy did not know whether it was simply a prank of young madcaps or a real punishment. Le Fare, a personal friend of the regent, commanded this expedition with a great deal of tact, order and precision. The marshal who made an outcry, cursing at the top of his voice, was shut in the first sedan chair at hand and then transferred to a carriage, which had been waiting for some time and was thus kidnapped, or rather forcibly taken, from the court before the king, the ministers, the regent, or even the marshal's own followers became aware of it. Several hours after this event the latter learned that their master had left for his country seat at Villeroy, which was just as surprising to them as it had been to the marshall himself.

But the next day the regent, Cardinal Dubois, and the whole court were in their turn thrown into just as unforeseen an embarrassment. The former bishop, de Fréjus, preceptor of the king, had disappeared from court and from his home without any one knowing what had become of him, nor did it appear what was the motive of so extraodinary a disappearance. The king, who began to show some kindly feeling and attachment for his governor and especially for this prelate, began to fret over their absence and also believed that Fleury was exiled. He never ceased weeping, refused to take any nourishment, and could not be induced to seek repose during the night which he passed in sobs, bitter lamentings and groanings. The Duke of Orleans and Dubois were already in consternation, they repented having exiled Villeroy without foreseeing the course of events. Couriers were sent into every corner of France to find the preceptor and to bring him back to the king, and to impose silence on the evilly disposed ones who already were spreading the rumors, some that he had been exiled, others that Cardinal Dubois had caused him to be kidnapped and put out of the way. This course was necessary, in fact, to impose silence on those who carried their wild clamors to the point of imputing the most atrocious calumnies to the regent. Happily for the repose of the young king, who had become ill as the result of these events, and for the peace of mind of the regent and of Dubois, who knew of no remedy with which to assuage his extreme sorrow, he was discovered at the home of Lamoignon, at Bâville, from whence he had already given instructions to some of his people to reveal the secret of his whereabouts. This discovery, which brought calmness to the minds of all, and satisfied the regent, caused Dubois to utter these words which were often repeated at that time: " The good man ran away to Bâville for the pleasure of having himself hunted up and to play the child."

The sequel of this affair proved that Fleury had not been to Bâville to do what Dubois attributed to him. The preceptor returned to the court where he enjoyed the complete confidence of the young king; and Villeroy, furious on learning of his retaining his position, sent word from Lyon, where he had just been transferred, that Fleury had betrayed him by returning to his office with the king, saying that there existed between them a mutual pledge, by which it was agreed that should one of the two lose his place the other should retire to his country place or to a convent, whence he would not come until the other had resumed his old position. And that each should use every effort in behalf of the other to secure his return to the king's good graces. Fleury could not deny the existence of this promise. He acknowledged it to his intimate friends several times when they reported the news to him; but he added that the great sorrow of the king, his despair at seeing himself deprived at once of a governor and a preceptor, whom he loved, being events that were unforeseen when they made the agreement, the critical state of the king suspended the force of the promise.

Such was the end of Marshal de Villeroy, worthy of being respected, both by Dubois and the regent, on account of his virtue. He preserved a quaint and venerable character in a court from whence all morals and all good taste had been banished.

Villeroy was tall and of fine physique, he had been a great gallant and still boasted of his conquests even in his old age. He was in disfavor as long as the Duke of Orleans lived and the decree of banishment was not revoked until the ministry of M. de Duc, who permitted him to return to court. The king, who had been told of this, received him coldly, which vexed him so much that he established himself in Paris. Under the ministry of Cardinal Fleury he desired to return to court and Maréchal, chief surgeon, undertook to bring this about. Villeroy asked for what was due him for his service as governor of the king's person and the payment of it in bank-notes. This amounted to six hundred and sixty thousand francs. He also asked that in the future his honorarium should be paid to him; that the Duke de Villeroy, his son, be created Marshal of France, and that the Marquis d'Alincourt be made duke and peer by re-establishing for him the Duchy of Beaupréau. The cardinal granted him the payment of his fees up to the time of his exile, but refused the rest of his petition. Villeroy was disposed to accept; but the king no longer mentioning him, he never appeared at court and died the 18th of July, 1730, without having received even the arrearage due him.

CHAPTER XV.

The licentious festivals mentioned by Mlle. Tencin, praised by Dubois, and celebrated in the presence of the regent at Saint-Cloud.

WE should not know what was the trend of morals of the Greeks and Romans, and how their primitive asceticism degenerated into license and corruption, if the historians of those nations had not preserved a picture of the customs of their contemporaries.

Livy Tacitus and all the worthy historians did their duty in this respect. We shall imitate their veracity, therefore; but we shall refrain from giving the scandalous details that shock modesty and prudence. In 1722 the court of the king was composed of his tutor, his preceptor, all pious individuals and men of edifying deportment, but the court of the regent was as licentious and depraved as this court was reserved and cultured; and although the regent, on account of his indulgence in pleasure, was prematurely old, his mistresses and his companions in debauchery sought new devices to awaken his passion.

The Cardinal Dubois, not at all knowing the dangerous nature of the poisonous humors that circulated in his blood and not foreseeing his early death, sought every means to get possession of authority that he might rule in France after the king had become of age, as he had ruled during the regency. He had been warned of the worthlessness of the Duke of Orleans, and he feared lest that prince, endowed with the knowledge necessary to administer all departments of the government, and born for glory, would abandon his reckless pleasure seeking life for affairs of state, when that period should have arrived in his life at which dulled passions cease to distract thoughtful men. Dubois had, up to that time, kept the Duke of Orleans interested in all the pleasures with which he had surrounded him. His schemes even included making work difficult and distasteful to him, presenting complicated business requiring careful deliberation and thought, that he might weary him. He knew the make-up of his pupil; he had studied him since youth, and endeavored, in concert with the *roués*, to constantly seek amusements of different kinds. The nearer the regent approached the period of indifference for pleasures, which nature establishes as a penalty for debauchery, the more the cardinal, ingenious and fruitful in resource, sought out new devices to divert him.

The court of this prince at that time went to Saint-Cloud, in preference to all other places, for its nightly orgies; for they began to fear the preceptor, Fleury, who was gaining control of the young king, and whose principles were too much opposed to these scenes of lewdness. It was, moreover, more becoming to be removed from the king and the capitol. Therefore they gathered at Saint-Cloud, whence they excluded all the valets. There were found women of the demi-monde, who were brought there at night blindfolded that they might not know where they were; the regent, his women and the *roués*, who did not wish to be known, were masked; but it was said at once that only the regent and Cardinal Dubois were capable of devising such amusements.

At other times they chose the most beautiful young people of both sexes who danced at the opera to repeat the ballets that the easy tone of society during the regency had made so wanton, and these young people executed these dances in that primitive state in which men were before garments were known. These orgies that the regent, Dubois, and his *roués* called *fêtes d'Adam*, were repeated a dozen times, for the prince seemed to enjoy them. The cardinal thus kept the Duke of Orleans busy. The king was becoming of age, and if he succeeded in accomplishing his object and should gain his confidence at the critical time, he had already formed a plan to remove the regent.

Orgies of a new character soon followed the *fêtes d'Adam;* the pen obliged to describe them hesitates and refuses to perform its function lest future ages might know the infamies of this period. Yet we recount them since reticence is a vice in history and candor is a virtue. We shall add that Mme. de Tencin, ingenious in artifice, knew the causes and the degrees of the premature old age of the regent and the necessity of keeping him busied and distracted in order to preserve the influence of Dubois. For this reason her skill devised new pleasures. She was the cardinal's confidant, his counselor, she ruled his house. Every day she gave Dubois new advice and pointed out to him all sorts of expedients to maintain his influence and to keep dangerous persons away. Therefore when the regent no longer desired a repetition of the dances, she suggested to the cardinal to propose the festivals and amusements of the *Flagellants*.

The next day each *roué* was provided with a dozen whips for this new game. The society of the *roués* was anxious to know what this was for and they were told in advance the number of actors that would be in the party; for each one showed his whip as an indication of the coming festival by trying the effect of these instruments on his hand. Let us spare details since we cannot hide the story. The whole court of the *roués* kept themselves in complete darkness. Let us permit the regent to inform us better.

This prince showed some remorse. He said one day to Cardinal Dubois who told it to Mme. de Tencin from whom Richelieu heard these strange stories: "What will history say; she will reveal the orgies of my regency in the same light that she did the festivals that we all know were held in the Court of Henry III. Our festivals will be made known to the world. Posterity will know every detail and artists will engrave them."

But he added if that is done, it will also be said that everything took place at the instigation of a cardinal.

Dubois had ordered Mme. de Tencin to write the *chronique scandaleuse du genre humain*. This story is still extant in manuscript, written by Mme. de Tencin for the use of Dubois and the regent, and the most voluptuous and infamous doings of the Romans, the Greeks, and the Italian courts, were either executed or at least closely imitated. Messalina and Cleopatra were played; they played Ninon, the memory of which was still more vivid; they caused the debauchees of the most remote antiquity to issue from their tombs.

Never did these orgies commence until every one was in that state of ecstasy produced by champagne. They never thought of commencing their orgies until every one was in a state of drunken indifference and when the company reached that moment, when the glasses leaped in air, when the joyous words, bachanalian songs, liquors, the recitation of all sorts of wanton tales that came from the mouths of women, had brought every one to a state of eagerness, then the repetition began. The regent at such times retired to a corner with some intimates from whence he reviewed and applauded everything done by this strange company. Women of every condition of life, but without distinction of rank, were received there, and the present generation would be greatly surprised to know that mothers and grandmothers were found there, for the most of them asked God's forgiveness for the rest of their lives for the part they took in these shameful scenes. The most licentious were sought out by the regent; they were urged on and made reckless by the infamous cardinal who gave them money, position, jewelry and notes from Law. Mme. de Tencin and Dubois together planned for the success of these assemblies, that amused the regent, and looked after the affairs of the government and thus they neared the period of the king's majority, the time anxiously awaited by them for the ruin of the regent.

Although this prince amused himself by these boisterous orgies nevertheless he had propensities that were peculiarly his own. After **all these** mistresses of whom we have spoken in the course of this work, he allied himself with the Marchioness de Parabère, young and pretty. She had been rejected by her husband, who given to drink, brought into society customs strange to our century, showing himself more attached to the bottle than to his wife. The nobles, according to the customs of the time, still loved to drink and intoxicating liquors were better known than our sweetened drinks of to-day, such as coffee and tea which came into use toward the end of this century.

Mme. d'Averne, who received at her home a choice company of young libertines at that time, was still regarded affectionately by the regent. The Duchess de Gesvres and Mme. de Sabran continued their mode of life with this prince. These ladies were neither jealous of each other nor inimical to one another; they invited and were mutually invited to festivals, rendezvous, they loaned one another their lovers and sought new mistresses for the prince. Mme. de Sabran even brought to her home Mme. de Nicoly who appeared on the scene, for a moment, at the beginning of the year 1722, but suddenly disappeared.

All these ladies met on terms of equality both Emilie who was cherished by the regent and his other theatre girls. The titled ladies talked with those who were not; old women, those of the former court (except those of religious leanings) longed for access to the interior of this court. The public, however, knew nothing of what transpired in these festivals, but they knew that the regent and his trusted ones amused themselves in common, although very secretly.

CHAPTER XVI.

Picture of the ministry drawn by the regent himself, after the regency. (This word-picture must have been made at the end of the month of July in 1723).

THUS it will be seen that there was left in intimate association with the prince none but debauchees, or ministers without talent, whom the Prince of Orleans openly ridiculed. He was one day applauded by all the company of Mme. d'Averne, his mistress, when he read a witty critique of his own character and that of his ministers. The description that he gave utterance to was of such a peculiar taste and so novel that all Paris admired his talent in the art of scornful diatribe. The evil disposed and the remnants of the ancient court always disconcerted by the witty sayings of the prince were especially annoyed by the one I am about to describe.

They would gladly have flooded the capital and provinces with the most frightful libels against him; but the indifference of the prince that drove him to despair, not only took the sting from their sarcasm but it also disconcerted the malicious ones, who saw how powerless was this means of accomplishing what they desired. The Duke of Orleans one day visited Mme. d'Averne, whose home was the rendezvous of the wits of the day. Surrounded by men of letters, distinguished artists and nobles of the court, he gave utterance in this aristocratic body to the most bitter criticism of his own government. He cited the case of a hypothetical pamphlet and said to the company that always eagerly listened to him: "Ladies, the French people are very malicious in writing libels against me in which I and all my ministers as well are torn to pieces; they pretend that the czar, having found the French government better than that of the other states that he had gone through, sent an ambassador to France for the express purpose of asking me to aid him with my counsels. The ambassador did me great honor by eulogizing me in behalf of his master to which I replied, His Imperial Majesty, sir, does me great honor in entertaining such a kind opinion of my capacity; I do not merit it. Jealous of me, Louis XIV. excluded me from his councils; my studies were limited to belles-lettres, chemistry, painting and music. My birth, it is true, called me to the regency, but I do not interfere with the government except to think over in the evening, when I and my companions in pleasure are drunk, of making decrees that annul those of the night before. I am sorry, sir, that I cannot be of assistance to your master in his great project. See Cardinal Dubois."

Cardinal Dubois to the Ambassador of Russia.

The ambassador speaking to Dubois, whom he had gone to find on the suggestion of the prince was thus addressed by the cardinal:—

"The Duke of Orleans surely was joking when he sent you to me, for where does he think I have learned to govern well. I am the son of a village apothecary; I commenced in the Sorbonne at Paris by being a doctor's lackey. Good fortune made me sub-tutor of monsieur, the regent. He overwhelmed me with dignities without giving me capacity. Moreover I am tormented by an evil which consumes me, and prevents me, though I would have the skill to deal with the affairs of France. Therefore I refer you to monsieur, the Keeper of the Seals, and the Secretaries of State."

The ambassador went to see all these gentlemen who replied to him as follows:—

"Monsieur D'Arménonville, Keeper of the Seals.

"Is it as Keeper of the Seals, Monsieur Ambassador, that you come to consult me or as financier? I shall tell you, sir, that I have never known anything beyond the state of my domestic finances; never those of the king, and as a Keeper of the Seals, I am told to seal whatever is to be sealed, without being even permitted to read the documents. I am only a good natured fellow."

M. de Maurepas, Minister of Marine.

"I would be charmed to be useful to His Imperial Majesty," said he to the ambassador of Russia, "but I trust that he will have the kindness to allow me to inform myself. I have intellect, desire to learn, love for the king and the state, but I left college and never saw anything in the marine line but a vessel that was ascending the Seine two years ago and those boats two feet deep that are made to amuse children of my age. However I do not despair in the hope of making myself useful some day to his Imperial Majesty; but I have only been an amiable rogue of a child engaged in playing pranks on the ladies up to the present time."

Monsieur de Breteuil.

"Whom are you addressing, sir? I am Secretary of War, it is true, but I never saw any other troops than the regiment that passed through Limoges while I was commissary there."

Monsieur de la Vrillière.

"Here, sir, these are our formulas for *lettres de cachet*; that is the extent of my knowledge thus far. Here is one used to imprison a poor priest in the Bastille. That is all that they have had me do and the only thing I know how to do. I will give it to you with all my heart. You can give it to your master, who sends his people to Siberia in the same way."

Monsieur Doden.

"I was formerly councilor in parliament and reported a trial very well; but Monsieur the Duke of Orleans made me comptroller-general, and as a matter of fact I know nothing of my duties."

"This," said the prince, "is how the ambassador, running from one minister to another, returned to his court as he went without having acquired any knowledge at all."

The pleasant thing in this story of the prince is that he aimed the pamphlet against himself, as well as against his ministers. This "joke" of the prince is printed here for the first time and, although he was by no means insensible to bitter and calumnious criticism, nor to the fabrications of malicious persons, the scorn or indifference that he, as well as the nobles, ministers, and princes who possess intellect, showed for these productions was the weapon by which he disconcerted calumny. Such has always been the pride of the greatest geniuses; Montesquieu, Rousseau, Buffon, like the Duke of Orleans, laughed at calumny and Frederick even allowed his printers to publish them. It is true Voltaire wished to combat calumny all his life; but this is because he was devoured by a life-long ambition to show the universality of his talent which attained sublimity in the art of humiliating jealousy.

CHAPTER XVII.

Greek orgies beneath the windows of Louis XV. at Versailles.

THE rage for orgies had already been introduced into France and conjugal and secret infidelities, double or triple extra-marital relations not only could no longer satisfy the spirit of libertinism of the nobles and princes of the court, but the perverseness of their hearts required boisterous and wild pleasures, acts of libertinism, done in public and in the presence of many people goaded on by the same necessity.

From one species of debauchery to another they went until they reached those of the Greeks and, although under the late king, who was easily offended by everything that was contrary to good taste, delicacy and nature, there were found courtiers who were guilty of these vanities. Although his own brother was accused of them and the monarch was obliged to punish him severely, Louis XIV. finally succeeded in making this vice rare and disgraceful. He caused it to hide its face, to disappear from society, so to speak, and to seek refuge in deepest darkness.

But under the regency, everything being permitted in the line of public immorality, the princes and cardinal ministers, themselves, setting the example, shameful scenes were increased to such a degree that one day a group of seventeen was formed right under the windows of the king. This happened during the heat of the month of August, 1722. Fontenelle, the Duke de Boufflers, D'Alincourt, the Count de Roye, the Marquis de Meuse, Champigni, captain of the guard, and several officers of the king's household were the ring leaders in this nocturnal orgie.

What they did, perhaps, under the very eyes of the king, what was seen in the light of the moon caused so many curious lords and ladies of the court to crowd about the windows, that all Versailles, even Paris, was thrown into great commotion by it. Fleury, the Marshal. de Villeroy, although his grandson was a member of the party, the Abbé Vitement and other attachées of the king declared that in view of the complaints and public clamor they would retire if the regent did not order the guilty ones punished severely. The Marshal de Boufflers and his wife, religious and even pious as in the times of Louis XIV., ordered their son to appear before them and with the crucifix in their hands chided him, for these ceremonies were still customary at that period.

The sensation that this orgie caused determined the Duke of Orleans, Dubois, Monsieur le Duc, and Marshall de Villars, to hold a council, to ascertain, as they said, "the means to appease the pious." The regent who enjoyed the joke contented himself with saying that it would be necessary to deliver a harsh lecture to these nobles and to tell them that they did not have the best taste in the world. As it was said that these gentlemen had already formed a brotherhood, he determined on its dissolution.

Dubois was more indulgent. He said that if these gentlemen were punished, every one would become so hypocritical and so circumspect that they could employ no one, and that as the affairs of state sometimes demanded people, who were free from every scruple, who could be used in many ways, he determined to let the matter drop.

Villars and Monsieur le Duc, made the observation that as this vice was not known to the people, a nominal punishment, such as a few days in the Bastille, would be sufficient. All these judges had a good deal to reproach themselves with, for they were both judges and accomplices. However they determined upon a slight punishment.

Fontenelle was sent to the Bastille and made application for a change of name; he took that of Rambure; he was the most daring and the chief of the guilty ones, having led his comrades on, planned the festival and determined on the details. D'Alincourt was banished to one of his country estates. De Meuse was compelled to leave for his regiment by a *lettre de cachet*. Let us tell the truth in regard to Boufflers; he suffered himself to be maltreated, rather than consent to any guilty deed; he was religious and of good moral character and because he threatened to cry for help he was tortured, persecuted and abused and accused of being a devout coward. He was punished by his father and mother only, who felt themselves outraged by his conduct.

Villars, who simply alludes to these deeds in his Memoirs, and who is circumspect, contents himself by telling the truth without changing it, simply saying: "A sorry adventure took place in the family of Marshall de Villeroy; he saw himself obliged to remove the Duchess de Ratz his granddaughter on account of loose conduct and the Marquis d'Alincourt, his grandson on account of youthful adventures, which caused a great sensation. The Marquis de Rambure, colonel of Navarre, was sent to the Bastille and the Marquis d'Alincourt was sent to Joigny."

The Marshal de Villars here confounds two very distinct events: the orgie of the garden under the windows of the king and the anecdote which has reference to the conduct of the Duchess de Ratz. The author of these Memoirs, writing the history of France, speaks of the orgie because it describes the morals of the time and is silent about the duchess, because that was merely a family affair.

CHAPTER XVIII.

How the police made use of prostitution to govern the capitol during the regency. Adventures of the celebrated Fillon. An experience of a president's wife.

FOR the purpose of finishing the history the morals of the court and of the nobles during the regency and to consider the results of the association of the police and the libertines, which D'Argenson, the lieutenant-general of police was the first to use in his department; to show the degeneration of social institutions of Frenchmen under royal despotism, we grant a place in history to the famous courtesan called Fillon, who was a type of many others of her age and played a large part in the secret affairs of the government. Fillon at the age of fourteen showed a decided penchant for libertinism; she was ravishingly beautiful and the artists said that there was something in her person that recalled the beau-ideal of the ancients. She was nearly six feet tall; her complexion was very white, her blonde hair fell almost to her knees; she could almost use it for a mantle. The regent conceived the idea of constructing for her a grotto illumined by rays of light directed on a bed of straw matting. Mlle. Fillon half covered by her beautiful blonde hair was accustomed to retire there and the regent came to do penance with her and to admire, as artist and amateur, the perfect proportions of nature's work.

Gallant and dangerous adventures in which Fillon showed character, genius and great ambition caused her to be singled out from all her fellow prostitutes by the lieutenant-general of police. D'Argenson, the skillful chief of spies, recognized in this girl original skill, firmness, courage and he attached her to his service. She succeeded in getting his confidence and securing from him the necessary authority for the establishment of a great house of prostitution. Marriage was part of her plan and she wished to have the most beautiful man of the capitol, whom she would choose from among all those she had known during her career, and this husband was to be the most celebrated man in France for his beauty, statue and strength. Her choice was the former Suisse of the Hotel de Mazarin.

Nothwithstanding the fact that la Fillon had promised to reform on marrying him, her libertinism continued always; she was ill-treated by him and complained to the Duke of Orleans, regent, who used to sup with her and who usually called her *sa commere*. This prince gave orders to the Suisse to be contented with the money that his wife gave him and not to disturb her; but the husband, to whom she had promised fidelity, never ceased tormenting her until he died, for he resented her unlawful conduct.

Saint-Laurent, first valet-de-chambre of Albergoti succeeded the Suisse and left his wife, who was always faithful to him. To attach him to her service she gave him more than one hundred thousand francs, which she received from the regent, from the ministers and from the young girls in her employ. They corresponded with her every morning; for she bestirred herself every day to discover some new secrets, intrigues or pamphlets that interested the government so much during the despotism. She served the ministry with great skill. She was of kind desposition, honest and naive, although shrewd and brusque in conversation. She made known without losing her credit during the regency that Cardinal Dubois owed his elevation to the ministry, and even the archepiscopal dignity of Cambrai to her. "No one will ever know," said she, "what I did that he might be cardinal. All that I can say is that at the bottom of the affair was a woman. As for the negotiations he had at Rome and Vienna they were but a matter of form. The great difficulty to be overcome was in the Palais-Royal." It is known that the regent held his court in the palace; and that he had to negotiate with nobles of the ancient court, who were often unyielding in regard to very many matters.

During the regency Fillon had for a long time the key of a little door which led from the street to the interior of the Palais-Royal and to the very chamber of the regent, relieving her from the necessity of passing staircases or antechambers that were in use, so that she had free access to the apartments of Cardinal Dubois. She received the young nobles of the time of the regency in her apartments and Marshal de Richelieu, who preserved many curious anecdotes of that house, anecdotes which assure us that the young courtiers went to sup and lodge at the home of Mlle. Fillon for one louis.

President Fillon, magistrate of the tribunal of Aleçon,

having come to Paris in 1710 to reside for some time, had an amiable, virtuous and pretty wife, who was called Madame *la présidente Fillon.*

The wife of President Baillet, an extraordinary woman, who only wished to visit prominent women like herself and did not wish to receive nor visit women either above or beneath her rank, had no sooner learned of the arrival of a president's wife from the province than she wished to call on her and asked her people for her address. They gave that of Mlle. Fillon.

Mme. Baillet who was very beautiful and virtuous was received by the courtesan as an interesting women who had quarreled with her husband, and Mlle. Fillon promised her the finest and most exciting adventures possible. The wife of President Baillet, astounded at the tone, the expressions, and the indecent conversation, was furious, and endeavored to escape from the house of the courtesan. Mlle. Fillon, redoubling her caresses and respectful deference, promised her great amusement and ended by telling her that very many other president's wives distinguished for honor, virtue and rank came to visit her.

The Duke of Orleans, who used to see Fillon, even during the life time of Louis XIV., was delighted with the anecdote, related it to every willing listener and never ceased to repeat it. Louis XIV. shrugged his shoulders at it; Mme. de Maintenon replied with some religious terms of disapproval and the young people of the court never called Mlle. Fillon anything but *la présidente.* The wives of the presidents of the sovereign courts remonstrated in vain against this prostitution of their title; d'Argenson, who needed Fillon, even during the life of Mme. de Maintenon, said to an indignant president's wife in one of these audiences: "Never disturb this *présidente* in her functions and she will never trouble you in yours." The President Fillon who was of austere character and who in a matter of joking was neither an adept nor appreciative, thought himself obliged to change his name and his place of residence. It was the same gentleman who afterward became farmer-general under the name of Villemur.

La présidente Fillon, courtesan, lost almost at the same time Cardinal Dubois, d'Argenson and the regent. She married a German, coachman of a Count of Saxony, a man vigorous and as handsome as her first husband. When he became aware that she had secret dealings with the police, he abused her and forced her to abandon her questionable understandings with the police, the revenues from which she remitted to the famous courtesan, Prevot, her protégée. Ill-treated by this German, having lost her fortune, and neither wishing nor being able to find for him any position, not even in domestic service, she induced him to enlist in the cavalry, and she established a new house which was still open during the first years of the ministry of Monsieur le Duc de Bourbon. The government had made new progress in brutishness since that period.

A lady of the court, an agent of the abolished regime, who detests the morals of free people and by whom liberty is to be found only in the license of former times; a genteel academician who regrets the times of the monarchy and the ceremonial during which it called to the Louvre effeminate citizens, who applauded the eulogies and principles of the academy unquestioningly; will find this expression atrocious and barbarous. But how can we characterize the third of the periods of political degeneration in the former government by any other words?

In its impotence, it had at first called in women of questionable reputation to assist the administration of the police in the capitol. After this alliance it demanded a portion of the gains of these courtesans.

Therefore I ask the academy to give me a French word capable of characterizing more accurately this revolution in our ancient customs; a revolution that elevated prostitutes to the rank of public functionaries in the administration of the police of the first city of the world, and which degraded the government to the point of sharing the pecuniary emoluments derived from the most disgraceful and shameful actions. Antiquity, in its most degraded age of dissoluteness, never offered such a combination of perversity and baseness.

CHAPTER XIX.

Death of Dubois.—Strange peculiarities.—The Duke of Orleans, prime minister.

TORMENTED for a long time by an unmentionable disease, Dubois passed an unhappy and wretched life. He carefully concealed his malady and he yielded to a fit of extreme passion when he heard that the public had learned of the causes which he had wished to conceal. The king held a grand review of the troops this year and the cardinal, who wished to appear in public for the purpose of recovering his shattered reputation, which had been injured by the rumor of this disease, mounted his horse. He caused him to prance in an effort to imitate the grace and nimbleness of a vigorous and healthy young man. This resulted in an aggravation of his malady and he became mortally ill.

The surgeons made a careful examination and the appearance of the affected part was such that in order to avoid sudden death, total amputation was unanimously decided upon, although at the time it was rumored that a different operation was to be performed.

This strange news drove the cardinal into a furious passion, but he had to yield, for he was told that death would be the result of a longer resistance. Then he allowed himself to be removed to his apartment in Versailles. There it was suggested that he receive absolution which he angrily refused.

When he saw the frightful preparations of the doctors and surgeons and especially of their instruments he appointed a Franciscan friar of Versailles his confessor. This friar came and talked with him for a quarter of an hour or more and this was his only act of repentance. The operation, however, did not give the surgeons great hope of lengthening the days of His Eminence; it was therefore determined to induce him to receive Holy Communion before being operated upon; but the sick man evaded the question by telling them that the priests of Versailles were not well enough acquainted with the ceremonial that is due a cardinal. Then uttering blasphemies against God and oaths against the doctors, he told them: "I do not wish to be operated upon." The regent came and begged of him to allow them to proceed with the operation and to affect his speedy cure. After prayers and anxious beseechings he determined to do it. La Peyronie performed the operation in five minutes, with great skill, courage and dexterity although he was interrupted by the sick man, who uttered invectives and curses with his last breath.

After the operation, the doctors and surgeons realized that Dubois had not long to live. He still had a clear mind and the energy of an indomitable will and the news that he must die increased his grief and threw him into a still greater state of despair, which ended in death. It is recorded that he asked to see what the surgeon's art had extracted from his body; and that the sight of it caused him to grind his teeth and produced the most hideous contortions in his face. Finally this dreadful scene ended by the appearance of a priest who brought the Eucharist. All the religious persons, who were in the room, had opportunity to be disheartened by the sight of instruments of crime mixed with those of religion, resting on the same table. The regent who observed the progress of the disease in the sick room wrote to Nocé, whom Dubois had exiled, as follows:—

"Dubois has finally consented to have the operation performed. You would have been as amazed as I, had you seen the distress of the priests, who did not know as much as we did about this holy man. The storm, which threatens, is going to take away my rogue and tomorrow, without doubt, you will hear from me."

The next day the regent wrote to Nocé: "The brute is dead and dead is the poison. I await thee this evening at the Palais-Royal. The dead body was carried from Versailles to the church of the Chapter, Saint-Honoré. He was buried in the first chapel, to the right, where libertines posted in passing satirical epitaphs that were worthy of this priest. His brother caused a beautiful mausoleum to be erected for him, without doubt to indemnify the canons for the burdensome legacy of such a corpse; but public opinion does not demand a false inscription to be placed thereon, neither for the present generation nor for future ages; it is simple, true and worthy of Dubois; an enumeration of his charges and of his dignities is made, and the epitaphs end with the wish that he may have a truer happiness.

An epitaph written by hand and placed over the door of the church, Saint-Honoré, was more expressive.

Cardinal Dubois was born with an intriguing mind; he understood character perfectly and he knew how to employ men for his own ends with great skill. It is but too authentic that successive crimes raised him to his dignities and to the rank of prime minister, which but few persons attain. Boundless and unbridled ambition to rise caused him to regard honor, promises, good faith, affection and gratitude as so many playthings. The great principle which he never lost sight of was that all men are born evil, that they all possess malice, to a greater or less degree, and that one's conduct must be in accordance with that idea, and that the different degrees of malice that each person is possessed of must be carefully estimated. His voluptuousness was great, but it was gross and brutal, devoid of any of those delicacies which even libertines sometimes know how to affect. Moreover his nature was incapable of any kind of friendly gallantry toward women.

In his heart he had no virtue, neither religious nor humane; nor did he have that sympathy with misfortune and pain, with which nature endows all sentient beings. Charged with the education of a prince he debauched him and got possession of his mind when he had made debauchery a necessity and a habit.

The finest moments of his life were at the time when he favored the ambition of the young prince, when it was necessary to deprive the Duke du Maine of the authority of the regency. Then he negotiated with parliament;

he flew night and day from councilor to councilor; he made promises; he was extremely active in making treaties with various members and by dint of this activity, he succeeded in winning the suffrages of the multitude.

From that moment on he determined to ruin the old Court of Louis XIV.; he delivered it over to the mockery of libertines and gloried in his triumph over parliament.

But when he had to prepare himself, far in advance, to treat with the Court of Rome for the obtaining of a cardinal's dignity; when he had to negotiate with the Molinists, who asked to be saved from the precipice over which he threatened to throw them as a recompense for their concessions; then he dragged the parliamentary party through the mud and helped the party of the Molinists to its feet; he opened the prisons of state and filled them with Jansenists in order to please the party which was to procure for him the cardinal's hat.

In the beginning of the regency he had concluded and signed two famous treaties of alliance with a great deal of dexterity and without great waste of time. Having succeeded to the ministry, he concluded the treaty between the regent and Spain with great skill; but in all these contradictory negotiations, the principle and end of all that he did was to satisfy his passion for ruling and to gratify his personal ambition.

The petulency of his character, which he had carefully restrained before he rose to eminence, was allowed to develop when he was clothed with complete power; from that time on he no longer cared for the decencies or the conventions of society. He treated women with the harshness of a vandal and his furniture, even his most important despatches, he cast into the flames when he learned some bit of news that was displeasing to him. Annoyed one morning for having worked four hours without having despatched a quarter of the replies to letters or to petitions, the regent found him near a great fire where he had thrown all the letters and petitions, he had not had time to answer; he told the prince that he was thus getting even with his work.

Always busy with espionage, which was the implement that he made use of most, he was in the habit of listening to reports of girls and women of the town, whom he received in his audiences with honest women, making no distinctions. All these vile means, these unworthy actions, were the stepping-stones that he used for his own preferment; he also used them to preserve his sovereign power.

Such was the portrait and such was the character of this celebrated minister; of him, nothing bad enough will ever be said, according to the expression of M. de Paulmy who had no reason to be satirical nor flattering to Dubois, and who thus expressed himself in a book which is published under the title of *d'Essais dans le gout de ceux de Montaigne.*

It was foreseen that at the death of Dubois the Duke of Orleans would ask to be made prime minister; but the king was prevented from giving the prince the power of signing financial orders. Some of his friends asked him to demand from Louis XV. this right; but Belle-

Isle, who was ubiquitious, told him that he knew from Fleury that the king would not grant him this favor and advised the Duke of Orleans not to insist upon it. The prince, however, spoke of it while working with the king in the presence of the Duke de Charost; but the king had been forewarned and did not reply. The Duke of Orleans insisted and the king preserving the same silence put his hands up to his face and fled to his anteroom. Fleury who arrived that very moment followed him there; he remained there with him for three-quarters of an hour and the king continued signing every order pertaining to the finances.

CHAPTER XX.

Portrait and death of the Duke of Orleans.—Monsieur le Duc, Prince de Condé declared prime minister.

NATURE had endowed the Duke of Orleans with a face that was interesting, gracious and amiable. He was not tall, but he had a noble mien, he was easy; his character was kind, facile, frank and especially candid. He had black hair; his complexion was ruddy and he had a temperament always more or less given to good cheer, to pleasures. and alas to brutal debauchery, the only cause of the mistakes of his life for which posterity will reproach him.

The Duke of Orleans also had a love for the beautiful, for all the arts, for the physical sciences, for mechanics and other branches of knowledge which he cultivated all his life in order to satisfy this penchant, and which made him the most amiable and popular prince of his time. Louis XIV. was jealous of his popularity and his victories in Italy and Spain, his talents, his skill in the profession of war, his courage in the midst of the greatest dangers had not a little to do with drawing upon him that disgrace in which he lived as long as the old monarch survived.

Louis XIV. was umbrageous and jealous of all the marked talents of others, not dependent on him, if they did not serve to increase his own glory; or if they did not seem to have been created by him.

The regent had that kindly disposition of character which seems characteristic of the Bourbon race. Neither pride nor scorn for others were part of his makeup; he was easily approached; he engaged in conversation with every one, only assuming a tone suitable to his rank when speaking with kings or with princes.

Too easy, because he was too kind, he knew neither the hatred nor the pleasure of vengeance. The conspiracy of Cellamare was met and conquered without the shedding of a drop of blood; and indeed if four Britons lost their heads by it, it was because he was deceived by Dubois, by Montesquiou, and by the courtiers who surrounded him and who kept telling him that he would ruin the state.

Posterity will reproach the regent only with his attachment and his yielding to Dubois, the vilest and worst of men.

But this cardinal who acquired the secret of dominating him from childhood, of surrounding him with his influence and who made use of his power over him in after years, made pleasure and debauchery alluring to him, and if posterity blames this friendship in the prince, which was at the same time his greatest fault and his greatest misfortune, it must at the same time accord him credit for a broad mind, for the impetus given to the arts and sciences, for the great leniency towards his critics and even indifference to calumnies which represented him to the nation as the assassin of princes that he might rule in their place. It will accord him credit, above all, for having taken as a model the merciful Henry IV. whom moreover he resembled so much that the similarity was universally recognized.

With his mistresses the regent was always rather amiable, but he was given to unceremonious and frequent pleasures in their company. He was never vexed by their lack of fidelity nor by their persistent fondness for him; he abandoned one, took up with another, then returned to the first one, then the third or the tenth as the whim seized him. Some few knew how to engage his affections for some time; they succeeded in doing it only by presenting to him an amiable and ease loving disposition and by dissipating the cares caused by his work for the state. Such were the ladies de Parabère, d'Argenson, and others whom he distinguished by his rewards. He was passionately fond of variety, novelty and frequent change, and he often boasted of his frequent and illustrious victories. This prince died on the 17th of December at six o'clock in the evening, in his room where he was conversing with the Duchess de Phalaris, his mistress. He died as the result of an apoplectic fit which left him in an unconscious state. Parisians in joking about the death said: "He died assisted by his wonted confessor."

A half hour after the attack the surgeon of the Prince de Rohan bled him. Fifteen days afterwards Charic, his doctor, urged him to try some other cure and Maréchal, the first surgeon, who was a great friend of his and who had rendered him some signal services under the late king, told him, three days before his death, that he was but a walking apoplectic; and that he would not be surprised to have it announced at any moment that he had died. These predictions did not affect the prince, who put off the suggested course of treatment until the following week and he never lived to carry out his physician's suggestions.

Calumny was renewed against him after his death. It was said that the vaults of the Palais-Royal were full of gold, and the prince had only suffered death because, having attempted to poison Louis XV., he, himself had, by mistake, swallowed the fatal potion prepared for his intended victim. His son found his inheritance encumbered with debts, which were paid only by making great retrenchments in the ordinary family expenditures.

The Duke of Orleans being dead, la Vrillière advised Monsieur le Duc to profit by the occasion and to ask for himself the vacant place of prime minister. Former Bishop de Fréjus was with the king when Monsieur le Duc entered, and asked the young monarch for the place left vacant by the Duke of Orleans. The king made no reply, but he looked fixedly at the Bishop de Fréjus, who likewise remained silent; a nod of the head, mark of his approbation, was the only sign indicating that it was a feasible plan. The prelate breaking silence said to the Duke de Bourbon: "You see, sir, that His Majesty grants your petition and makes you prime minister." Bourbon immediately took the usual oath of fidelity.

CHAPTER XXI.

The results of the Spanish queen's ambition to rule in France.—Abdication of Phillip V.—Reign of Louis I., his son.—The unseemly conduct of the daughter of the regent, Queen of Spain.—Phillip V. reascends the throne.

A SHORT time after the death of the regent, France was agitated by the strange news that Phillip V. had abdicated the throne of Spain and that he had retired to Saint-Ildephonse with his wife, abandoning the kingdom to the prince of Asturias.

This action was not at all surprising in a person like King Phillip, who was every day becoming more melancholy, reserved, sombre, taciturn, and even flighty. This monarch had for a long time been wearied with the duties of the throne. His shrewd wife left nothing for him but the empty shell of power, whilst constantly busied with cares for his health, and tormented with the fear of losing it, he knew no other charms than the physical pleasures of conjugal love, without which his passionate temperament could not exist. Another pastime was long and frequent conversations with his confessor on subjects pertaining to his conscience.

But it was a matter of surprise that the queen, who dominated him, who constantly surrounded him with her influence, who permitted no mortal man to approach his sacred person, who guarded all the affairs of Spain as easily as she did the head and heart of her husband, should thus permit him to abandon his crown to a young prince utterly incapable of transacting any business of importance. To explain the enigma let us follow the thread of the ambition of this princess.

The plans of Alberoni having been frustrated, she had abandoned the unfortunate minister, who was merely the tool of her ambition. One part of her fleet having been dispersed and the other destroyed, she had been reduced to the necessity of abandoning force, and had to resort to petty ruses in order to carry out her ambitious schemes. Therefore she proposed to the regent the marriage of her daughter to the prince of Asturias and offered a mere babe, three years of age to Louis XV. who was ten or eleven years of age, and in spite of its tender age, the child was sent to France.

The queen thus retarded the birth of a daughter and gave herself a longer respite in which to plan the success of her schemes of aggrandizement.

But when after the death of the regent she saw Monsieur le Duc clad in supreme power, when she learned of the hatred of this prince for the house of Orleans, when Monsieur le Duc had assured her that he would favor the house of Phillip V. in case Louis XV. died, then, always consistent in her plans and crafty in the choice of means she made use of, always Italian in her external conduct relative to her great plan, she permitted the whims, the scruples, and the love of the king for quietude, to take their course and apparently consented to go to Saint-Ildephonse and be immured, but with the secret design of soon issuing from that resort with still greater power.

Moreover she abandoned a throne rendered almost insupportable to her on account of the discontent of the Spaniards, the hatred which she bore them, their resentment and the scandalous affronts they had been guilty of toward her.

It was then that she emptied the coffers of the king, that she might not be dependent on either the good-will or the pity of his successor; she accumulated at Saint-Ildephonse the revenues of the current year and for two years in advance, so that Louis I. would find the treasury empty.

Thus the Queen of Spain and Phillip V. retired to the country only in the hope of the early death of Louis XV., a hope that for a long time had held the houses of Orleans and all the European powers in a state of anxious suspense. They all had kept their eyes fixed on the frail health of the young monarch; every day they expected news of his death; and beheld with regret European peace endangered by the struggle between the house of Orleans and Spain contingent on his death. The queen, who continually incited his ambition, was so sure of his cause and its success, that she always had her treasures packed in trunks, all business concluded and all her jewelry put in a small casket, so that she could depart with the least possible delay at the slightest signal.

Was she aware of the colds and of the fits of indigestion of Louis XV? She was seen to open her beautiful eyes and gaze steadfastly into the eyes of those about her. She constantly asked for the latest news concerning Louis XV. and kept herself in readiness to immediately enter a carriage with her husband, to leave a detested people and, it may be added, a people that in turn detested her.

The daughter of the regent, wife of Louis I., when she ascended the throne of Spain, had received at the Palais-Royal, too liberal an education not to scorn the etiquette of the court of Madrid.

As long as Phillip V. and the queen reigned the young princess of Asturias, restrained by respect and filial submission, had been obliged to comport herself with prudence and always according to the orders of the king and the advice of his court, although in the beginning she was capricious and not at all submissive.

Her conduct underwent a complete change when she became queen and saw Phillip V. and his wife relegated to Saint-Ildephonse.

Then she gave free reign to all her passions and indulged in amusements that her sisters permitted in the Abbé of Chelles. She yielded to too great intimacy with the ladies-in-waiting, who knew how to please her and who participated in pleasures the very mention of which caused the retirement of Sancta Crux, her major domo, who did not wish to lend an air of decency to such scandalous scenes.

The old countess, d'Altamira, the chief lady-in-waiting, jealous of the other ladies, and uneasy at seeing herself kept away from evening parties, for she had passed the age when these pleasures were suitable, first spoke of the hours of retirement, which Spanish ceremonial did not permit of change.

The young queen made her an object of derision. She did not stop here but even made the countess's interpretation of Castilian etiquette ridiculous. Altamira therefore took revenge by informing the king, her husband, of all that passed secretly in the presence of the queen and her ladies-in-waiting.

The king loved his wife, but he learned with indignation of the reports of Altamira and he dismissed the guilty ladies-in-waiting. On the other hand he left in the queen's service only those who could not be suspected of being guilty of pleasures demanded by her tastes, on account of their youth and their virtue and he imprisoned the queen in a castle for eight days.

This young monarch, born in Spain and speaking Spanish, had already received Spanish principles and Spanish morality in his education and he was well grounded in them; he loved his country; he admired it, and felt himself wounded to the quick on learning of the shameful practices of his wife; he believed that it was his duty to punish her with firmness and to make her do penance. The queen submitted to the chastisement, succeeded in pacifying the king and by the show of respect and wifely affection, once more obtained his favor.

Twelve of the court ladies, however, were dismissed permanently, a thing which did not prevent the young queen from occasionally indulging in the same youthful pleasures with ladies of her own age.

Her husband died, a victim of smallpox, at the age of seventeen years, and there is every reason to believe that those who proposed to marry his widow, to the brother of the late king and heir of Phillip V., would have succeeded, if this princess had not lost the esteem of the Spaniards. They had been informed of the orgies of the queen and of the nature of the amusements she had indulged in. Therefore she returned to Paris and lived there in the strictest seclusion.

CHAPTER XXII.

The ministry of Monsieur le Duc, of the House of Condé.—Character of the prime minister.—Customs of the time and anecdotes of the court.

M. LE DUC was endowed from birth with strange passions, but, nevertheless, though courage and the military spirits are rarely found in alliance with vices of this nature, I must say of this prince, then chief of the House of Condé, that from his earliest youth he had given proof of personal bravery in the presence of the enemy, whose fire he had braved with so much coolness that it was said by witnesses that he would be the fitting heir of the military talents of the princes of his house.

The anxiety of his mother, her prayers and her remonstrances finally prevailed and brought back the young prince from his follies and Mme. de Nesle, a coquette, libertine, accustomed to the princes and fops of the time, soon learned to give this prince the tastes that were natural and decent and carried her success far enough to have several children by him. But unfortunately for France and for the duke, fate willed that he should meet two masked ladies at the ball of the opera, one of whom allured him so much and was enabled to please him in spite of her mask, that he was inspired with the desire to know her.

Two days after, these ladies, who perceived that they had been able to please him, met the prince again wearing the same costume and he again became a victim to their allurements. M. le Duc succeeded in recognizing Mme. d'Aussi, but he could not recognize her companion, who would not unmask. They therefore devoted themselves in an emulous manner to the purpose of increasing the curiosity of the prince and to make themselves still more interesting. They finally promised to reveal their identity at their first ball, if he still desired to make their acquaintance.

The duke did not fail to keep the appointment and the ball having commenced they continued to excite his curiosity by concealing their identity. After the thousand coquettish ruses a witty woman is capable of, the Marchioness de Prie, whose maiden name was Berthelot, (the wife of our ambassador at Turin), made known her identity. This lady was pretty, witty, shrewd and somewhat of a mischief-maker even at that time. She did not hesitate to carry on a conversation, seductive, bold and even lewd; she was ambitious and had brought to France all the voluptuous customs known to Italian women, so different from the customs of French women and yet so seductive to their lovers and to their husbands. The wife of the ambassador was so alluring that M. le Duc abandoned Mme. de Nesle and became passionately fond of her; the ambassador, who arrived from Turin, was neither angry nor jealous and was so much of a simpleton, or at least desired to pass for such, that he boasted in society of the kindnesses of M. le Duc and of his intimacy, which went so far, he said, as to lead him to eat and sleep in his home.

Mme. de Prie, who knew how to govern her husband, also knew how to enchant M. le Duc in every sense of that word. She induced him to engage in affairs of state during the regency; she associated with the Pâris brothers whose financial skill in the department of finance was universally recognized, and judging that the Duke of Orleans would live but a short time on account of his lax life, she predicted that M. le Duc might one day fill his position; and scarcely had the Duke of Orleans passed away, when she had all the affairs of state of France under her control. From this moment the ministers, chosen by Dubois, all of a shrewd character, sought to ascertain what they must do and be to please the favorite. La Vrillière, who had no other talent than the shrewdness of blindly following the dominant party, was well satisfied in executing the wishes of this imperious woman. D'Arménonville an unscrupulous man and versatile courtier was keeper of the seals. He was unscrupulous enough to do underhanded tricks and was devotedly attached to the service of Dubois, having secret understanding with the Jesuits in all parts of the world. He did not hesitate to become equally devoted to Mme. de Prie. Morille was more talented but of the same character, and indeed a man who was even bought and sold by the English. He enabled Dubois to draw a pension from the Cabinet of London. As to Breteuil, minister of war, he had other means of pleasing her, being skillful enough to make her unfaithful to the duke, and the baron indeed had more influence over her mind than any of the other ministers and if the latter had her confidence in their ability to execute her wishes in the routine work of the ministry, Breteuil obtained her confidence from the first to such a degree, that he was given the direction of state affairs. Breteuil was not a man of genius but an honest man whose only real fault was his too great complaisance with Dubois. He was the creature of the House of Orleans and having become minister under M. le Duc, he conducted himself honestly in a trying position where his loyalty might be questioned by both of the rival houses.

Dodun was a still more important man than all of these to Mme. de Prie for he was minister of finance; he was more submissive and more devoted to the favorite than all the other ministers; moreover she was prudent enough to openly protect the famous Duvernay, whom she could at any moment elevate by disgracing Dodun if he were not in harmony with her. Dodun, who did not regard Duvernay as a vain bugbear, was a man of extreme and peerless humility, utterly void of personal will, the most servile " errand-boy," and servant even of Mme. Berthelot de Prie, who had accustomed him to the functions of a simple valet-de-chambre.

These were they, who governed the affairs of France in 1724. Dubois had formed the ministry with all these mediocre characters; the regent had not hesitated to cover them with ridicule even in public, as we have noted above; Mme. de Prie made them her clerks; and we shall see shortly what bagatelles these great statesmen devoted their attentions to during the ministry of M. le Duc.

CHAPTER XXIII.

Rivalry between the Houses of Orleans and Condé.—Continuation of the picture of public morals.

THE rivalry between the Houses of Orleans and Condé broke the monotony of a pitiable ministry and the son of the regent, who had been initiated into the affairs of state for some months, could not endure the thought of being dominated by M. le Duc, whom he regarded as a prince beneath him, both in rank, talents and in intellect. The regent, however, skillful in the art of estimating men's characters told him plainly enough that he would never be a very distinguished man. He even told him one day distinctly and in the presence of the whole assembly in the Palais-Royal: "Remember, my son, that you will never be anything but an honest man."

In spite of this horoscope, the Duke of Orleans betrayed publicly jealousy of M. le Duc, prime minister, and refused to treat him any differently than he did during the regency of his father. He consistently conducted himself as etiquette dictated to the first prince of the blood and if M. le Duc did enjoy power in the conduct of governmental affairs, the Duke of Orleans kept him strictly within his rank of prince and even in the most minute details he maintained himself in all his dealings with the duke as one conscious of his eminent position as first prince of the blood of France, heir presumptive governed by chiefs, who having derived their customs from the former court and seen the danger of the vicious examples of the regent pass by, had maintained themselves pure in life and character, free from all the depravity of the following generation. On the other hand there were only a few of the parvenu families elevated and enriched by the political revolutions, who persisted in the evil tendencies of the courtiers of the Palais-Royal.

to the throne, and forced him to come to him in order to inform him that he had been chosen prime minister.

Thus everything had become trivial and petty in the court. The great pageantry and the imposing tone of Louis XIV. had disappeared. The politics of the regency, engineered by arbitrary and vicious ministers, no longer stirred men's minds; the great pre-eminent characters, good or bad, were no more. Young princes without talent, beautiful princesses, witty, amiable, but debauched; legitimate children of Louis XIV., all in a state of consternation at the brilliant *coups d'etate* of the regency; a young king fourteen years of age, weak, without energy and without will power, governed by an old devotee of religion. Such is the sad picture of the French court at this time.

The culture of Louis XIV., the general rules of decorum and deportment, however, still existed; but these things were scattered only in a few select societies; they were not found, however, in their purity but were sullied by the noisome atmosphere which dominated society after the beginning of the regency. This was true for instance, of Rambouillet, where the young king was to be instructed in the first principles of good taste and of genuine gallantry, which were to be admired in his court during the ministry of Fleury. There the decent, delicate and natural conduct, all relics of the time of Louis XIV., were admired. The houses that were specially tenacious of the rules of the old court were des Luynes, des La Rochefoucauld, des Mourtmart, Sully, la Vallière, la Feuillade, etc. All these houses were governed by chiefs, who having derived their customs from the former court and seen the danger of the vicious examples of the regent pass by, had maintained themselves pure in life and character, free from all the depravity of the following generation. On the other hand there were only a few of the parvenu families elevated and enriched by the political revolutions, who persisted in the evil tendencies of the courtiers of the Palais-Royal.

CHAPTER XXIV.

The sequel of the rivalry of the Houses of Orleans and Condé.— Marriage of the Duke of Orleans.

IN the chaotic state of morals and social customs the heir-presumptive to the throne and the prime minister, chiefs of two branches of the same house, soon drifted from rivalry into open quarrels and indiscreet discussion. These were wrongly reported by valets or by courtiers and from sullen disputes, hatred, then calumny, resulted. The regent had procured for his son the patents of the colonel-general of French and foreign infantry and colonels-general had had among other prerogatives, that of working personally with the king. M. le Duc, inflexible in his determination to humiliate, as he said, the Orleans family asserted that this claim was preposterous and extravagant. Mme. of Orleans also desired to have her son at the head of two regiments. She sustained Le Blanc, a minister of whom we shall speak presently, wishing to retain him in position, because he could not be devoted to M. le Duc, who persecuted him; and she not only desired to obtain his pardon directly from the king but she was even bitterly opposed to receiving any pardon for him, if it were to be received through M. le Duc.

Thus when a distribution of the apartments of Versailles was made in 1724, she refused to accept those that her son desired because the assignment was made by M. le Duc, but she obliged her son to ask for the apartments directly from the king.

M. le Duc, on the other hand, was continually seeking means to avenge himself for the haughty attitude of M. and Mme. of Orleans and not slow in driving their creature from the administration of police in order to displease them. D'Argenson governed the police with less talent than his father, but with more circumspection and with more deference to men's opinions and feelings. This position, having become more important and delicate, was of so much inportance that a prime minister had need of having an administrator of it, who was entirely in sympathy with his wishes. This was especially so since the position had been administered by d'Argenson, père. Thus Mme. de Prie, who had all the curiosity of her sex, and M. le Duc, continually excited by suspicions that always torment narrow minds, called a man to this position whom they could be sure of. This was a relative of Mme. de Prie, the famous d'Omberval, known by his monopolies, and who had scarcely arrived and taken up the duties of his office when he was suspected, and not without good grounds, of being guilty of favoring the monopolies of a chosen few.

Mme. of Orleans was furious, for they also had dismissed from the lodgings in Versailles the gentlemen whom the regent had placed there and who were the support of their faction at court. Belle-Isle, Clermont, Simiane, and the *roués* lost their apartments. The ruin of the faction created by the regent, her husband, and the elevation of interminable quarrels in France the Orleanists and the faction of M. le Duc had a lively quarrel concerning all these trifles. The king who finally intervened requested his minister to yield and M. le Duc was compelled to have the instructions drawn up for the request of the hand of Princess of Baden and to choose for this purpose a titled person; but always full of secret resentment, and not daring to refuse the instruction nor the choice of a titled person, he selected a person who was unfriendly to the Orleans family and gave the commission to his creature, the Marquis de Matignon. As to the request to be made in the name of the king, he ordered Matignon to simply pay an indifferent compliment and not to make a request according to the old time custom. The Matignons, under the duke, began to be favored with all sorts of benefits and as usual drew upon themselves the jealousy of the courtiers.

CHAPTER XXV.

Richelieu ambassador to Vienna.—He was first taken for a spy.—He challenges Riperda, Spanish Ambassador.—His useful and gallant conduct towards the Countess Badioni, Mistress of Prince Eugene.

WHILE the inner court of France was thus agitated, parties being formed, and parliaments making leagues, and while Fleury was silently watching the minister, whom he secretly hoped to supplant, Duke de Richelieu, made ambassador to Vienna, was preparing to treat with the emperor.

Charles VI., the thirteenth and last emperor of the Austrian House, had inherited ambition, pride, the determination, even of the principles of his family. In him ended the males of that superb Austrian family that by its pride and despotism had long ago ruined Switzerland and Holland, that had made the imperial throne almost hereditary in its family for three long centuries, notwithstanding the fact that it was constitutionally elective. This family had incorporated in its possessions so many kingdoms or sovereignties, either by right of conquest or voluntary submission, and its influence on the Courts of the Empire was such, that all Germany trembled, especially under the three last emperors. Dangerous to the liberty of Europe, it had demonstrated how unvarying conduct and principles consistently followed out by sovereigns, in the long run, dissipate all national assemblies and triumph over the multitude, which does not bear anything but the fickle and transient opinions of the centuries, which skillful princes can always modify when they are dangerous to their success. In Spain, Austria had destroyed the power of the Cortès and the Grandees. In Hungary she had worked for the same end, and was even endeavoring by means of small, almost secret attacks, often renewed, however, to rob Flanders of its privileges and to tire out the adherence to public freedom. Such was the genius of the house of Austria, which was dying out. Charles VI. was forty years of age when the Duke de Richelieu reached Vienna. He was born in 1685; (by his wife, the Princess of Brunswick-Blankenberg-Wolfenbuttel), he had only two daughters: the celebrated Maria-Theresa, then eight years of age and Maria Leonora born in the year 1718, and a third who died at the age of two years. He was of a sombre and melancholy disposition, harsh towards his generals and his courtiers; there was nothing but pomp and ostentation in his court; there was no easiness and still less gallantry. He was a stranger to generosity, to compassion, and yet he was better than the majority of his predecessors in principle and character; for his severity was rather political than the stamp of his own character.

As to the Court of Charles VI. the scrupulous etiquette and ceremonious despotism were observed there with the most extreme exactness. Religious devotion reigned there in ostentation, and as the emperor was a religious devotee, every one was obliged to imitate him. Here is the letter that the Duke de Richelieu wrote to Cardinal Polignac on this subject. This will convey an idea of the inner workings of the Court of Charles VI.

"I have led a very pious Lenten life, during which time I have not had a quarter of an hour's leisure a day and I confess that, if I had known what kind of a life an ambassador must lead here, nothing would have led me to accept this ambassy, where under pretext of invitations and of public functions and chapels, the emperor causes himself to be humbly followed by the ambassadors, as if they were *valets-de-chambre*. Only a Capuchian friar in the most robust health could withstand the strain on his constitution during Lent. To give Your Eminence an idea by actual count I have spent since Palm Sunday until Tuesday after Easter, exactly one hundred hours in church with the emperor. The Count du Luc, who has been here eighteen months, nine or ten of which passed before he had his court reception and the rest in sickness, left us in entire ignorance of this treasure of piety which I have just discovered to my expense. I confess it is my opinion that devoutness and the unheard of constraint, that is approved here, yet is found in no other court in the world, is something simply unbearable."

Cardinal de Polignac answered the Duke de Richelieu from Rome in these terms:—

"As to the word painting that you have made of the way in which you have fulfilled your Lenten duties during the Holy week and Easter, I believe that I can do no better than to felicitate you on having passed it; it is quite likely that you have never experienced this in your life. Imagine a cardinal at Rome doing exactly the same thing. It is true, however, that we are paid for our trouble."

Such was the Court of Charles VI. It may be seen that it resembled somewhat the court at Rome.

The new ambassador did not wish to appear in Vienna unless in the most resplendent apparel and imposing magnificence, being persuaded that rich equipages with a numerous and superbly liveried retinue should announce the representative of the greatest king in Europe. No one had, up to that time, displayed such luxury and for the first time he satisfied this penchant, which he had always had for magnificence. He had brought with him a large number of gentlemen, pages, squires, foot-soldiers, couriers and footmen, the servants of his chamber were very numerous; indeed he neglected no opportunity to dazzle Vienna by his ostentation. Notwithstanding the pomp with which the Duke de Richelieu surrounded himself, he was at first taken as a spy from the Court of France and he was very poorly received; he was even told that he was too young to be an ambassador (he was only twenty-nine years of age at that time). He informed the Bishop of Fréjus of some annoyances that he had suffered; but the latter replied by cautioning him to be patient, and above all to remember the necessity of being extremely prudent.

The Emperor Charles VI., proud and haughty, was surrounded by the most scrupulous etiquette. This prince was a devout religionist and Richelieu was obliged to seem to be one. Worn out by the unending church duties, he bore witness of his weariness more than once to the women, with whom he corresponded and especially in his letters to the duchess—who carried on a correspondence with him. Likewise he gave the same impression to the Marquis de Silly, who informed him of everything that transpired in the Court of France.

The ministers of the empire were vexed at seeing the young duke arrive. There was no love lost between them, and Prince Eugene, especially the object of their jealousy, gave them more umbrage since he seemed to be on better terms than ever with the emperor for having materially contributed to the conclusion of the treaty with Spain. The emperor regarded it as his own work and he had determined upon the marriage of the archduchesses with the heirs of the Spanish throne.

In such circumstances the ambassador of France had to exercise great skill and firmness of character. He played a very subordinate rôle. The Court of Vienna, entirely prejudiced in favor of that of Spain, intended to put the Duke de Riperda in possession of the chapels, claiming that if one of the two were once there the other one would have to wait, since the first could not be dispossessed without insult. In every manner the Viennese Court endeavored to humiliate the Duke de Richelieu, who received orders from the court to postpone his entry. Richelieu made a vigorous representation that he ought to make entry at once and contend with him for the honor even though he should arrive; at the same time he sent word that the latter would return prime minister to Spain.

He made the observation to M. de Morville, chargé of foreign affairs, that it was necessary to assume a haughty tone in order to destroy the idea that these people had of our weakness and of the timidity of our government, assuring him that if they would take the advice he proposed, they would succeed in making this court do just as France wanted it to, and that they could propose to the court to be our mediator with Spain, which was thought incredible at that time. He added that the emperor was fearful of war, that his greatest desire was to establish his daughters in life and that the fear he entertained of France could alone furnish the lever with which we could work.

According to this plan in spite of the advice of the French minister, who still wished to temporize, the ambassador wished to assume the manner which he thought most effective in dealing with the ministers of the emperor and in a short time he received assurances from them of the desire that their master had to live in peace with the king. Nevertheless, M. de Morville rejected every plan of reconciliation with Spain, if brought about in concert with the emperor, wishing no other mediator than the King of England through whom they expected much. He claimed that the emperor was not dealing in good faith; that he had direct interest in preventing the French aims and that his only object was to sow suspicion and distrust between the King of France and the King of England. Nevertheless the duke received permission to proceed with his reception at the Austrian Court.

Riperda, who had his tools everywhere and who shared the hatred that his court felt towards France, thought that he could assume haughty airs towards this young man, who was making his début in the career of diplomacy. He had arrogated to himself the precedence and thought that he could maintain it; but Richelieu, who inwardly regarded him as a scoundrel, did not long tolerate the tone that he assumed. He endeavored to avoid engaging in any business that would put the two courts in an embarrassing position, but at the same time he assumed that it would be entirely permissible for him to pick a quarrel as between ambassadors. The occasion was not long in presenting itself. One day the Duke de Riperda, wishing to precede him in going into the presence of the emperor, was still on the stairway. Richelieu more alert passed by him and in passing elbowed him so vigorously that he caused him to fall back on the stairway. Thinking that this event would have a serious issue he betook himself in the evening to the house of Riperda, who had the announcement made that he had gone out. The next morning Richelieu sent to inquire about his health. The footman returned without reply; finally he encountered the ambassador on the street and expressed his astonishment at his not having sent him news of his condition, after he had presented himself at his home and sent messengers there for that purpose; the ambassador stammered a few words and abruptly left him; the Duke de Richelieu shrugged his shoulders.

His rank was no longer disputed. Sometime afterwards Riperda was recalled.

Richelieu had sought every means to ally himself with Prince Eugene, who had shown great friendship for him, but this friendship only consisted of vain and frivolous appearances. Prince Eugene was not communicative and the ambassador could not derive the benefit that he had hoped to derive from it. As usual he called love into his service; he had already made use of love in bringing about his own promotion and he still thought that it could do service for him. The Countess Badiani was being courted by Prince Eugene, whose entire confidence she possessed; Richelieu, remembering that he had often succeeded in pleasing the gentler sex, endeavored to gain the good will of this woman so essential in his plan of campaign.

Entirely devoted to business, he bent his whole attention to the success of the undertaking, which had been intrusted to him; he flattered himself with having penetrated, unaided, the secrets of the government of the Empire, and having a curiosity to assure himself of this fact, he thought no better plan presented itself than that of winning the intimate confidence of the Countess Badiani. The success that had always followed him in France did not abandon him in Austria. His rival was Prince Eugene, a man celebrated for the victories won over Louis XIV. and over the Turks, but a man whom age could not always assure success in love. Richelieu appeared before Mme. Badiani with the advantage of youth and ease, and the countess, full of discernment, could not refrain from secretly giving him preference. Very adroit and insidious he soon shared her favors with the prince, and acquainted the countess with the merits he possessed. Astonished at his gallantry and at the many proofs that he had shown of it, she finally judged that the ambassador was as much an adept in the art of loving, as he was in the art of diplomacy and conceived for him a most ardent esteem.

Confidence followed esteem; all the secrets of Prince Eugene were wrested from her heart by the new lover, who in this manner, prevented operations contrary to the interests, with which he was charged. It was thus that our skillful ambassador learned of the determination of the emperor to postpone the day of giving his reception, and that he learned that the Duke de Riperda, who had publicly announced his departure, did not really wish to leave. Then he was seen to redouble his activity and to speak more openly than ever before; but Prince Eugene and M. de Zinzerdorf assured him that the emperor could not be induced to act by importunities.

CHAPTER XXVI.

Public reception of Richelieu in Vienna.—Adventure of the sleighs with the Princess Lichtenstein.—The sequel of the adventure.—He causes the cardinal's cap to be given to the Bishop of Fréjus.—He is made chevalier of the order of the Holy Ghost before being eligible on account of age.—He concludes his negotiations and returns to Paris.

FINALLY, after a thousand new bickerings and infinite pains, his public reception was set for the 7th of November, and his public audience with the emperor for the following day. It was on this occasion that the Duke de Richelieu displayed all that magnificence and pomp which he loved to be distinguished. Never before had an ambassador appeared with such a retinue. In satisfying his taste, he thought it was necessary to overawe the Court of Vienna. He had sixty-nine carriages drawn by six horses each, and six others of still greater magnificence, also drawn by six horses. The carriage of the ambassador was lined, within and without, with crimson velvet, covered with a golden embroidery in relief, with golden fringes; the four panels were decorated with the coat-of-arms of the ambassador, embroidered in relief with medallions. His crest, likewise embroidered, filled up the small side panels. The great rear panel presented some more beautiful embroidery in relief, as did also the imperial, the velvet of which was covered with large golden branches of golden embroidery, which, meeting above in the middle, formed a sort of flower. The horses were bay, the harness crimson velvet, covered with plaques of gilded silver and Spanish points in gold, and the aigrettes were crimson plumes mixed with golden ornaments.

The second was decorated with velvet of the same richness, with designs symbolic of peace; the horses were dapple gray; the harness was embroidered in gold, as was the velvet of the carriage; the plumes were blue with golden ornaments.

The third carriage was decorated with green velvet, embroidered in gold with fringes of the same material; the imperial was provided with ornaments of bronze-gold; the horses were dun colored, with a harness of similar color, embroidered green plumes with gold decorations.

The fourth carriage was in jonquil velvet, all covered with silver embroidery with silver fringes. On the imperial of the coach there appeared figures of Prudence, of Secrecy, etc. It was drawn by six black Italian horses; the harness, similar to the velvet decorations within, was covered with plaques and embroidered with silver; and with jonquil plumes mixed with silver ornaments.

The two other carriages were, one of flax-gray velvet, embroidered in gold, with harness to match; and the other of rose velvet, embroidered in silver; the horses drawing this carriage were chestnut, with rose-colored harness provided with plaques of chased silver, mixed plumes and aigrettes.

The retinue was equally brilliant; six couriers clad in red velvet entirely laced in silver; the rest of their outfit also being in silver cloth and fringes.

Fifty footmen followed clad in scarlet cloth, with grand livery of purple and silver silk, embroidered caps provided with white plumes and silver swords. And after them came twelve foot soldiers, holding silver staffs in their hands; and twelve mounted pages clad in red velvet embroidered in silver, with everything in conformity. Then came the governor of pages, lieutenant-governor, squire, sub-squires, Suisses, twenty-four grooms, half mounted and half leading horses. This magnificent pageant left the Faubourgh called the Landstresse, and entered the Italian gate on the way to the Rue Saint-Jean, where the palace of the ambassador was.

Another very extraordinary circumstance distinguished this entry of the duke for all time from that of all the other ministers. The horses of the duke's carriage, the saddle horses and those of the retinue, led by hand, were all shod in silver; the shoe of silver was of two parts and was held only by a very small horseshoe nail, so that on the journey all the horses cast their shoes and the people were permitted to keep the shoes as souvenires. The next day the ambassador had his public audience with the emperor, the reigning empress and the Empress Amelie; the same pomp marked this function. The duke appeared in his French attire that day and in vestments similar to those used by the peers when they go to parliament, and he introduced the same custom in all public gatherings. There were in his palace numerous tables; five hundred covers were laid; the gentlemen of the papal legation and the Archbishop of Vienna were invited; all the officers of the government were invited; and in order to give more freedom to the people, who gathered to witness this festival where everything was provided in a prodigal way, the ambassador opened all his apartments and did not enter until night.

That day was also signaled in a remarkable way by the precipitate departure of the Duke du Riperda.

Richelieu was saddened but not surprised when he learned of the exile of M. le Duc and of Mme. de Prie. On his arrival at Vienna he had been a witness of the hatred of the duke existing there; every day presented some new story or some insulting song aimed at him, and he had not the least doubt, but that he would be sacrificed. Moreover he had been instructed by the duchess of the measures pursued by the Bishop de Fréjus. Sure of his ground, he profited by the complaints accumulating against the prime minister and his favorite to groom himself for the place.

The duke received the orders of the king, through M. de Morville, not to make use of the mediation of the pope and of the English king, in the belief that the emperor would never listen to this plan. The Duke de Richelieu who was persuaded that the contrary was true, and who had always believed that in endeavoring to overawe the Austrian Court, he would succeed in securing Austrian mediation, had to combat the opinions of the Council of Versailles and the plans of the Court of Vienna. His whole manner of life was changed. It was no longer that of a man whose whole life is devoted to dreaming of pleasure and nothing more. Twelve, yes fifteen, hours of work a day no longer appalled him; he even worked long into the night and his nights, which formerly were taken up by love episodes, were now devoted to most serious matters of business.

This change in his manner of life, and the important negotiations he burdened himself with, caused a breakdown in his health. At Vienna he became troubled with indigestion; and in the midst of his anxiety, regarding himself, he discovered by quite an extraordinary event that almost omniscient man, Damis, whom he had mourned for so long in France. His joy dispelled his fears; but it was not complete, for this man told him that he had made a vow to renounce the philosopher's stone. He would have to devote his whole attention to medicine and after having prescribed some ineffectual remedies, he advised him to use tea, which was very beneficial and which he used for the rest of his life. He studied medicine with him and applied himself to the work of gathering a multitude of remedies which, judging by their labels, were all very wonderful.

The magnificent pomp in which the ambassador lived in Vienna caused him to incur many debts; he received but little money from France and was reduced to straitened circumstances. Not finding it easy to obtain credit from the Germans, he was obilged to have jewels and diamonds sent secretly from France, to be used as pledges. Seeing that they would not give him all the money that had been promised him, and seeing that he had been opposed in his diplomatic negotiations he threatened to ask for his recall. Moreover the emperor did not invite him to any private fêtes, except those of the chapels, where he was overwhelmed with functions, and where his position was very embarrassing and very annoying.

He complained of his position to M. de Morville and the Bishop de Fréjus, and received the following letter from him:—

RAMBOUILLET, May 4, 1726.

"I received, sir, two days ago, almost at the same hour the two letters of the 10th and of the 17th with which you honored me. It is true that we have noted in your despatches quite a decided desire to leave Vienna, and that you have no doubt but that you will receive an order to that effect. M. de Saint-Saphorin was of the same opinion and there was every reason to believe that such would be the case two months ago. There has been no ill-feeling towards you here, and it is very natural that under the conditions you find yourself in, you are anxious to return. You may be assured, sir, that this has made no bad impression and that, if your recall would not have a bad effect in the present circumstances, the scorn that the emperor manifests at every act of regard, by leaving you a simple resident there, would be a sufficient reason for us to consider your request.

"Although we are not perfectly acquainted with M. de Saint-Saphorin, we can but believe, that if you are intimately associated with him, you have used your talents to advantage and you are certainly to be praised on your conduct. You described perfectly the character of the Court of Vienna, and we depend upon you with entire confidence and are pleased with the manner in which you are treating with that court. The great promises of the Duke de Riperda may have given them a desire for war; but the emperor thinks, in his stubborn way, that he has deceived him, and that the King of Spain, himself, is in need of money to pay his troops and his expenses. Thus all these ministers are more humble and protest that they do not desire war; and they have recourse to the most flagrant artifices in their endeavors to cause us to break with England, a thing in which they will not succeed.

"Nothing is more just, sir, than your anxiety at not being able to pay your debts, and M. de Morville is making every endeavor to send you money. Let us hope that there will be more in circulation than there has been for some time past, and that the king will soon be in a position to pay you. It is very important that you conceal the extremity to which you are reduced and I, on my part, will preserve it as an absolute secret.

"It does not appear to me that anything has been hidden from you nor that you have not been accorded the implicit confidence that you merit so well. We are in a bad crisis but it will in the end come out to our advantage, for surely Europe is in too violent a state of agitation now, to have the present status quo continue.

"I beg you, sir, to be assured of the respect and the perfect affection with which I am yours, etc.,

"A. H., Bishop of Fréjus."

We see by this letter that he was not promised immediate succor and his embarrassment increased day by day. Moreover he learned that it was expected in France to bring about the reconciliation with Spain through the mediation of the pope and England, and he was very much vexed, that his constant protestations, that reconciliation could not be brought about except through the influence of the emperor, had not found general acceptance.

His agent, charged with the duty of procuring money for him at whatever premium, sent him sixty thousand francs, which sustained his courage somewhat. The Duchess de ——, that ever faithful friend, having become a widow and mistress of her own fortune, presented him with four letters of credit of twenty-five thousand francs each, which enabled him to await the money, that M. de Morville kept promising him constantly, without ever sending it.

The appearance of things soon changed. M. de Richelieu redoubling his activity, everywhere sustaining the dignity of his character, finally saw an opportunity to begin negotiations. The Counts Zinzerdorf and Staremberg seemed to invite negotiations; but Prince Eugene spoke with warmth against France, and, thinking that he would intimidate him by his haughty scorn, he exhibited, at the same time, all his animosity against the English king. The duke, who was not accustomed to being treated so haughtily, restrained himself and preserving his coolness in the conversation, bested his antagonist. He detected through all the ministers of Prince Eugene, the fear that he entertained lest there might be war and how unwelcome it would be to him; he was somewhat disturbed by the Vice-Chancellor, who, on account of a private opinion, desired to complicate matters. However, Richelieu was very skillful in calming the prince and was not long in re-establishing friendship with him.

He learned that the other ministers were deceiving him continually, and it was during a sleigh-ride that he learned all the secrets of the Court of Vienna while least expecting it. The emperor, who, as we have already said, never thought of the duke except in regard to religious services and always forgot him when pleasure or amusement were in order, invited him finally to a magnificent sleigh-riding party. Richelieu believed that he ought to appear there with his ordinary magnificence and was invited to escort the Princess de Lichtenstein. This lady was very pretty and very intimate with all the ministers. After the usual compliments she said to him during the course of the ride: "M. Ambassador, the zeal that you show in carrying out the wishes of your court, honors you, and you will allow me to give you some advice, since I have taken a deep interest in your case."

We may believe that this mark of confidence was received with gratitude by the duke; he begged her to enter into the greatest details and he knew that moderation should not be followed in this instance; he learned that the increase in the armament of the emperor was not a sign of war, but simply a means of intimidating France; and the French policy would be to arm likewise, in order to give the world to understand that she did not fear the war, with which she was threatened. He also learned that people had a very poor idea of our government, and that its weakness alone justified the emperor in his bold attitude towards Richelieu; finally he learned that the choice of the pope and the king of England as mediator between France and Spain was not well received in France because the emperor alone could bring about the reconciliation that was sought for.

The Duke de Richelieu was more than pleased to learn that the secrets which had been concealed from him tallied exactly with his own opinions. Positive that he was right and that it was necessary to follow the course that he had already marked out to terminate this great negotiation, he redoubled his importunities to the French ministers and replied to those of the emperor, who threatened him with war, that France was ready to undertake it; that she had simply begun negotiations to avoid the shedding of blood, but that neither money nor men were wanting. At last he was fortunate enough to have his ideas adopted in France and his penetration and his policy were justified.

His enemies, always jealous of his successes in love, still more jealous of his employment in the important negotiations with which he was intrusted, caused the most harmful detrimental rumors to be started concerning him. They implied that he had sold secrets of state; but the penetration of the duke and his success imposed silence on them. People were astonished that such a dissipated young man could be gifted with qualities necessary in the successful ambassador.

The Princess de Lichtenstein, who had shown marked interest in him, was well worthy of being the recipient of Richelieu's gratitude; she was well disposed toward the duke, whose wit and amiability she had already admired. The latter was not bound to the Countess de Badiani with very strong ties; he believed that he could form new ties with the princess. This liaison was a diversion which was very welcome to him, as he was overwhelmed with work and needed recreation. The mystery which surrounded her made the pleasure still more interesting; he could only visit the princess at night, as otherwise he might compromise her and excite the suspicions of the ministers of Vienna. He was accustomed to visit her without a retinue, clad unostentatiously and on foot. He entered her palace through a concealed door which opened at a secret signal. One evening as he was leaving her home in this unusual dress, he encountered, near the home of Mme. de Lichtenstein, three men of his, following, very drunk who did not recognize him. They saw a man who was trying to conceal himself and they wanted to ascertain who he was. The day signal was to clap the hands three times. The duke had already begun to signal, when they accosted him; he passed to the other side of the street; his men did likewise; he retraced his steps; they imitated him; finally the duke, disconcerted, knowing that he was dealing with three of his footmen, struck the one that was nearest him with his cane, ordering him away. The servant, who could not believe that it was his master, became angry and shouted that the livery of the Ambassador of France was being insulted. The others came to his aid; passersby crowded about; they were about to arrest the duke; and he had scarcely time to give his name, for they threatened to handle him roughly. Being recognized, the scene became still more disagreeable for him, for his footmen, on their knees, plead for pardon, using the words, Highness, Excellence, Monseigneur. The duke, who wished to preserve his incognito, regretted the necessity of being named as much as he did being insulted. The people assembled; he was obliged to retire and it was more difficult for him to evade the excuses of his servants than it was to avoid the wrath of the crowd. The next day the princess was told of this unfortunate event and a rendezvous was fixed for the same day in which love indemnified them for the annoyance of the night before.

The Duke de Richelieu was thus consoled for the insults which he endured in his negotiations. His persistence and constancy were crowned with success; and the treaty was signed in favor of France. It is the duty of historians to enter into all the details of this negotiation; we shall content ourselves with saying that it was brought to a successful issue by the talents, the careful tact and the shrewd common sense of Richelieu. He had not limited himself to the work of negotiating this treaty. He had also assisted much in winning the cardinalship for the Bishop de Fréjus. This bishop, even though seeming to be unconcerned in the matter, had caused the king to sign the degree banishing M. le Duc, and it was on this occasion that the monarch showed that dissimulation which never honors a king, an example of which was shown by his predecessor in dismissing Fouquet. Louis XV. showed marked friendship for M. le Duc, even on the very day that he signed the order for his retreat to Chantilly; the latter did not receive it until the moment he was about to leave for Rambouillet. It is sad to see the Cardinal de Fleury accustoming his pupil to deeds unworthy of the head of a great nation. Doubtless M. le Duc merited his dismissal; all France was complaining of him and especially of his blind attachment for Mme. de Prie, who really governed France. He had acted as all ministers have acted, who, on beginning their public duties, destroy the good or bad works of those whom they succeed; they want plans that are their own, and the people are always the victims of this experimenting: but nothing compelled Cardinal de Fleury to have the king play this miserable comedy, the outcome of which was foreseen by all reasonable people. Afterwards he informed Louis XV. that he abolished the functions of prime minister and as if the young prince had desired to administer his realm himself, he caused him to write to Cardinal de Noailles, that not confident of being strong enough to undertake the government he asked him to offer public prayers to God to obtain from him grace necessary to govern his states. Incense was burned in all the churches and the people, always inclined to believe the good that is told them concerning their kings, showed excessive joy in learning that their sovereign was going to see to everything for himself and to work for their welfare.

During this time the modest Bishop de Fréjus, who had carefully kept all his rivals at a distance and caused the important places to be given to his tools, who had kept his pupil away from all important affairs, accustoming him to avoid work, gradually usurped authority. He knew well that his master, who had been brought up as if the throne were strange to him and ignorant of everything, was unable to take a single step without consulting him. He reigned in his stead without ever having the appearance of doing it. In a little while his conduct could not be mistaken; he wished to be prince of the church, and without having the title of prime minister he exercised the authority of that office in every sense of the word. This mild prelate, moving as slowly as the proverbial turtle, never lost sight of the goal he intended to reach; he reached it at the age of seventy-three and he preserved rare tact to the very end of his career.

Fleury had none of those brilliant qualities that go to make a great minister but nevertheless France was happy during his administration. The kingdom soon assumed another appearance. Exhausted by the system of Law, the cardinal thought that he possessed in himself resources enough to repair the losses occasioned by that charlatan. Like a skillful physician, who knows the weak temperament of his patient, and who, not daring to give any strong remedy, abandons him to the care of nature, that gently brings back to health, the cardinal, who did not like war, who had qualities unsuited to carry on war, who wished to be at peace, bought peace at any price. And this peace caused commerce to flourish and brought back abundance to the French fields and homes. It was thus that Fleury accomplished much by doing nothing at all; he was timid and dared not undertake any great enterprise; on the other hand being very economical, he regarded the state as a large home to be governed accordingly. He repaired French losses by giving France peace. Genius had nothing to do with her fortune; Fleury was incapable of grasping great ideas, but his administration is sufficient proof, that an honest man in establishing tranquillity in a realm can make it flourishing; that a state like France does not need a minister who has vast and sublime ideas; that if he does not place the country's resources in the hands of rascals and at the mercy of schemers, he is doing his country a great service. The ministry of Cardinal de Fleury, who, as we very easily recognize by his conduct of affairs, was not a great man, was a pattern for all succeeding ministries.

The Duke de Richelieu saw with great pleasure the success of his negotiations, his health was failing and his one desire was to return to France. He was mentioned favorably as ambassador to Spain and in fact this was the only ambassy that could have tempted him; but he desired, before deciding to accept it, to pass some time at Paris. Weary of public duties he continually wrote to his mistresses and to the Marquis de Silly, his friend, that he had no other ambition than that of obtaining a good government where he could be master of an important office at court. His presence was still necessary at Vienna and he expected to be nominated premier plenipotentiary to the congress; but Cardinal de Fleury had reserved this place for himself. We can see by the following letter, that he was very sure of his authority and at the same time he was doing justice to the Duke de Richelieu.

RAMBOUILLET, June 26, 1725.

"I reply, sir, to the letter of the 14th inst., with which you have honored me and which gave us the signature of M. de Bournonville in the name of the King of Spain and consequently the conclusion of the important matter, with which you were charged. I understand your eager desire to leave a place trying to your health, detrimental to your domestic interests, and where there is but little more for you to accomplish. And since you ask for your dismissal with so much urgency, the king is too well pleased with your services to refuse you your request. The only question for us now is to give you public marks of the king's satisfaction which you have so well merited, and to choose some one who may be able to maintain the good feeling established by the signing of the preliminaries between the two courts. I believe, sir, that I can assure you in the name of the king, that he will bestow on you the *Cordon Bleu* in the month of January next; but awaiting his majesty's expressed wishes concerning it, I ask you, if you please, the same question that I have also asked of your plenipotentiary, the Abbé de Saint-Remy. It would be quite proper to nominate you plenipotentiary to the congress; but I beg you to make the following reflections and consider them very seriously.

"*First:* I shall have the honor of informing you, that the king will name me his first plenipotentiary because he believes that my presence there might be valuable, and I do not know whether you would in that case feel satisfied in being nominated as second and whether M. the Dukes your confrères would agree to it on their part.

"*Second:* It is possible for congress to be very long and very burdensome. Its length and all the trivialities of the negotiations of an assemblage of so many different nations, most of them very indolent, might weary you and not be to your taste. I would not be exposed to that ennui, should the king do me the honor of nominating me, because I could be present at the congress only from time to time, when important matters demand my presence.

"*Third:* You without doubt know that the English do not think that you are very loyal to their interests and they look upon you with suspicion; there might perhaps be some difficulty and embarrassment for you by being exposed to the intrigues which would result from this prejudice, and it would be more difficult in that case to bring them to that conciliatory attitude, which would be indispensable to a complete pacification.

"You will have the kindness, sir, to reflect on these three reasons and make your decision. I beg you, however, that this decision be immediate; for we cannot defer the nomination of a plenipotentiary. If you do not care to be of the number, the king might nominate you anyway and you, on the other hand, might petition him to allow you to decline the honor, for the good reasons that you will present. The king would be the only one to know of it, and perhaps this refusal would do you no less honor than the nomination itself.

"I have assured the Abbé de Saint-Remy that I would let no occasion pass by to bring about your honorable dismissal from Vienna, and that he has but to suggest the methods to me.

"As for your successor we can dispense with the nomination of one for Vienna, as the emperor has been three years without nominating and without having an ambassador here. I think that it would be sufficient to nominate a minister plenipotentiary for that court. The choice is not easy to make and we are laboring over it continually.

"You are not mistaken, as to the inclinations of the Court of Vienna and you have been justified by all that has happened. M. de Grimaldi brought me your letter of the 14th of April ten or twelve days ago, and you can assure his uncle that I shall endeavor to accord him, in the person of M. his nephew, all the esteem and consideration that I have for such a distinguished prelate. I entreat you to bear witness to Prince Eugene (he had contributed in causing him to be honored with the dignity of the cardinalate) that I do not at all forget the obligations under which I am to him and that independently of his most kind conduct and the politeness with which he treated me at Fréjus, I honor his probity, which is more marked in my estimation than all his other great qualities.

"No one in the world, sir, honors you more or is more faithfully attached to you than I.

"CARDINAL DE FLEURY."

The Duke de Richelieu was very satisfied in receiving news of the fact that he was to be made chevalier of the Order of the Holy Ghost, although he was not as old as the statute prescribed. This favor was still more precious to him on that account; he refused to be nominated for congress and restrained all his desires to see Paris again or to experience the new pleasures that awaited him. He was still uncertain whether he would accept the Spanish ambassy, and it was in Paris that the king's favor caused him to abandon his career. From the news he was continually receiving, he was of the opinion that Louis XV. would be a weak prince and that the most skillful man would succeed in guiding him. From this time on he formed the plan of having a share in the good graces of the king and we shall see that he not only had the ability to obtain the favor of the king but also to retain it.

His nomination by the king to the *Cordon Bleu* reached him at the end of January, 1728. As he could wear it before the ceremony of decoration, the usual announcement of the fact was made at Vienna in the presence of Cardinal Kollonits, on the 24th of February. Prince

Eugene, Count de Zinzerdorf, the chancellor of the emperor, father of Tournemain, his Jesuit confessor, were witnesses. Richelieu was but thirty-two years of age at that time, and every one knew that the required age was thirty-five, for admission to the Order of the Holy Ghost. He was admitted to the order at Versailles, January 1, 1729.

Finally the time for the departure of the Duke de Richelieu arrived. The Princess de Lichtenstein did not leave him without shedding tears and the Countess de Badiani was pained at his departure. This last liaison had cooled the friendship between him and Prince Eugene, who was jealous of Richelieu's many visits to her. They left each other quite coolly and it was only some time afterward that their friendship was renewed on account of their absence from each other.

CHAPTER XXVII.

The dismissal of the Infanta.—How Mlle. de Vermandois lost the crown.—Louis XV. married to the daughter of Stanislaus.—The irritation of Spain.

THE anger of Mme. de Prie at the Orleans family was as energetic as it was concentrated. Neither pardon nor kindness could cause the first prince of the blood to yield. Mme. de Prie and M. le Duc determined to make war on the dearest interests of that prince. The health of Louis XV. was still very delicate; he had frequent attacks of illness and M. le Duc had everything to fear for his own well-being and for his credit, if the king should die. Bitterly jealous of the House of Orleans, goaded on by his mother and by Mme. de Prie, M. le Duc determined to negotiate a marriage between his sister and the young king who was then in the beginning of his fifteenth year. Although he was of delicate health, nature had already made him capable of having children as the valets, pages, and young lords of the court bore positive witness. Mme. the Duchess constantly urged M. le Duc to marry the young monarch. As the regent and the Queen of Spain had married the young king according to their own interests and for very shrewd political reasons, M. le Duc, who had penetrated their designs, annulled the marriage for the same reason.

Mlle. de Vermandois, sister of the prime minister, was

beautiful, amiable, modest, pious, somewhat proud and witty though sincere; her beauty was enhanced by gentle lineaments and by that freshness which the innocence of youth possesses; her modesty was natural, she had not been tainted by the corruption and utter lack of principles that characterized society during the regency, neither was she spoiled by that tone of abandon of all propriety at that time. She was proud, for she had compared the difference between her name and the other *pensionnaires* of the convent and she enjoyed their regard, as each one eagerly endeavored to be agreeable to her. This was why she had a way with her that might excite displeasure and a frankness in her conversation, which gave proof of her independence. Mme. de Prie was heartily in favor of a marriage between the sister of her lover and the king; but she desired to know the character of the princess thoroughly before its consummation and intended to exclude her from the throne if, after conversation with her, she should discover in her any indication of a dictatorial spirit. In that case she intended to seek for the young king, Louis XV., another princess, whom she might more readily influence. Thoroughly imbued with this ambition, Mme. de Prie disguised herself, changed her name, and assumed the name of a titled lady, that she might have the privilege and better means of studying the young princess, who was at the Convent of Tours. Therefore she went to ask for her in the name of a lady who was traveling and who had letters and commission from M. le Duc. Mme. de Prie stated that she was well known and brought news of the court; she was so skillful in conversation and enriched it with so many details that Mlle. de Vermandois spent a long time with her.

From one subject to another Mme. de Prie led the conversation to the point where she could easily ask the young *pensionnaire*, if she had ever heard Mme. de Prie, the favorite of her brother, spoken of in the convent. Then the princess began to tell her all sorts of abominations concerning Mme. de Prie herself, who was not disconcerted by it. She said that she knew this wicked creature only too well; that every one in the convent spoke of her with the utmost contempt; that it was to be regretted that her brother should have for his mistress a woman who should cause him to be detested throughout all France and who caused him to commit follies, and that it would be well if his friends should counsel him to abandon the woman.

Thus Mme. de Prie heard her sentence pronounced by the young princess, who naively reported everything that was said of her throughout the whole kingdom. Full of scorn and anger, she said, so that the princess could hear it: "Go, you will never be Queen of France."

Having arrived at Versailles she rehearsed her journey to the prime minister and assured him that his sister had every quality suitable for a Queen of France; she said that the princess was very amiable; she even urged him to bring about the marriage as soon as possible; but at the same time she spoke to Pâris-Duvernay in an entirely different manner regarding the subject. This gentleman enjoyed the confidence of the prince and through it had control of the most important state affairs. She observed to him that when this marriage was once concluded with Mlle. de Vermandois he would have five masters instead of one ; i. e., the king, the queen, Mme. la Duchesse and Lassay, (who as was well known had complete sway over her) and M. le Duc. Duvernay influenced this prince so that he changed his purpose, he informed the court, which was aware of the journey of Mme. de Prie, that the marriage could not take place because of the refusal of her sister, her modesty and her piety forbidding her to accept that great honor. It was resolved therefore to look elsewhere for a suitable wife for the king as soon as possible ; for the dismissal of the Infanta had been decreed.

The impossibility of finding for the king a princess of French blood being quite well proven, they cast their eyes on the sovereign families of Europe. None could give us a Queen of France. M. le Duc did not wish a princess of Lorraine on account of the close relationship with the Duke of Orleans. A Portuguese princess was spoken of, but poor blood and the suspicion of a strain of insanity in the family caused her to be excluded. They searched all the courts of Germany and found either blemishes in the families or mediocrity in the sovereigns.

There were at Modena three princesses of an eligible age but they were also excluded on account of Mlle. de Valois, daughter of the regent who had married the hereditary prince. The czarina had already offered her daughter Elizabeth, but it had been observed that her birth was of dubious origin and her conduct suspicious;

and such was the idea that was entertained throughout Europe of the family of the czars, then so little known, that for a long time it had not been thought fitting that it should be allied with French blood. The King of England was informed that one of his grand children would be gladly welcomed as Queen of France, but his most confidential ministers told him that if he favored this alliance he would arouse the jealousy of the English and would violate the laws of Great Britain. The King of England, nevertheless, was very favorable to it; he was a kindly gentleman, a father who appreciated the value of this offer and who, ever after had closer confidential relations with us, although this relation had an ulterior motive which was to the prejudice of our marine and French commerce. Therefore a princess was sought who was governed by no one, who was of a tranquil character, and who had no other support than that of M. le Duc and Mme. de Prie; they took the royal almanac, giving a list of princesses of Europe but none was found. Then Duvernay, who had become acquainted with the King of Poland by lending him money at Würtemberg, proposed the daughter of Stanislaus. As they wished to have a princess without credit and a daughter of a sovereign without power in Europe, they found the necessary qualities in this princess, the daughter of a dethroned King of Poland. Moreover Pâris assured them that being of a timid disposition and kindly character, she would never have any other will than that of M. le Duc, on reaching France. This King of Poland wished to have the princess marry at any cost so as to withdraw her from the presence of her mother, who could not endure her. For sometime he had commissioned a cavalry captain called Vauchoux to negotiate her marriage with M. le Duc. If he could not succeed in it he was to treat with M. de Charolais and thus from one lord to another, even to M. de Courtanvaux.

The proposition had been made during the life of Mme. the Princess who was formally opposed to it, and requested the Abbé Mongin, preceptor of the duke to prevent this marriage after her death, saying there were enough princesses in Europe for her grandson, without giving him the daughter of a dethroned king. Stanislaus thus saw all hopes of marrying his daughter vanish, when Vauchoux came to announce that his daughter had been chosen as the king's wife. He was on the hunt and Vauchoux had sought him in the fields to acquaint him with the glad tidings, which caused him to swoon in his carriage. He did not recover consciousness until they reached Weissembourg where he said: "I desired to reascend the throne only to establish my daughter in life, but I no longer think of it now, as this marriage is the climax of all my desires."

Meanwhile the opinions of the courtiers, who were called to the council by M. le Duc, to consider the dismissal of the Infanta and to give the king a fertile wife, were extremely divided. If M. le Duc, if Cardinal de Bissy, if Marshal de Villars, Morville, and la Marck were in favor of dismissing the Infanta, the Bishop of Fréjus and some few others stubbornly resisted it. The

Marshal de Villars insisted upon it in vain, but with politeness; the most powerful reasons for dismissing the Infanta were useless. Fleury was opposed to it without making any reply, and the others, displeased with his conduct, left the council. The majority of votes was in favor of it; but Fleury was determined. They were very much embarrassed because of his influence on the mind and will of the young king, and for the lack of honest reasons as well as practical ones for the dismissal of the princess. Some wished to treat directly with the Spanish Court; others, more bitter, with M. le Duc at their head, wished to dismiss her without delay and without preliminary negotiations, which might retard the carrying out of the plan, or might make it less practicable or more dangerous for the councilors by exposing them to the resentment of the Queen of Spain, who wished to postpone her plan of attempting to rule in France or give us her daughter as a sovereign.

This princess always kept up secret liaisons in France; she maintained a large number of old courtiers, faithful servants of Louis XIV. who heartily espoused her cause and who looked with sorrow on the change of principles and the rapid succession of unexpected events which brought about such frequent revolutions in the ministry. She was therefore warned of the designs of M. le Duc; and seeing Marshal de Tessé, our ambassador, recalled by the court, because they wished to spare him the sorrow of imparting the news that we were to give to King Phillip concerning the matter, this princess, to assure herself of our plans, sent courier after courier with the purpose of impressing us with the necessity of hastening the betrothal of Louis XV. with her daughter.

It was in circumstances like these that Abbé de Livry, French minister in Portugal, was commissioned to communicate to her the news of the necessity of our breaking every preliminary of the proposed marriage. The abbé, according to his instructions, was to ask first for an audience with their majesties; after having obtained it he was to hand them the letter from Louis XV. without acquainting them with the contents of the despatches. By this means the king and queen would have given some reply to the minister. But the abbé, instead of literally following out his instructions, on obtaining an audience, began by throwing himself at the feet of the king and queen. He spoke ambiguously and hesitatingly of the approaching dismissal of the Infanta, which at once threw the king and queen into a restless state of uncertainty and then into such anger that they absolutely refused to receive the letter from King Louis XV. They immediately ordered the ambassador to leave the castle and Spanish territory, including Mlle. de Beaujolais, daughter of the regent in the disgrace. The latter had already come to Spain to be married to the queen's son, Don Carlos. Finally the sensitiveness of the Spaniards was such on receiving the news of the dismissal of their princess that Frenchmen were publicly insulted in the streets of Madrid, by the Spanish populace. The queen, herself, set the example by dismissing the French Consuls and ordering them off Spanish territory and by recalling her ministers from the French

Court. She also permitted troops scattered along the Spanish frontiers among the Pyrenees to made incursions into French territory. She insisted that Baron de Riperda, her minister, should conclude his treaty with the emperor on whatever condition he could, forbidding all mention of the agreement with the Court of France, and all attempts to diminish in her eyes the enormity of the insults that the French Court had visited upon her and from which she intended to derive a glorious satisfaction, as she said.

CHAPTER XXVIII.

The house of the queen is prepared.—Different word-paintings.—The young queen is astonished at the presents that France makes her.

AFTER having searched *carefully* it was found that the wife of Marshal de Boufflers had the qualities and requisite virtues suitable for a lady-in-waiting; from this it can be inferred to what a state of corruption the sex had fallen; how the regency had favored scandalous libertinism and to what a degree they had forgotten the rules of decorum of the times of Louis XIV.

It is for these reasons that they chose the Countess de Mailly for lady of the bed chamber; for she was neither capricious, intriguing, nor ambitious. Her character on the other hand would readily adapt itself to that of the queen, with whom she had a great deal of sympathy. Moreover Mme. de Mailly had a kind disposition. She was of an even temper, well-known uprightness and great modesty. They were not so careful in selecting the twelve ladies-maids. It would have been too difficult, said Massillon in his Memoirs, to fill these positions with ladies of spotless character.

Among the other gallant women admitted into the court of the queen, Mme. de Nesle and Mme. de Gontaut were also noted, ladies who had feelings of affection for the Duke de Richelieu, less interested perhaps but more natural than those of Mme. de Prie for M. le Duc. Mme. de Nesle was bright, courageous, active. There was on the contrary more intelligence and reflection in Mme. de Gontaut. The behavior of the ladies of the queen's palace was therefore quite varied. Lastly the other ladies of the palace were the wife of Marshal de Villars, the Duchesses de Tallard, de Bethune, d'Eperhon, ladies d'Egmont, de Chalais, de Rupelmonde, de Mérode, and de Mapignon suspected of some flirtations less bold and more secret than those of the other ladies.

As to the officers of the queen's chapel, Fleury, after many excuses, accepted the position of chief almoner. Tavannes, Bishop of Chalons-sur-Marne, afterwards Archbishop of Rouen and cardinal, was declared first almoner.

The Polish princess being on the way and her home being prepared for her, the king had to be instructed as to the duties of married people. The cardinal had inspired in him so great a respect for morality from his very childhood, that he wept the very day of the arrival of the Infanta then eleven years of age. From that time on he had demeaned himself with the most exemplary modesty.

CHAPTER XXIX.

Attempt of the queen and M. le Duc to get rid of Fleury.—Triumph of the prelate.—Character of the Duke de Mortemart.—Facts about the court.—About Mme. de Prie and M. le Duc.

FLEURY burned with an ardent desire to control the affairs of state, but we must acknowledge that, if he cherished this secret ambition to rule, he also wished to work for the welfare of France, which had been distressed by so many revolutions. He wished to deliver his country from the ministry of M. le Duc, swayed too much by the evil influence of that wicked woman Mme. de Prie. In vain did this prince leave to the prelate the direction of ecclesiastical affairs and the greater part of the distribution of benefices, of livings and of pardons; Fleury wished to enjoy all the power and drive out the favorite whose cunning he feared.

One day she spread a net in order to ruin Fleury and cause him to lose his place at court; the adroit prelate avoided it and turned it into a triumph and an example which was to overawe his enemies and all the ambitious persons who sought to rob him of the confidence of his pupil.

As a matter of fact, Mme. de Prie, directed by Duvernay, one day inspired M. le Duc with a stratagem to dismiss Fleury from work with the king, work he was always accustomed to do, and to withdraw him from all influence over his affairs and compel him to retire.

In order to succeed in this it was determined that at the next period of work with the monarch, the queen should beg him to call on her, that the king should be occupied a long time with M. le Duc and that, in thus establishing work with the princess, they would leave Fleury.

Thus, Monday evening, Dec. 17, 1725, they were gaming in the queen's apartment. She appeared but a moment, returning to her own apartments where she met M. le Duc. Then she sent for the king who was in his apartments with M. de Fréjus, and at that moment all the doors were closed not to be opened until eleven o'clock.

M. de Fréjus had gone out at half past eight. Impatient at the non arrival of the king, but without seeming to be moved, those who passed the evening with him did not notice anything out of the way. The king himself had not been advised of his departure until the evening of the 18th on returning from the chase; for he had not yet read the letter that M. de Fréjus had written him on the following morning, as no one had cared to hand it to him. The prelate said in this letter that he was going to Issy, and that his majesty would never see him at court again.

The same conduct on the part of Fréjus had formerly grieved the king and had caused him to weep bitterly at the time of the disgrace of Marshall Villeroy, his governor. At that time this conduct on the part of the king had succeeded so well with Fleury that he had to go and seek him, and right quickly, in order to mollify the sorrow of the king and quench his tears. Fleury going this time in a fit of sulks to Issy, the king did not seem to be less grieved, and he went to his vestry to sulkily complain to M. le Duc, and wept continually for his preceptor.

Fleury's party at court was loudly indignant and members of it gathered in little knots here and there, and even people who would have approved the disgrace of Fleury, if it had been the work of the king, courageously stood in his defense. The Duke de Mortemart a man of decision, of magnificent character, and attached to the young king on principle rather than on account of his official position as first gentleman of the chamber, was at that moment engaged at the court. He determined to speak to the young king of the flight of the prelate, placed himself at the head of those displeased with M. le Duc, took the letter of Fleury and carried it to the king. This act of generosity was so well received by the court and even by the party of M. le Duc, that Mortemart gained from it a reputation of being a virtuous, decided and loyal man, whilst the rest of the partisans of Fleury lost time in deliberating or making indecisive, confused and cowardly efforts. Mortemart, seeing the regrets of the king, did still more; he courageously said to him: "But is not His Majesty the master and the one to recall his preceptor? As for me, I assure you that if His Majesty ordered me I would go to Issy to get him, and I would bring him in my carriage. I would do still more," he added; "I would go to M. le Duc de Bourbon himself, but always in behalf of His Majesty, and order him to send a courier at once to the Bishop of Fréjus and request him to return."

In his trouble the king, who was still shedding tears, felt comforted and consoled by the offer, and agreed to everything that Mortemart suggested to him. The Marquis de Silly, who did not write about everything that transpired at court, but still informed Richelieu of a great many of the anecdotes of the court, wrote him a letter, saying that the king had shown great feeling and a determined will, himself pronouncing the word "*J'Ordonne*," and of his own volition too. He added that after he had given this order, Mortemart spoke to the king very plainly in regard to Mme. de Prie and Duvernay, and instructed the king as to the real sources of the evils that had come upon the state.

However it may be, Mortemart himself, that very moment, sought out the Duke de Bourbon and told him that the will of the king was that he should recall the old Bishop de Fréjus from his country home. M. le Duc, who could not restrain his anger against Mortemart, told him that he was engaged in a sorry commission, yet at once ordered a courier to notify the prelate of the orders of Louis.

Fleury returned therefore to the service of the king, in triumph, and the most extreme consternation was observed in the party of the Duke de Bourbon. The queen herself was embarrassed at it; she was neither false nor deceitful nor shrewd; the measures that she had adopted with M. le Duc were, as we have seen, very puerile.

As to the Duke de Mortemart he was an honest man

who exhibited a decided character at the Court of Louis XV., and moreover he retained the customs and decorum of the former court; he was of an amiable yet respectful gallantry toward ladies, whose respect he sought; he was esteemed by nobles on account of his character, and was devoted to his wife, of whom he was fondly jealous.

Mme. de Mortemart, on the other hand, showed other tastes and rebuffed him so vigorously that in 1736 he had to plead against a suit for separation. The Duke de Mortemart was, nevertheless, passionately in love with her, and it was only on account of his excessive love that she had an aversion for him. This ardent passion on the one hand and aversion on the other caused such exciting scenes in the Mortemart home that mutual friends had great difficulty in concealing them from the public. The quarrels ended when Mme. de Mortemart retiring to the Convent of Cherche-Midi to plead for separation, realized after some months of privation her need of a husband and appreciated her true happiness, in having this man for her husband. The duke always in love sought her at the convent, brought her back with him and both of them called on the President de Nassigny, their judge, and asserted that they were reconciled and good friends.

However, after the adventure of the Bishop de Fréjus, Duvernay and Mme. de Prie became the object of hatred of all France. The Marquis de Silly wrote to the Duke de Richelieu: "M. le Duc is more determined than ever to uphold these two personages; he believes that his honor is at stake and the frivolous and ill-concerted plot that Pâris, Duvernay and Mme. de Prie imposed upon the queen and him with reference to M. de Fréjus, discredited them even among their friends, so that the epithet *tête de papier* will cling to them, if they are not careful.

Here is the picture of the situation at court. Let the reader judge these events.

"All credit and the consideration for the queen seem to be undermined; the interest that the king seems to have for her is merely conjugal, and I do not know what will become of her if she does not soon become enceinte.

"Since the court has been established at Marly the king is more talkative than usual. People begin to say that he is witty; I have thought it a long time, you know; he is, if I am not mistaken a machine, very slow in developing, very difficult to start in motion but which can move, and will show marked merit when once started. The example of M. de Fréjus is the proof of it.

" M. le Duc is always in a state of anger against M. de Mortemart. This, however, did not prevent the king from asking him if he would not return to see them at Marly when he took leave of him at the end of the year.

"Chabannes, a man very much devoted to M. le Duc and having the reputation of being a very honest man, has lost favor with him for having spoken.

"After all this I am not very sure about deciding on a definite prediction as to the future. A new retirement of M. de Fréjus would not surprise me at all; nor indeed would I be surprised at the fall of Mme. de Prie and Duvernay. Many people have more faith in the latter event; as for me I suspend my prophecy. I believe, however, that if evil fate comes to these two people it will be sometime hence.

"You have no need of advice; but it seems to me that this violent fermentation need not cause you to change your present conduct, and that you ought to regard all this as impending without entering into any explanation with the belligerent parties. The thing for you to do, it seems to me, is to remain in a neutral position.

"The contraction of the currency will be followed by an expansion, this is but a simple operation of finance, the evils of which are indispensably necessary in order to sustain it; a violent operation resembling an emetic given in cases of acute illness. It is to the four Pâris brothers that the public is under obligations for having brought the state to the verge of ruin.

"It is not at all true that Mme. d'Egmont has received her dismissal. M. le Duc loved her more than ever when the court left for Marly; I do not believe he has changed toward her. Mme. de Prie has scarcely sojourned at Marly at all. Paris has been her usual place of abode, and the opera, the ball, and the comedy her daily amusements.

"The reconciliation between Mlle. de Charolais and M. le Duc has caused a great sensation. According to my personal knowledge of the circumstances, this reconciliation is only a simple matter of regard, with the understanding that no exactions would be made from either one as regards their friends, their acquaintances, etc. It was M. d'Antin, who did most to bring about this result; for some time past he has had the confidence of M. le Duc and had had many private conferences with him. No one in the world understands better than he, how to manage the goat and the cabbage; it is a good way to acquire a reputation at court, if one can succeed by over-reaching another. Do not be surprised, if you hear him spoken of soon.

"The Duke de Noailles is very shrewd in his conduct, especially so with regard to his Jansenism to which he is devoted. It is perhaps an obstacle that will block his career some of these days. The king treats him very well; he often converses with him and shows a marked affection for him.

"I have some fears that you are too little acquainted with the ideas you express concerning the Duke de Gesvres; those who know, believe that the king is no more intimate with him than with others, and that his intimacy with him is less founded on affection than on the fact that he enjoys listening to his tales and his conversation. However, I think as you do, that he is a man that we must look out for and who is perhaps a man who will have great influence on the times, probably in the near future."

The Marquis de Silly was a fine man and a wit in his day; it is interesting to know what his opinion of the Spanish situation was: "The Chevalier Dubourg is still at the Court of the Queen of Spain at Vincennes; whether these later events occupy the public mind or whether he has had no dealings at all with our minister or with M. Duvernay, absolutely nothing more is said of him; but I have always believed that the Spanish Court had other objects in sending him here than that of establishing well-ordered etiquette in the house of the dowager queen. I think that he is more or less of a spy of the Spanish Court and especially charged with examining the feeling of people here and predicting their future disposition. The articles of the treaty of Vienna confirm me in this opinion. Since the dismissal of the Infanta I have regarded our quarrel with Spain as an evil. The treaty of Vienna, which resulted from it, rendered it a still greater evil on account of the difficulty of remedying it now. This is the result of drawing the government into treaties, whose consequences may be embarrassing, and which we might have dispensed with in the present instance. I am a born Frenchman, and I feel love of country coursing in my veins. I feel myself hurt and pained at stipulations, so devoid of honor and so humiliating to us, and which seem to confess great weakness, we might even say that it revealed a very disgraceful fear for a kingdom as powerful as this; for in spite of what the Pâris brothers have done for its degradation, two months of good administration will bring it back to health and vigor."

Sometime afterwards Richelieu received a letter from the Marquis de Silly which informed him concerning the inner life of the Court of Versailles. It was dated April 30, 1736. "M. le Duc who for three weeks has been reading continually has scarcely any leisure for the most important affairs.

"Morville declared his mind to me concerning the news given to M. le Duc, that you had asked for your recall and predicted war. That gave me occasion to argue with him concerning this subject and I have, I believe, sufficiently convinced him of that which he was already persuaded of; i. e., that you have never committed any indiscretion. He assured me that M. le Duc never believed that you had demanded anything essential; but they have been very much displeased with the rumors of war that have been prevalent in Paris because M. Duvernay persuaded his Most Serene Highness that, it is these rumors of war that contract the currency, and I would not answer for his not warning the duke of your supposed indiscretion in order to base an argument on general affairs.

"The English fleet, destined for the Baltic sea, has set sail and if the wind has been favorable, it may at the present time be anchored at Sund. Twelve vessels of the King of Denmark are to join this fleet and the presence of these thirty-three ships may put an obstacle in the way of the negotiation of Rabutin with the czarina and stop the Russian fleet. All preparations for war are being continued here; almost all the regiments have successfully filled their complements. Militia is being mustered and munitions of war are being gathered. Everything passes off finely up to the present time, but this is not true concerning financial questions. Circulation has been curtailed and almost completely suspended in several of the provinces; poverty is increasing on all sides. In spite of this the realm is intact; remedies are visible and we may add that they are even easy of execution, but the Pâris brothers, maddened by the ruin of the whole people, by the immense profits which they, Bernard and their associates are making, oppose reform with all their might; it is at least public opinion that it is their determination to hold the government dependent on them both now and for the future, by endeavoring to make themselves complete masters of all money in circulation and all the credit.

"Mme. de Prie continues to speak of a journey that she is to make to Normandy, but I do not know when this is to take place nor how long her stay will be. The aversion that the king has for her is almost at the breaking point; he not only refuses to speak to her but he ignores her and it is easily seen that her presence pains him. She sees the queen less than ever and she only sets foot here during her week of service; she passes most all the rest of the time in Paris; she is present at all the shows, promenades, etc. It does not seem, however, that M. le Duc is losing confidence in her, but it is, on the other hand, plain that he could get along without her more easily now than he could have done six months ago. His affection for Mme. d'Egmont has always been very strong. In regard to Duvernay, I believe that he stands as well as ever with his Most Serene Highness, although he has affected, however, for sometime, to show himself but twice a week and to appear not to engage in any affairs outside the restricted limitations of his own office."

After the great event of the flight of Fleury the true friends of M. le Duc have done everything in their power to induce him to get rid of the two persons so odious to the public and who were plainly seen to be leading him to his ruin.

M. de Fréjus himself made use of every possible means, reason, mildness, suggestion, and it seemed that M. le Duc was going to defer to his opinion; for Mme. de Prie left for Normandy, Duvernay appeared less frequently at Versailles and he and his brother had ignored the increase in the circulation of money. Alarmed at not having been consulted and at the little confidence that M. le Duc had in him at this time, Duvernay had sent a courier to Mme. de Prie, who left at once and in the greatest haste, arriving unexpectedly in Versailles Saturday, June 1. M. le Duc, the premier, was surprised at her entrance. Two days afterward Duvernay reappeared and spoke with his customary imperious tone. The conspirators opposed to them were indignant, and his reception of Duvernay and Mme. de Prie hastened the catastrophe which we are about to recount. M. de Fréjus had been assured that it was M. le Duc who had sent a courier for Mme. de Prie; but what will appear singular is that since the last return of Mme. de Prie, M. de Fréjus had a two hours' interview with M. le Duc, endeavoring to persuade him to give her up entirely, and it is known that M. de Fréjus himself, was determined upon retiring two months before. It was thus that the prelate and M. le Duc were on their guard.

Here are some observations made by Mme. de Prie; it was her usual custom to mix gallantry and sometimes something more than gallantry in the letters that she used to write to the Duke de Richelieu. She said to him: "The Marchioness de Villars had a retinue that I could only describe to you in several volumes; four alone would be necessary for the four matters that to-day make up her occupations and her pleasures. The public has it that, without in the least injuring her relations with the great prince with whom she has become reconciled, she stands very well with M. de Guébriant; M. de Dombes flatters her vanity and indeed claims that it is only a rest, since he has dismissed Mlle. de Charolais, who is inconsolable. The marchioness in spite of so many important cares has not ceased to use her influence on M. the Count de Clermont for whom she dishevelled her hair with the Duchess de Boufflers. All this does not ward off the butterflies, among whom M. the Duke of Orleans is numbered. Be discreet about all this and do not cite me, I beg of you. The Count of Bavaria preferred a new love affair to an old incident; it was M. de Saint-Florentin who caused him to make this reflection. If I were to speak of myself to you I would not find such gay subjects; but I will not say anything more except that my love of country must be very strong to induce me to remain in a land where I have just experienced the most extreme horrors through those whom I have served best, and where I have no other consolation than that of seeing my enemies compelled to lie to injure me. Although this may be a triumph, I could be more proud of a retreat, and in spite of the violent insistence which the queen, M. le Duc and my friends wish to force upon me as to this resolution, I believe that you will understand that I have been most prudent. And when I no longer excite envy, I will no longer show him anything but the real facts about my conduct, and will soon obtain the esteem of honest people and the justice that is due me. I shall have peace of mind and tranquillity, moreover, they will not impute to me the governing of people, who are not in a humor to be governed, and whose firmness of character ought to be well known. When their glory has been my sole object in life, I do not wish to find myself to-day the pretext with which they wish to weaken it. I speak to you as to a friend; I hope that you will make no other use of this than that of being touched by my confidence, and that in whatever situation I am you will devote as much loving thought to one who thinks nobly in the city, as you would to one who patiently suffers the injustices of the court. It is not a very satisfying favor to show you a recluse, but it has the merit of uniqueness, for I will share it with but few people.

"Duvernay is as unhappy as I am, and M. le Duc thinks his honor is at stake in retaining him; and he suffers not less than I in this determination and even more; I know that he is his own master and that I am free in my position if one can be free who is bound by the ties of affection and friendship. If you are curious and discreet, two qualities rarely found together, I will tell you more another time." The Duke de Richelieu who was much attached to Mme. de Prie wrote her concerning all the rumors that had reached Vienna. He was under some obligation to her; and besides he was grateful to her. He desired her to discontinue her interference in every matter of business that could have the least relation to the government; she answered him as follows:—

"After a year's justification, I am at the present moment in the position I long for. I shall never abandon my place as court-lady, but I shall fulfil it by serving my week and remaining in my home at Paris the rest of the time. In a word I wish to banish everything that is constrained in my position and only preserve that which is natural to a woman of quality, who does not wish to interfere with anything. I am not the person to be twice asked to give an account of my conduct. I find nothing to reproach myself with but a foolish negligence of all my own interests. M. le Duc is too firm, too enlightened, and I daresay too headstrong to follow me with the slightest complaisance. I find all the obstacles in the world in the way of carrying out my own will; I still have more merit in following my will since people only seek to deceive it by chains which seem to be flowers; but which may conceal serpents, of which the whole court is full. I have seen nothing so black, so base, so false, and so despicable as all that which I am seeing now. M. le Duc alone seems to-day to be worthy of all my veneration and of all my affection for him; firmness, friendship, truth have marked all his conduct toward me. They are the virtues which have made him complete master of my life for all time. I would joyfully give up my life in his service. This also presents the only regret that outweighs the joy that I shall have in withdrawing from court, and the difficulties which I find that he presents to my plan are the only ones that affect me. After this I shall have his esteem everywhere; nothing can cause me to lose it; this assurance gives me power to resist him.

"I shall not reply to what you say to me in regard to the choice of my friends; I can not believe that you were foolish enough to think that because they have come to my house and I have sought to render them services, they were my friends on that account; I wish to say as Harlequin in Timon, 'I know well that they were not worthy of the desire I had to oblige them; but I myself was worthy of the desire of doing good.' For those, whom I have called my true friends, and the few which my situation had permitted me to depend upon, they are the same; I am not deceived in them and they will remain true. I am overjoyed to think that you are of the number and you shall see in the future if you can find any one who can possibly merit friendship more than I, provided that these two qualities blind you as to my faults, and I shall ever be sure of your friendship.

"I shall tell you, in regard to the admission to the order of the Holy Ghost, that for thirty-six reasons the queen has not been able to get it for M. de Nangis and M. de Tessé, and she was obliged to submit to the obstacles she found in the way of fulfilling her desires. Therefore do not complain; there is no intention whatever to treat you unfairly for they are very well pleased with you.

"I am surprised that you accuse me of not writing you

in the letter that you wrote me on the 16th of March; I have written you a volume in which I said that everything was entered in customary order or nearly so. At the time I am writing now, I have more leisure and am much happier than I have ever been. I have broken all the chains that have bound me; I have only kept that bond which binds me to my friends, and to my place at court. I am no longer annoyed by anything; I pass a fortnight at Paris, wherever I please and a week of service at Versailles. I am no longer a dog in leash; I take pleasure in often leaving the place that I never loved, now, when I might remain there with the greatest enjoyment to myself, and when the queen and M. le Duc and my friends show the greatest desire to have me remain. M. de Fréjus has said no more, because, in truth, I have not given him occasion to say anything. M. de Mortemart has fallen into deepest discredit with the king, with the public, and even with M. de Fréjus. As for Duvernay, of whom you speak in your letter, he is situated about as I am. He has a greater affection for me than ever, and I have never had reason to do otherwise than love and esteem him. Be sure that everything that is sent you from other sources are idle stories, and I, alone, impart to you the simple truth.

"Poor Voltaire excites my deepest pity. In the main point he is right, but in presenting it he has blundered in an inexcusable way; he has been in the Bastille for three days through his own fault. If he had simply remained away from Paris he would not have been taken; he has the Bastille as a prison, and yet he receives his friends there. I sent him your letter yesterday. I could not get it to him earlier, not knowing where he was living.

"There is a furious quarrel going on here which is stirring up the whole court. The royal princesses have demanded the right nave of the chapel, that is to say, Mlle. de Clermont and Mlle. de Charolais: for Mlle. of Orleans and all the princesses have always taken the left side and left the right side to the ladies-in-waiting of the queen. So they wanted the nave occupied by the ladies of the palace, and, as they desired, after the ladies of the queen had been seated, the latter withdrew to the benches in the rear to make way for the princesses, who, not contented with that, desired their ladies-in-waiting to be seated at their sides, in front of the ladies of the palace. They claim that the naves are like the boxes in the theatre, where they can have their retinue and their company according to their rank. The ladies of the palace reply that the queen, then, is the only princess of the realm whom they refuse to obey, and who is without retinue and without company; that without a dispute we will give our places to the princesses; that it is with pleasure that we render them due respect, but it is not thus with their ladies, who have no right to separate us from the queen and be seated in front of us. You can imagine that this affair caused a shocking disturbance, and that every one is talking about it, because, as a matter of fact, the ladies-in-waiting of the princesses oppose us in everything, and are invading our rights, as far as they can. But as far as I am concerned I was not there when the quarrel happened. I shall not be there when it is settled, and where the eleven ladies are, I shall be found to be the twelfth. Thus I shall not interfere nor trouble myself in regard to this any more than I have with regard to anything else that is transpiring of which, thank heaven, I know nothing."

This is the language of Mme. de Prie, but the truth will come out in the next chapter.

CHAPTER XXX.

Exile of M. le Duc, prime minister, and of Mme. de Prie.—Character of the king and Fleury.

FLEURY and M. le Duc continually watched one another, but finally the crash came, and Fleury caused the duke to be exiled. The prelate told the king that this prince was the object of the scorn and indignation of all France; that he was the cause of all the calamities of the realm, and that it was time that his majesty, who had natural talents and sufficient and necessary intelligence, should govern the kingdom himself. The details of this disgrace were sent to Vienna to the Duke de Richelieu by the Marquis de Silly and by several other nobles of the court. Their descriptions will be preserved in these Memoirs.

"The king, who was not to go to Rambouillet until the 12th, gave notice on Monday, June 10, after dinner, that he would leave at eleven o'clock on the morning of the 11th; but the ambassadors and the Council of Finance detained him so that he could not take his carriage until three in the afternoon. On leaving he told M. le Duc that he would await him at Rambouillet, whereas the young monarch had already exiled him to Chantilly, and had given all the necessary orders.

"It was also observed, some days before, that the king was driving with M. le Duc in a very familiar manner without giving him any idea of what was being plotted against him, the king preserving his usual gayety.

"M. le Duc was engaged the rest of the afternoon working with Breteuil and Dodun, who did not leave until eight o'clock. M. le Duc left almost at once to enter his chaise which was awaiting him at the foot of the queen's staircase. Then Saint-Florentin presented himself with a portfolio; but as the prince wished to reach Rambouillet in time to dine with the king, he put the matter off until his return.

"The Duc de Charost, who had awaited the end of the work of the comptroller-general, then begged M. le Duc to return to his office a moment with him, and it was here in the office that he handed him the letter from the king.

"Charost had received from Fleury two letters from the king notifying him of the disgrace of M. le Duc. One was very mild, the king saying in substance that he wished to know the details of his own personal affairs, so as to be able to govern himself, adding that he found it necessary to save the expense of a first minister, and that accordingly he desired M. le Duc should pass some time at Chantilly.

"In the second letter the king spoke as a master who wills and orders, in case the first letter did not produce the desired effect. Charost, either by a blunder, or as some assert, voluntarily, gave the harsher letter to him first, and M. le Duc was so astonished by it that he expressed his surprise that his majesty should give his orders in such a peremptory tone to one accustomed to respect the king and to set an example of submission. Charost took the harsh letter and gave him the other.

"M. le Duc at once wrote to the king and entered his chaise in silence. On issuing from the courtyard he ordered his postillion, who was going to turn to the right, to go straight ahead and told him to take the road to Saint-Cloud from whence he sent a page to Saint-Denis, to have the post-horses in readiness, and continuing his journey he arrived at Chantilly an hour after midnight. The news was not known at Versailles until midnight. M. de Fréjus went to announce it to the queen at eight or nine o'clock in the evening. It is said that she wept bitterly, and that when he had gone, she sent for Mlle. de Clermont and Mme. de Prie.

"At Rambouillet not a word was said about it; the king supped very gayly and enjoyed a game of cards which did not draw to a close until late in the evening. Mme. the Duchess received a letter from M. de Fréjus at four o'clock in the morning announcing the news in the most suitable terms. The king had written five or six lines to her in his own hand at the foot of the letter, using very flattering and even tender expressions. She left Saint-Mour at once and reaching Paris she received a note from her son in which he expressed himself as a man would who regards his downfall as the beginning of tranquillity and repose, which he said he seemed to feel. At four o'clock she left for Chantilly.

"Let us return to Versailles. The queen had sent for Mlle. de Clermont and Mme. de Prie after M. de Fréjus had left her. The result of the conversation is not known; but a moment after it was finished Mlle. de Clermont entered her carriage and took Mme. de Prie with her.

"M. de Fréjus also despatched a courier to M. le Duc of Orleans, to his mother and to the Prince de Conti. On the arrival of the courier at the home of the Duke of Orleans, it was given out in Paris that he was to receive a great and important position, and as he left at that time, it was believed that he was going to Rambouillet. But he went no further than Versailles where he stopped. He had Maurepas come to see him in the morning and worked with him a long time. Finally that we may better estimate the whole course of events, and the ministry and M. le Duc, we shall here publish a letter which Richelieu wrote from Vienna on the 3rd of August, 1726, to Cardinal Polignac, his friend.

"My regrets at what has happened to M. le Duc cannot be more sorrowful nor more sincere because I know his good intention, and I would have wished with all my heart that he could have remained in the closest intimacy with M. de Fréjus, as I am persuaded he had good intentions toward him, and I believe that this union could only have been of a salutary effect for the state and for every one concerned.

"But it was impossible for it to exist after the manner they have used those who had the regards of M. le Duc; and third persons have carried things from one to the other to such a point that one of the two must needs oust the other. It was the greatest folly for the party of M. le Duc to believe that they were more powerful, when they realized the situation in which they had put the prince in the kingdom, in the court and in his relations with the king. I know very well that all this was done contrary to the advice of the great Pâris, who has an excellent head, very different from that of Duvernay, who has been the chief cause of the ruin of M. le Duc after having been the ruin of the finances, although he had the best intentions in the world. But it is a rare thing indeed to find a bourgeois capable of thinking great thoughts.

(NOTE BY THE EDITOR.)

I would never have suspected that a man of intellect such as M. de Richelieu would think it was necessary to be of noble birth in order to *penser dans le grand.* I would gladly know whether the United States of America, for example, who have taken for the foundation of their constitution the noblest and the highest truths, truths which the human mind hither to never attained, asked for the advice of some *gentlemen to penser dans le grand.* I would ask again if the nation assembled in 1789 called to its aid the French nobility to establish a constitution which elevates human nature far beyond the point attained within the memory of historical times, since it establishes our rights from the very primitive times of man, before castes began in society. Certain it is that the French and American bourgeoisie has for ten years past thought sublime thoughts.

Without doubt the bourgeois of ancient times in France thought petty thoughts; for the people were only soldiers, priests or lawyers. Command of armies was destined only to a few families who were accustomed to think sublime thoughts; the offices of prelates were destined to gentlemen's sons, whom the care of souls and the administration of sacraments (petty functions) would have dishonored. The high magistracies also were the heritage of distinguished families. To administer public affairs, proofs of nobility were necessary in Burgundy, Artois, Languedoc and in Brittany.

Proofs were necessary to gain admission to the persons of our kings, as if the monarch were not the approachable father and the king of all without exception. I have heard it said (in the presence of the Archbishop of Narbonne, then president of the clergy) of a vicar-general who directed a whole diocese whilst his prelate lived in Paris in the midst of pleasures: 'That grand-vicar is a man of merit to be sure, but he is not a man of birth.'

And it is because his bishop, who was a fool, was man of birth that he had this prelacy with the salary of one hundred thousand francs, and that the vicar-general, who was only a man *de merite*, had obtained as a favor after ten years of work, two thousand francs income.

I am not surprised therefore if the nobility of France said with Marshal de Richelieu that the bourgeoisie only thought petty thoughts; nor am I surprised that the French bourgeoisie, outraged and driven to despair, gave proof that it could think sublime thoughts. If I am not mistaken this is one of the causes of the revolution of 1789.

Continuation of Richelieu's Letter.

"We were saying that it was rare for a bourgeois to be capable of thinking sublime thoughts; we might add that it would be still more rare if at the same time he would have to have knowledge of a court as particular as ours. The poor fellow never had any confidence in my advice and had no idea of the court. He imagined that by winning over all the valets of the king he would get control of the master. He devoted all his dexterity and skill to that end, without taking on good faith what I have told him several times; that it was true that the valets of the king would advise him of all that was passing, but the nobles would be the ones to ruin him, and as long as he had none to take his part and to justify his undertakings, all his little schemings would only serve to forewarn him of his ruin some days before it occurred. I was mistaken on this point alone, for he did not even know it the night before.

"Mme. de Rohan who had found favor with him had enchanted him by her insipid and honeyed words and Mme. de Prie did so still more easily. They soon established themselves in the confidence of M. le Duc. But, as I explained plainly concerning them, and as I more than once positively asserted when I discovered this intimacy, they could no longer count upon me for I have watched others take the same course. Nevertheless I have learned many things concerning this intimacy, especially since I have been in Vienna, and although I do not believe that it was absolutely through them that M. le Duc was ruined, yet I think that the advice of these gentlemen, who would have wished to rule alone in the ministry, always kept away those who might have had a share in his confidence and induced him to do what was fair and right, thus enabling him to secure honest people for his service. For indeed without falling into that prostitution in which M. of Orleans threw all his virtues, he might have been able to avoid falling into excesses on the other hand, and not expose himself to the loss of his place, bearing with him the regret of having sought to pay homage only to the Matignons. The self-reproach which he experiences now must be too poignant to justify us in wantonly adding to it by making complaints of him."

Such was the letter written by Richelieu to Cardinal de Polignac.

Richelieu also wrote to Mme. de Prie, because he could not bring himself to utterly forsake a woman in her disgrace after having been intimate with her when she was in favor at court. She was still interesting in her misfortune and behaved with a certain haughtiness, as did M. le Duc. She said: " I rarely have occasion to receive letters and still more rarely to write them, therefore do not look upon my infrequent letters as negligence. I should certainly be pained were you to do so and I find the greatest pleasure to-day in seeking how to thank you for the marks of your remembrance and the assurances of your kind friendship; they are most dear to me, as is also the brilliancy of your mind; however, I do not think that they could have altered events. My conduct has always been what it should be; but it had no influence whatever on events, of which I was totally ignorant. My affection has been my ruin and the part which I took in what was transpiring had no effect on the result. For ten months I have not lived in a manner to warrant my being suspected of meddling in state affairs. I am enduring my condition without sorrow; I am pained only in my sympathy for the persons in whom I am interested; I am nearer happiness than I have been for eight years. I have nothing to reproach myself for; I have, moreover, nothing to regret, for this is a country that I have never loved; I am therefore very much at ease and am planning a quiet life for the future, to be passed, with a small circle of friends. I hope soon to attain it, because with patience and a conduct irreproachable as to past, present and future all I have to await is but the dues of justice. I shall be charmed to count you in the small number of my friends, and I flatter myself that you will be a dearer one than you have ever been. You do not understand me thoroughly; the situation, in which I was, concealed me to a large degree from the world and made me somewhat of a mystery. I suspected this, I had suspected very often, that this mask was between me and the public but people did not realize their mistaken notions in regard to me; thanks be to God I now look clearly into faces and I can see what I really am. Surely I shall acquire a true knowledge of my friends through frank and disinterested conduct; moreover as they will say nothing that may lead me to deceive myself and as I shall see only people who will prove to me their true friendship, I shall be relieved of the sorrow of mistrusting those with whom I live, which in truth has been the greatest misfortune of my position, for nothing is more distasteful to me than deceit."

Such were the sentiments of Mme. de Prie who, in spite of her beautiful philosophy, died some time afterward in Normandy in sorrow and remorse. She never saw M. le Duc again.

Does not the love of truth demand that she should be painted without prejudice, and that we permit her to exculpate herself?

CHAPTER XXXI.

Character of M. le Duc.—How the woman De Prie, Duvernay, and Dodun deceived the prince.

BEFORE the incident which gave M. le Duc, Bernard, Duvernay and Dodun the nickname of *Têtes de papier*, Mme. de Prie, who had been somewhat less officious in the conduct of affairs of late, was very much interested in every detail. One day Dodun and Duvernay planned the most singular stratagem to convince M. le Duc of the wide knowledge possessed by Mme. de Prie, for the purpose of increasing the confidence he had reposed in her. This gives a very good idea of the character and of the mind of these courtiers.

Dodun was working with the prince one day when Mme. de Prie entered as if unexpectedly, and after the usual greetings remained with them, listening to a very complicated report of some financial transaction, which she had been shown to in advance by Duvernay.

The business seemed to be very embarrassing to M. le Duc. Dodun pretended to be undecided. Mme. de Prie took the floor and repeating the lesson that she had learned with great ease gradually laid bare the only course which could be followed. Dodun, who pretended to be surprised at the depth of insight of Mme. de Prie, with enthusiasm cried out: " The spirit of the great Colbert inspires you, madame."

M. le Duc was obliged to admit her great sagacity. M. le Duc had that kindness of character and that worth which is a well known to be a trait of the princess of the House of Bourbon. Like them he had been poorly educated, and it is seen how he permitted himself to be dominated by women and what the ruses were by which they sought to deceive him. He was credulous, he had his limitations and although not well educated, yet at the same time he was an honest man; and even though truth compels us to state his faults and his mistakes and to draw a picture of the calamities which he caused to France, we must acknowledge that he was continually deceived, and that in this respect he was less at fault than was the regent, because the Duke of Orleans received from nature all the qualities that could have prevented his being deceived. We must therefore distinguish in these Memoirs the minister, who like Dubois was a deceiver, from the minister, who was deceived as was M. le Duc; and again we must distinguish these two ministers from the regent, who, on account of his rare qualities, his genius, his talents, his sagacity could have avoided his own errors, and could have prevented the deceptions of his ministers, yet had the weakness to abandon France to all the perfidies that distressed her, especially toward the end of the regency.

As to Mme. de Prie she conducted herself so it would appear that she really loved M. le Duc only when she was disgraced; women detested her and the partisans of the old time rules and decorum of Louis XIV. added their scorn and hate. They could not endure her tresses flowing like those of the Bacchantes during her morning negligee; nor her schemes, now indecisive, now bold; nor her ogling and immodest glances; nor her shouts of unexpected laughter. Her equivocal manners were characteristic of her morals and her deportment at court. Her character, it is true, did not permit her to indulge in atrocious or cold-blooded actions, but she was skillful enough to use *lettres de cachet*, exile, imprisonment and sometimes even judicial trial to ruin those who had the misfortune to be distasteful to her. Usually she was content to refuse pardon to those whom she hated, and her partisans who wished to defend her, could say nothing more favorable to her than that she had never countenanced poisonings nor assassinations. Licentious, witty, skillful in procuring lovers and changing them without harm to herself, it was said of her in relation with the *Cordons Bleus* that several men had been granted this favor by virtue of talents that she alone had discovered in them. Finally her licentiousness was the cause of a shameful malady which she communicated to M. le Duc.

Mme. de Prie then began to complain bitterly and indignantly cursed all the frightful infidelities of the prince; she described the ills that she was suffering, she was angry with him; and at the same time she was sensible enough to be secretly treated by Mme. de—— who sometimes accorded her favors to the prince at random, and it was agreed that she should acquaint M. le Duc with the fact that the immoral life of her husband was the cause of the common accident, and that it could not be imputed to Mme. de Prie, his usual favorite. For this reason the duke could not become angry with Mme. de Prie, to whom he made many excuses. And he could not hold any grudge against Mme. de —— who seemed to be both innocent and trustworthy. And Mme. de Prie had influence enough to insert in the list of persons to be rewarded with the *Cordons Bleus*, M. de ——, for his wife wished to be remunerated for her complaisance in this matter.

In retirement at Chantilly, M. le Duc suffered at the hands of the cardinal, all those petty acts of vengeance which mediocre spirits are capable of. He was deprived of the privilege of the chase; this was denied him under various pretexts. The prince, therefore, was obliged to devote his time to investigations in chemistry and from that time on he began that famous collection of natural history which Bomare has since enriched, substituting, however, in the arrangement of natural productions, a systematic order in place of the chaos which reigned before he interested himself in this collection. The prince had entertained at his home all manner of alchemists and charlatans, who came to interest him in the philosopher's stone.

In his exile M. le Duc made his vassals the object of all sorts of beneficences at his hand. His testamentary will proved that he loved well-doing, that had he been trained more carefully, he would have been more popular and the minister of the king and of France, rather than that of Mme. de Prie. M. le Duc, rich, powerful and a royal prince had no other distracting interests.

After his retirement, Fleury, who called Morville and

Marshal d'Huxelles to assist him in the management of foreign affairs, as well as calling the ministers of other departments to assist him in the ordinary routine of business, determined as far as possible to remove the royal princes from the ministry. He wished to force from the Duke of Orleans his resignation as colonel-general of infantry. Silly wrote to the Duke de Richelieu saying that they were endeavoring to find an equivalent position to satisfy her royal highness, Mme. of Orleans, but it was not an easy matter. They had several schemes, and among others that of establishing a distinguished rank for the other princes of the Orleans branch of the family. "I think I know," said he, "and this is a great secret, that the Orleans family will not yield anything *de proprio motu*; that they will not enter into a negotiation; that they will obey if they are ordered. As to an equivalent, I think that I also know that they will not accept a rank which will only be fictitious, and which might bring them into litigation forever with the other princes of the blood.

"Besides this I am almost convinced that it is the desire of the present government to remove without any exception both the princes of the blood and the legitimated princes, from the administration of public affairs, and to reduce their influence simply to their own personal merit,—to the same footing in which they were at the time of the late king.

"M. d'Antin left yesterday evening for Compiègne, where the king intends to go next year; he himself has marked out on the plot of the forest the new roads that he intends to have built and the arched bridges over the marsh which separates them. As regards the castle, he has ordered it restored to the condition in which it was when the late king visited it for the last time. They suggested to him wood floorings and ceilings; he laconically replied that he preferred the paving to a wood flooring, and the beams and joists to a ceiling. His majesty went to Rambouillet to-day, and he will return very late Thursday and go back again Sunday evening; it is not known for how long. It is sure that his sojourn there pleases him, and that he is more at his ease with Mme. la Countesse de Toulouse than with the other ladies. Shrewd people, who carefully note these things, are not inclined to have great respect for the influence which she has and may have over the king. It seems very probable that he will reduce himself to a sort of familiarity with her which she may make use of according to her character, in venturing to propose things that will influence him indirectly in certain contingencies, and serve her brother for whom His Majesty shows a great liking; but I do not know his opinion of his ability, and that is the chief point to be considered, for I recollect that the king would formerly have been keen to judge men and principally those whom he saw most intimately, and I have heard it said that they do not gain much by it. Don't you think that it would be wise and prudent to remain away from the king and await an opportunity when business, occasion and necessity give good reasons for approaching him seriously? The queen plays a very sad and a very pitiable rôle; the semi-estrangement of the king for her is plainly seen; the poor lady seems to be embarrassed and wrong in everything.

"Up to the present I have not learned that Spain has had any direct influence in the change which has just taken place in our ministry; I do not even believe that there has been any other correspondence than that between the Abbé de Montgon and some Spanish underlings. They forwarded the news of the changes that have taken place by the papal nuncio who is here, and the nuncio addressed himself to his colleague, Aldobrandin, who did the same duty in Spain. I am told that the whole nation manifested extreme joy, and that the king was also extremely pleased and praised M. de Fréjus; but I am inclined to believe that it is rather a feeling of vengeance against the duke and his confidants than sincere love of France. Nevertheless, it is quite probable that it may open some way to a reconciliation, and that the grandees of Spain and the Spanish ministry would not be displeased to see us have great influence in their country, which might then be delivered from the tyranny of the imperial government,—of course always being assured that they would not fall under our influence, and that they be permitted to govern themselves. But how can all this be adjusted? If I am right in my conjectures I surely would believe our reconciliation was at hand. Nevertheless, I will do my very best to unravel what is passing; but it seems difficult to me. M. de Morville maintains a secrecy which borders on the mysterious, and it is only indirectly and by accident that I can learn the hand he is playing. I must keep it secret, in order not to alarm our allies by the treaty of Hanover. For however good a face we put on the matter the allies are certainly uneasy, in spite of the positive and reiterated assurances given them by M. de Fréjus and M. de Morville that they will adhere exactly and conscientiously to all the conditions and all the promises made them by the former ministry.

"Morville, since the fall of M. le Duc, has ingratiated himself very carefully to the new comers. He understood, as well as his friends did, that Desforts and Le Blanc were scheming to become masters of the situation. Morville's and Maurepas' game will be to join forces. Besides there are natural, mutual inclinations on their part, and liaisons of friendship and mutual esteem; but the premier has no predilection for that which seems to be partisan, and the latter has for a long time been quarreling with the keeper of the seals. Moreover he is inclined to use his own wings in flying; (he is only twenty-four years old;) he has a bright intellect, talents, friends, family and a good game to play." Such was the inside history of the court.

CHAPTER XXXII.

Picture of France at the beginning of Fleury's ministry.—The court.
—The king.—The queen.—Beauty of the king, his timidity in the
presence of women.—Character and expressions of the queen.

FRANCE finally had complete repose.

The military reign of Louis XIV. had not only stirred up from centre to circumference the whole continent of Europe, but this monarch, hungering for glory, conquest and renown, had not ceased during his interminable reign to torment his people in order to satisfy every whim of his desire to build castles, enrich his courtiers and multiply his conquests. The secret ambition of Mme. de Maintenon and the interested schemes of the legitimated children had long ago prepared storms for the regency. And the Jesuit, Le Tellier, confessor of Louis XIV., had introduced dissension in the church of France by his guidance of the king.

During the minority, a prince endowed with rare good quality governed France; and if it is indeed true that Cardinal de Noailles, archbishop of Paris, repressed the terrors of armed Jesuitism, which disposed of the liberty of citizens who were odious to the order of the Jesuits by *lettres de cachet*, by exiles, or imprisonment; if it is true that at the beginning of the regency, Noailles, and the councils repaired to a certain extent the financial chaos, it is also true that the ministry of the

Dubois, of Le Blanc, of d'Argenson, of Law, which distressed the state in another manner, succeeded them. The ceremonial of the reign of Louis XIV. was based upon a supposititious system of morals, though it did not produce them, whilst the élite of the debauches surrounding the Duke of Orleans during his regency, substituted the boisterous libertinism which preverted our morals and lead finally, toward the end of the regency, into such scandalous conduct, that there was a general tendency to imitate it in the private societies of the capital, whence it extended into all our provinces, and even passed into the ephemeral Court of Louis I. of Spain.

The conspiracy of Cellamare, or rather of the legitimated princes and the Queen of Spain, against the Duke of Orleans, afterwards was a disturbing element to all ranks in the kingdom toward the middle of the regency, and the constituted authority spared neither force nor strategy to maintain itself. Being victorious it attacked the magistracy and dispersed it, only to maintain the follies of the system and the other plans of Dubois, Le Blanc and d'Argenson.

These internal strifes had great influence on foreign affairs and Europe no longer knew what her actual relations with France were, since it had been governed for so long a time by such changeable policies. Louis XIV. had given a king to Spain; yet the Duke of Orleans made war upon him; the Queen of Spain signed a treaty of peace with the Duke of Orleans by giving her daughter in marriage to Louis XV. but M. le Duc dismissed her.

We were in alliance with England it is true, but that nation used every effort to keep us estranged from Spain, in order to dominate us as a maritime power, divide the two monarchies which might have been able to aid each other, and maintain for itself exclusive commerce.

The emperor and the German princes did not have the opinion of France that she merited; they were devoted to Spain; yet we were also bound in a close alliance with the pope, whose policy was going to be triumphant, the Bishop de Fréjus never ceasing to favor ultramontane rights, so odious to France. Such was the state of foreign affairs and the internal state of the realm when Fleury was declared minister. This is how he brought up the king, and the use this monarch made of the happy disposition, nature endowed him with.

The health of the king, Louis XV., which was a matter of vital importance to the peace of all Europe, became stronger, but still it was somewhat delicate. The royal house of Spain watched the progress of affairs, especially those of Orleans, very carefully.

As to the moral qualities of the young prince, he seemed modest and reserved, although he had a full realization of his power. He had no other will in the affairs of state than that of Fleury, his favorite minister. His education had been neglected. No principle of national law, of literature or of history had been given him by his preceptor and governor, Villeroy and Charost; in fact these two gentlemen did not have the necessary training themselves, therefore could not impart it; on the other hand, there was a great desire to make him exacting in regard to etiquette, and in the belief and the practice of religion; they often frightened him, from his earliest childhood, with pictures of death, the devil and hell. These first impressions, which remained with him through life, were renewed at Easter, and especially on hearing of the death of some noble of his court or some of his friends, so that there was a perpetual struggle between his passions and his principles; and this struggle lasted to the end of his days.

The king in his youth was fond, neither of festivals, nor pomp, nor magnificent ceremony. He learned this reserve and this taste for solitude from Fleury who had kept him aloof from all pomp from his earliest childhood. Eager to make him submissive, and desirous of concentrating in himself complete power, he only allowed him to engage in the hunt, for which he had a boundless passion. Fleury had made him silent, melancholy, reserved, and capable only of showing the necessary attentions and the particular politeness suitable to the manners of a sovereign, avoiding the puerile actions customary to his age.

At the age of seventeen years the development of his whole body and every muscle was so perfect that he was reputed to be the most beautiful youth in the realm. Nature had forgotten nothing, neither in details nor in the ensemble, and this great temperament which we all know him to have possessed in his old age was peculiar to him when he was but fourteen.

Nevertheless timid toward women, avoiding them "*comme la peste*" to use the expression of a courtier,

Fleury had taught him that the majority of them were without virtue and that all had been corrupted from the beginning of the regency. Thus the king was beautiful as a cupid and yet his affections were fixed on no woman; he was pursued and he fled. At Rambouillet he sometimes affected voluptuous manners but without any special desire. Women showed their love for him, and he never even gave the slightest sign that he had a heart that was susceptible to love, except toward Madame the Countess de Toulouse, whom he distinguished above all other women. He gradually withdrew himself from the society of youths of his age and especially from that of Gesvres and de La Trémoille, who by secret instructions and by the diversions of that age had developed his passion.

Thus married to a woman, as simple and as modest as he, they at first mutually feared one another and they only visited one another ceremoniously and without passion; the valets even add that in their most intimate intercourse this couple were as reserved as if in public, and although the king knew from that time on the true charms of nature, no woman had been able to attract to herself his charming glance. It was seen from the beginning of his marriage that he was returning to the society which had secretly formed around him under the ministry of M. le Duc and the manners of which he never lost until he was finally excited by the charms of Mme. de Mailly, one of the famous sisters. His beautiful eyes, however, and the charm of his manners, attracted women. His charming disposition emboldened them; plans

Portrait of the Young Louis XV. Exhibited to the
Royal Family

From the painting by J. Dumont

rtrait of the Young Louis XV Exhibited in the
Royal Palm.

were formed, and some even proposed to him; but the young monarch, always timid, answered the corruptors, "She is not so beautiful as my wife," whilst Fleury put obstacles in the way of the efforts and intrigues of those who wished to destroy the influence of the Countess de Toulouse and the daughter of Stanislaus.

This princess, naturally modest and simple, was like the king, subject to the constant surveillance of the adroit cardinal, who was jealous of the harmony which reigned between this married couple. She wished, on one occasion, to assume the power of the preceptor; but we recall the famous note, which this prelate caused to be written to her in which the young king told her: "You will execute the orders of the cardinal." This letter caused such an impression on her mind that after having lamented the occurrence for a long time and wept over it, she finally imitated the action of the late queen, wife of Louis XIV.

Deprived of M. le Duc, who had elevated her to the crown; of Mme. de Prie, who had been charged with the details of the marriage; and of the ministers one and all, she was continually dominated by this devout, favored minister, who had not yet forgotten that she had been in league for a time with M. le Duc. She might, therefore, win the confidence of her husband, and like the Queen of Spain, profit by the necessities of the monarch and overcome that coolness toward her, which she had not yet overcome. She might even render him amorous as it often happens with young married people; but an old Jesuit, her confessor, who had become a courtier and reflected well on the nature of his religious advice, pointed out to her that heaven was continually wroth at the coquetry of women, and at the pleasures of married people, on account of the sanctity of the sacrament. The reserve on the part of the king continued. Finally the confessor persuaded her that the angels would never leave the nuptual bed, as long as chastity remained; and this princess, who had come to France entertaining an idea that a terrestrial crown might cause her to lose a heavenly one, to use her own expression, continued to live with the king as she had begun.

Amiable in repartee, ingenius in the precision of her replies and conversation, having an upright heart, excellent and even popular, tried by the misfortunes of Stanislaus, cherished by this virtuous father, who had imparted to her the kindness and candor of an honest monarch, hating expense, suffering real torments and great pain, when she learned of some public calamity, such were the qualities and virtues of her soul. She regarded all Frenchmen as her children; she loved the nation; never ceasing to speak with admiration of its deeds, its wars, its expeditions, its customs; she never mentioned the name of Louis XIV. but with profound respect, she always treated her husband as his first subject, always speaking to him in a humble and submissive tone, loving and adoring him as an earthly divinity.

Always truthful toward Fleury, even bold rather than deceptive toward him, she rarely abandoned this state of indifference in which she lived and reproached him but mildly for the little obstacles that he put in the way of a complete understanding with the king; she smiled somewhat maliciously, disconcerted him sometimes and then assumed the tone of the Queen of France. She told him that it was on his account that she had received such a cool treatment from the king, but at once showed him that she would suffer these tribulations for God's sake, and continually attacked him in his religious life, for she was dominated by it, having been brought up by her father in the strictest religious principles. These principles were so well grounded in her that at the death of the cardinal, she wished to have her nephew almoner at the French Court.

She regarded the grandeur with which she was surrounded as a burden; she lightened the duties of her servants and the length of her toilet; she hated rouge and fashions and especially their constant changing. It was a veritable torture for her to be surrounded by so many ladies-in-waiting, and their constant endeavors to please and serve her were irksome to her. Her character changed in this regard, however, as she grew older.

Having failed in her plan to dismiss the prelate, she made up her mind in regard to her course in the affairs of state, ministries and favorites; and she maintained the strictest reserve on all these questions and avoided asking the smallest favor.

She remembered the refusals that she had suffered at the hands of the prelate; she remembered how vainly she had reiterated her prayers in favor of a noble of her family and she never forgot that somewhat ungallant remark of the king, who invited her to do as he did; i. e.,

"Ask no favors of the cardinal." This reply she had often heard repeated since; therefore she feared to solicit favors and she forbade members of her family to do so, fearing the obstacles in the way of it. Finally her peace of mind was such that as long as she lived, she gave occasion for none of those petty intrigues, which make the history of courts so curious and so interesting. Up to the time of her death she abstained entirely from all affairs of government. Always even tempered, always herself, always inclined to ascertain what might please the monarch, rather than the husband, her only amusement was concerts. She took a profound interest in art. She did not love dancing nor dramas, and as her father had the same reserve and the same principles, she entertained him by concerts rather than the opera when he visited her at Versailles.

She regarded the expenses of the court as a terrible burden on the state, and frequently asked, "How much did this cost? Money is the product of the sweat of the nation," she said. She loved economy, and privations did not affect her. She devoted large sums from her private purse annually for the solace of the poor; she paid the dowries of poor girls; she granted bounties to wounded officers, to true nobility and poverty. Military service and wounds, sick people and old men, the education of youth and the apprenticeship in the crafts, were objects that were always sure to obtain her favor. Finally, devoting her attention to the very lowest class of citizens, she established homes, and founded workrooms in the parishes, and charity schools. Such was this queen that Rome would formerly have held up for the veneration of the nation, and to whom the academy, compelled by the state to devote all its energies to eulogies and compliments, would have accorded high praise, if the mistresses of the late king had not put a stop to such an audacity.

CHAPTER XXXIII.

Curious details about the princes and princesses.

THE Duke of Orleans, son of the regent, had neither the virtues nor the vices of his father. These two individuals were opposite in character, and whatever trait was found in one you could be sure it was wanting in the other. The Duke of Orleans' father was ingenious, witty, a lover of novelty, lascivious, irreligious, but his son had a mind both limited and bashful. He loved only his wife; he was religious; the former was devoted to his *roués*, the latter abandoned himself to his religious companions. The Duke of Orleans made all parties his toys, while his son wrote volumes to defend the authority of the papal Bull. Ready wit was one of the intellectual faculties of the Duke of Orleans; stubbornness and opposition were the basic principles of the character of his son; the former enjoyed dramas, noisy and tumultuous pleasures; the latter was an ascetic. The latter finally withdrew from society, going to Saint-Genevieve to discuss with his monks the Bull and papal authority, and to do penance there by confining himself in a little cell.

M. le Duc is well enough known by the innumerable sketches that we drew of him in the history of his ministry; we must add, however, that, being free from Mme. de Prie, he did not survive long, and died the following year in exile at Alençon. He was devoted to the

Countess d'Egmont, whom he had always loved somewhat, and who succeeded his first mistress; but the latter, in order not to be dismissed entirely from the court as had Mme. de Prie, resigned her place as lady-in-waiting. The disgrace of M. le Duc ended in 1729, and he was invited to return to court. Mme. la Duchess up to that time had not been able to induce the prince to marry again, the prince not being able to abandon Mme. de Prie; but what she could not obtain during the reign of this mistress, she succeeded in doing very easily through the influence of Mme. d'Egmont, who readily assisted her in this project. The prince in 1729 married the princess of Hesse Rheinfelds, sister of the Queen of Sardinia and grand-niece of mademoiselle, without losing his attachment for Mme. d'Egmont.

After M. le Duc we shall speak of the Count de Charolais, a vicious and wicked prince, whose youth was very disorderly. Every vice was in his character except what the nobles of that time still called *des bassesses*, such as robbery, swindling and the other vulgar crimes which we have seen permeated all ranks of society at that time. Charolais had genius and talent, but his heart was cruel and his actions were sanguinary; he took pleasure in killing dogs and pet animals, a thing which led him gradually to much more barbarous pleasures. Debaucheries of every kind were successively and then all together to his taste. He was of an active disposition and had great originality; but because his education was ruined he abused these good qualities.

His brother, the Count de Clermont, had neither his

talents nor his genius, neither did he have all his depraved tastes nor his brutal character. He was even amiable and decorous in society. It was to him that this century owed its first idea of the seraglio, which he filled with the prettiest girls he could find. He was brave in his army career, he was a born military man, but he was infatuated with the name of Condé.

The Prince de Conti, unhappy on account of his wife, by whom he was detested, and whom he adored, had only the ordinary virtues of mind and heart. He never had been able to please his wife, whom he constantly shadowed with spies, who caused her to endure a constant martyrdom and drove her to despair by their secret reports. Mme. de la Roche, who was careful to keep him informed of her conduct, tormented her and aroused her jealousy, and finally the husband dismissed her. Conti was of an amiable disposition; prodigal rather than liberal, brave and gallant, but misunderstandings and jealousy of his wife made him unhappy. As to the legitimated children of Louis XIV. they lived in seclusion at Sceaux and at Rambouillet; exile and prison had taught the Duke du Maine and his wife a great lesson and it had the effect of weakening a character, which nature had fitted for intrigues rather than for great deeds. The Court at Sceaux was still in a state of consternation and kept itself in unobtrusive seclusion, although it saw the triumph of Fleury and the ruin of M. le Duc, who had declared himself so openly against the legitimated princes. His brother, the Count de Toulouse, who had experienced no change in character, continued to love his wife. His pure morals and his charming society were the delight of Rambouillet. He enjoyed the kind consideration of all parties which he had gained by his character, and his earnestness when the late king gave him the rank of prince, when the Duke of Orleans deprived the Duke du Maine of his title and when the latter was elevated anew under the ministry of Fleury. His peaceable character, his charming wife, and his pleasant influence over the king increased the esteem in which he was held. He had just principles, his morals were pure, and his mind, without being brilliant, was not lacking in grace nor in bright qualities.

The princesses of that time are well worthy of a few strokes of the crayon.

Mme. de Duchess de Bourbon, proud, even haughty; determined, loving strife, pomp and ceremonial, visited the court but seldom, and was not over-well received there.

Mlle. de Charolais, who was brilliant in intellect and often somewhat malicious, and full of vigor, and even haughtiness when she was opposed, could not endure her mother and desired to be treated by her as an equal. She was wont to enjoy all sorts of pleasures, outside of her guardianship. This princess was very much sought after by the young king, whom she endeavored to captivate. She was an amateur poetess and a thousand trifling skits from her pen, and many songs of her composition were in circulation at that time. These were mostly productions describing intrigues of the court. She was subject to woman's capriciousness, and often passed in the twinkling of an eye from liveliness and vivacity into a state of sadness and melancholy. She had been beautiful in her youth; having arrived at the age of twenty-two years, she still had that solid and permanent beauty that certain faces preserve until their thirtieth or fortieth years and which disappears very gradually. She came to Rambouillet and for a long time she was the life of that court, on account of her brilliant conversation, her beauty, and her shrewd incisive intellect. Her coquetry, never being overdone, increased the pleasure of a court presided over by Mme. de Toulouse, who desired that in her home at least the external life should be in conformity to decorum, good usage and the tone of the ancient court.

Mme. la Countess de Toulouse, naturally of a proud disposition, was endowed with a kindly heart, a charming character, and a delicate mind. She had deep, brown eyes, a calm and dignified glance, a somewhat stout figure, a penetrating voice, a pretty mouth and she was reputed with good reason to be the woman, who had done most to develop the king's mind. She had lived only three years with her first husband, Gondrin. She knew how to attract and seduce the heart of the Count of Toulouse, legitimated son of the late king, who first married her secretly. France never saw a happier marriage; for thirteen years this married couple never experienced a trouble nor a cloud. The life they led at Rambouillet, the principles which ruled there, were so exemplary that this court gave a new tone to society and introduced a reforming influence that counteracted the total depravity of the regency. An air of magnificence preserved there the ostentation of the preceding reign, and the religion which ruled there, void of bigotry—which had been driven from the court during the regency—sought Rambouillet as if seeking an asylum. Here Mme. de Toulouse exacted its narrow observance. In vain did troubles, crimes, libertinism, seek to destroy piety during the regency; it was preserved in this castle and Mme. de Toulouse was careful that it should be permanent in her family.

It was into this society that Louis XV. first came to learn the usages of the world, social duties, and the decorum of polite society, which he well knew how to preserve for the rest of his life. Here his penchant for the fair sex began to manifest itself, and as the young monarch readily became devoted to persons who combined domestic virtues with an aristocratic tone, he found at Rambouillet all that could please him in this regard; and the cardinal, who feared nothing from this court, was charmed by the fact that the king frequented this home.

A single son was the result of this happy marriage. Mme. la Countess de Toulouse, who loved him as she loved her own life, inspired him at an early age with that piety which distinguished him through life. He was very delicate in childhood, and his mother was a thousand times alarmed at seeing him on the verge of the grave. It was then that, terror stricken, she strove to mould his character, and abandoned herself to misgivings.

The Court of the Queen of Spain, who had returned to France, after the death of Louis I., her husband, was just as disorderly as that of Rambouillet was religious. Public flirtations having obliged the queen in 1726 to dismiss several persons from her home, Du Bourg, her squire, who was displeased by this dismissal, persuaded Prince de Robecq, that the queen could not dismiss any one without his permission, since the major domo (a Spanish title which he had preserved) had the right to dispose of all the household offices.

The Prince de Robecq did more; he wrote to Spain letters detrimental to the queen, and obtained a letter from Marquis de la Pax, secretary of state of foreign affairs, which ordered the Prince de Robecq to fill the vacant places.

The queen, offended at the idea of being governed and subjected to her officers, who became independent of her authority, dismissed the Prince de Robecq, grand-master of her house, and the Spanish Court, to show its disapproval of this dismissal, ceased to send the pension of six hundred and sixty thousand francs, which it had promised. The queen was therefore obliged to retire to the Carmelite Convent of Rue Grenelle, and, in fact, to the same apartment that her sister had had prepared for her when she did penance there. The Duke de Nevers was the cause of this great quarrel. A nephew of the Duchess de Sforza, favorite of Mme. of Orleans, wished to supplant the Prince de Robecq, who made complaints to the Spanish Court; and this court, always despotically governed by the queen, took this opportunity to refuse the pension to the dowager queen; however, in 1732, it sent a hundred thousand francs as a part of the expense of reuniforming her guards, who were almost naked.

CHAPTER XXXIV.

Portrait of Cardinal de Fleury.—His character.

WE have seen by the foregoing the uncertain state in which foreign affairs were when M. le Duc was exiled. Finances were in disorder; commerce was languishing, the public credit was gone, the Court of France was without esteem and without influence in foreign countries. Religion was in danger, public morality ruined, and the whole nation wearied and worn out by the shocks which Louis XIV., La Tellier, the legitimated princes, the regent, the *roués*, Dubois, d'Argenson, Law, Mme. de Prie and M. le Duc, had in succession visited upon it.

In the midst of all this chaos, there arose an old man whose mind possessed nothing more than petty ruses and subtleties as the power that would enable it to succeed in great world matters. Timid in his actions, he was patient in awaiting the success of his aims and the restoration of the state, which undertaking he even dared to begin at his age of decrepitude. Disinterested for himself and his family, his only hope was to finally restore welfare and tranquillity to his country, and he suffered by the calamities which had come upon France, which he loved as he loved his own soul. He undertook to cure her ills, and succeeded in accomplishing his object almost by inaction, by leaving her in repose, and keeping intriguers from the affairs of state.

Amiable in society, especially toward women, and capable of quiet coquetry, he covered his whole ambition with the most simple exterior. There was not seen in him and in his conversation the open-hearted man who reveals truth or tears away the veil from his plans with assurance; but the adroit courtier, who presents to the gaze of the public only the thin shell; nevertheless he rarely deceived, for deceit was not a part of his character and only manifested itself on three or four occasions in his life,—as for example when he had to remove the ministry of M. le Duc. He prepared this court revolution by petty ruses and deceptions, which he practiced and caused his pupil to practice. It was seen even in this instance that he did not deceive M. le Duc, because that prince had offered to retire, but the young monarch, his pupil, for he persuaded him that he had reached the age when kings, who have the talents of his majesty, ought to take the reins of government themselves, and dismiss the prime ministers, especially when the people were so discontented with them.

But caution and timidity, rather than knavery, were the resources of his intellect; for he showed in society, and even in his work with the different ministers who were under him, only part of truth, and he never permitted himself to reveal to any individual, the whole of his schemes in regard to general affairs. He was, in reality, never known to commit himself; if there were artifice in his conduct, external peace of mind was the foundation of his habits and his actions, a precious quality both for ministers and for courtiers; for it is a quality that maintains them in position for a long time.

In spite of his imperturbability, Fleury did not live in a state of absolute indifference. Devoted to the faction of the legitimated princes of the former Court of Louis XIV., he carried on secret negotiations with this party and was sustained by it before he governed the state as a minister. His great power, especially during the regency, consisted in his studied appearance of incapability; he was afraid of the new court, he was even terrified by it, and if he succeeded in eluding the results of its rash deeds it was because he understood how to appear as a nonentity in its presence. He knew how to live in a state of perfect indifference to its riches, and in such simplicity that the court of the regency, whose evils he escaped, believed him not only unskillful in business, but utterly guiltless of any desire to interfere with public affairs.

We cannot understand how the King of Prussia, who has spoken so justly concerning this prelate, sometimes paints him in false colors, even though he was such a careful student of character. Frederic II. says of Fleury that: "If Richelieu and Mazarin succeeded in exhausting all that pomp and pageantry could give of glory and consideration, Fleury on the other hand built his greatness on the foundation of the simplicity. He preferred," says the King of Prussia, "negotiations to war, because he was powerful in intrigues and because he did not know how to command armies; bold in his projects, but timid in their execution, those qualities rendered him a useful servant of France."

Fleury is not well described by these observations.

It is not exactly because Richelieu and Mazarin had distinguished themselves by ostentation that Fleury wished to appear great by his simplicity, but because this virtue was a quality of his heart, which he never belied in all his life. This simplicity followed him everywhere; at Fréjus, at court, in the seclusion incident to his rôle of king's instructor and when he was cardinal and minister. Fleury was the ideal of simplicity; simplicity was depicted on his beautiful countenance, it was with him in his equipages, in his home and even in his beautiful hair which he allowed to flow loose and unarranged. Instead of a country home he had a small apartment at Issy, as if he were in a seminary. And if there were any virtue in his great character, we must say that it was this grand and noble simplicity, which he always revealed. "He preferred," it is true as the King of Prussia says, "negotiations to war," but it is not because "he was strong in intrigues and did not know how to command armies," but rather because he wished to leave the state to repose in quietude; because he feared war, and regarded the most successful war as a curse.

Fleury would have been better described, if it had been said of him that he feared both intrigues and war, that he feared equally those two curses of the welfare of nations, and that to have peace, he allowed the navy of France to fall into disuse, and drove intriguers from the ministry.

As to the boldness of his schemes and the timidity of their execution, I think on the other hand that boldness characterized their execution and that timidity was rather the marked characteristic of his projects. As a matter of fact, the cardinal was unimaginative; he even prevented the planning out of new affairs, because the state was suffering and because former ministries had done too much planning; but on the other hand, when this prelate had a well conceived idea that he determined to carry out, firmness seemed to rise out of this timid and weak soul, and he triumphed always over obstacles that opposed him. Fleury, in this, was like all pusillanimous and naturally weak men; for the courage which accompanies the first wish in a prompt and decided genius, the first perception and so to speak the initiative of undertakings, is only found in men who are weak by actual execution. This is the beautiful side of the cardinal. Let us consider the other side of his character.

This man, so precious at that time to France, was not faultless; he even had great faults of soul. He was a priest and an intolerant priest at that; and he had a confessor named Polet, who merits our execration for his sacerdotal and secret intrigues, which caused Fleury to commit the most astounding imprudences. He also had, in the monks of Saint-Sulpice, counselors who were dangerous to the peace of the realm, because under external appearance of peace, they suggested to him at Issy the matters relative to the papal Bull, acts of authority and despotism which threatened the state with civil war and, "which must end with bloody battle," wrote Cardinal Polignac from Rome, "which will be fought between the parties on the plain of Saint-Denis." The dawn of philosophy, which appeared in France about the year 1740, dissipating these monastical quarrels, relegated them to school benches and to the halls of Saint-Sulpice or of Saint-Magloire, and exposed them to such ridicule that Fleury and Beaumont la France heard no more of them.

Such was Cardinal Fleury, considered under every possible aspect. His first conduct of affairs in the ministry gained for him neither the eulogy of the capital city nor that of the court. It was openly said of him, that he had not developed the qualities of a great character; some even prophesied at that time that there would be nothing remarkable in his ministry.

CHAPTER XXXV.

Courtiers disgraced and the reasons therefore.—M. le Duc does honor to his retirement.—The Court of Madrid.—An illness of Louis XV.

As a matter of fact, the day of his elevation to the ministry, which ought to have been the triumph of his virtue, since it placed him in authority over his enemies, was only the triumph of his petty vengeances. On the one hand he recalled the enemies of M. le Duc from their exile and bestowed his confidence and friendship upon them; and on the other hand he exiled the friends and partisans of that prince, or removed them from office. Desforts was made comptroller-general, and Le Blanc, minister of war, to the prejudice of Dodun and Breteuil who were dismissed. The former, foreseeing the animosity of the prelate, himself asked for his own dismissal as soon as he learned of the fall of M. le Duc, but the latter awaited the moment of his disgrace, which was accompanied by a pension of sixteen thousand francs.

His vengeance even went to the point of ordering Maurepas to write to Mme. de Prie, whom Mlle. de Clermont had given an asylum at Chantilly, to ask her resignation from the office of lady-in-waiting and to exile her to Normandy. In vain did M. le Duc write to obtain permission for her to remain with him; she had to leave Chantilly where she had sought refuge.

The Pâris brothers; who had conducted financial affairs

under Dodun and under La Houssaye; who had contributed to the fall of Law's system of finance; who, under M. le Duc, Dubois and the regent, had always been consulted; who had established a certain system in finances by means of the journals which Desforts did not fail to abolish; were imprisoned or exiled as a reward for their services and because they were at that time devoted to M. le Duc. The eldest Pâris was sent to Dauphiné, his fatherland, Duvernay was sent fifty leagues from Paris and Montmartel was exiled to Saumur.

M. le Duc had selected choice persons to associate with and to amuse the monarch; Fleury deprived him of their services. The Duke de Gesvres, who had formerly been somewhat more than a friend of M. le Duc, and who, on that account, had succeeded in gaining the good will of Louis XV., lost favor at court.

Mme. de Nesle, a voluptuous, intriguing and pretty woman, amorous of the king and of all handsome men, and whom M. le Duc had placed in such a position that she might captivate the king, also lost favor. De Meuse, who still maintained the position with the king that the Duke de Gesvres had, and the other young courtiers of his ilk lost their influence. The king seemed to forget his former tastes and diversions and to become devoted to Mme. la Countess de Toulouse alone. The Sunday following the exile of M. le Duc, the king caused a memorial to be read in his council, in which he declared that he would henceforth take charge of the government of his state. Each minister came to work with M. de Fréjus and henceforth worked in his presence with the king. The old Marshal d'Huxelles, whom the prelate provided for, because they both had grown old in the same principles and in the same party, came to his home when Morville worked there. The king was more interested and took more pleasure in the details of foreign affairs than that of any other department, and Fleury did not fail to acquaint him with the fact that Europe approved of the revolution in the ministry.

As to Desforts, he resumed the former system of finances; he made an estimate with the receiver of finance which obliged them to furnish five million francs a month, and received from the Farmers General the submission of twenty-four millions, the result of the contracts. The fixed revenue of the state was then one hundred and forty millions, exclusive of the postal system, the incidentals, the rent of royal domain and the free will offerings of the clergy; a revenue of from fifteen to twenty millions was drawn from these sources. The total revenue of the state was therefore about one hundred and sixty millions, which was at that time a very impressive object lesson to all Europe.

The dismissal of the friends of M. le Duc and the recall of those, whom he had disgraced, was a great surprise to the observers of all these events. They saw the return of the chevalier and Count Belle-Ilse. La Jonchère, Sechelles, and Le Blanc, to whom the ministry was turned over at once. This Le Blanc had been in most sad circumstances. Created minister, because in the absence of Dubois he had been purveyor of pleasures to the prince, he had been driven from place by this same Dubois, who enjoyed supreme power as prime minister. La Vrillière the eternal signer and server of *lettres de cachet* sent him thirty leagues from Paris.

Persecuted by M. le Duc, but having succeeded in justifying himself as he alone could, Le Blanc had obtained his liberty and had retired to one of his castles afflicted with the diseases he had contracted in the Bastille; this was the place whither Fleury sent to notify him of his appointment to the ministry. Then, victorious over Dubois, and M. le Duc, he would have been nobler and grander in scorning his second class enemies who had simply been the tools of M. le Duc; but Le Blanc was only a man, and a mean and passionate man, even in the zenith of his glory. He attacked Arnaud, whom M. le Duc had made master of petitions, the certain reward of magistrates who knew how to obey ministers implicitly. He relieved him of his office and sent him into a sort of exile at Angoulême because this Arnaud had prevaricated when being interrogated on the progress of his department.

As to his new conduct in the ministry it was such, that associated with Mme. de Tresnel, his daughter, they determined to enrich themselves whenever the occasion arrived, and Le Blanc, incorrigible in spite of his misfortunes, never failed to accord favors and pensions with extraordinary liberality that won for him the protection and the good will of courtiers. The Duchess of Lévi and Mme. Dangeau, for a long time intimate friends of the prelate, seemed to be in league with him. This was especially true of the former, her husband being cousin germain to Belle-Isle, who was implicated in the affair. The Luynes, the Chaulnes, the Mortemarts, the Charosts, the d'Humieres, Saint-Simon, Luxembourg, Berwick, and especially Blouin, governor of Versailles and all those who were in alliance with their families and who had contributed to the exile of M. le Duc, showed themselves attached to Le Blanc and to the Bishop de Fréjus. The Rohans invariably turned to the side of the reigning power, and Noailles, who came for the purpose of sounding the status of affairs, showed himself for a moment and then disappeared. Villeroy, who had not yet expended all his bile against his preceptor, instead of visiting Versailles went to Chantilly to visit M. le Duc. To indemnify him for the loss that he had sustained and to silence him by interesting him, after the fashion of the revolution, they gave Mme. de Prie's position as court-lady to Mme. d'Alincourt. As to the most strict persons of the court, the Villeroys, the Sullys, the La Rochefoucaulds, they held themselves aloof from Le Blanc; they did not believe that he was sufficiently purified and simply kept to themselves.

The life of a courtier and even that of a prince is a strange thing, in the court of a despot. As soon as the favorite minister is installed the relatives of the disgraced princes, even in their most bitter misfortune, must go to pay him their compliments, and even show their submission. We see even Mme. the Duchess, and the king himself, coming to Versailles to treat him with respect; both of them, however, preserved a discreet silence in regard to this last event. The princes then went to visit the queen and remained a long time with her, and Fleury himself visited the duchess in the evening and remained in conversation with her for three hours. These perfidious visits seemed strange to the multitude; yet bold lying is the spirit and the vital atmosphere breathed at court. Ceremonial and etiquette continually stifle natural feelings; one is accustomed from childhood to dissimulate. Fleury possessed the art of dissimulation in a remarkable degree; he had always maintained a calm, serene composure in the presence of Louis XIV. and the regent, of Law and of d'Aguesseau, and also in the presence of Noailles and of Dubois.

In the revolution which ruined M. le Duc, the king seems much more interesting than Fleury, on account of the humane and tender feelings he displayed; but he also revealed the fact that his weak devotion to his minister or to his mistress would one day get possession of his mind. He sent a lieutenant of the royal body guard as far as Chantilly to watch and report to him the actions of M. le Duc. Louis XV. was so touched at the story this officer told on his return that he could not repress his tears and entered his closet to weep, whilst the cardinal, alone, seemed firm in his vengeance, listening to the base plaudits of the crowd of courtiers, who, without true hatred as without true devotion, had been the slaves of M. le Duc and now were the slaves of the new minister.

M. le Duc, alone, displayed nobility of character in this misfortune, which he bore with pride and with great composure. The Marquis de Silly, who went to see him at Chantilly, noticed and informed the Duke de Richelieu that he was engaged in hunting and caring for his gardens; that he was gay, tranquil, and contented in this the most beautiful place in the world. Instead of attributing his misfortune to Mme. de Prie, by whom he was always enchanted, and to the Pâris Brothers, he said that he himself was the cause of their misfortune, and when the prelate was mentioned he smiled, shrugging his shoulders.

The foreign ministers, who soon learned the weakness of Fleury's character and who perceived the meanness of his soul, endeavored to dominate him. The Duke of Savoy had not ceased to cultivate his friendship since he had been the preceptor of Louis XV., foreseeing what he would become later on. His minister was ordered to constantly remind him of his devotion.

The English minister, who wished to keep up a secret entente with France from the time of the regency, and, who, during his exile at Issy, had gone there for the purpose of persuading him not to abandon his place, endeavored from that time on to get control of the prelate. The Court of Spain alone, still irreconcilably injured on account of the dismissal of its Infanta, had no dealings with him, although Fleury before his elevation was in correspondence with that kingdom. Although the cowardice of the minister caused the angry, revengeful and haughty queen to fear some new and unexpected alliance, the first undertaking of Fleury, when he became minister, was to acquaint the Spanish Court of the news by courier. We did not have a minister at that court, but the Papal Nuncio was addressed with the request to impart the news to the Nuncio at the Spanish Court, who bore the despatches from the minister of France to the king and queen. They refused to receive and to open them; nevertheless they learned of this great news with satisfaction, for they blamed the Duke de Bourbon entirely for all the quarrels with Spain. But all this did not prevent Spain from preparing provisions, munitions of war, troops, and an artillery train of such a size that it was believed at Versailles that we were on the eve of a war. These warlike movements were made principally at Roussillon and Catalonia. They had learned then that Fleury did not wish to secede from the treaty of Hanover; they knew that he was in alliance with the English, and they pretended at the Madrid Court to be more irritated at it than they were in reality.

This Madrid Court, always extremely ambitious of establishing itself in France, was constantly watchful of the health of the king, who was getting stronger month by month.

The House of Orleans and its party also kept a careful watch on events. They kept a keen lookout, although with more reserve than the Madrid Court, on the pleasures of the king which might contribute to undermine his health, and all Europe, which had carried on for so long a time a disasterous war over the Spanish succession, feared that it might see the quarrel renewed over the succession of Louis XV., if that prince should die. A sickness of Louis XV. alarmed all observers, and the king was so carefully watched that we publish the following letter, written by the Marquis de Silly to the Duke de Richelieu, in Vienna.

"Tuesday, July 23rd, the king arose at eight o'clock, and, dressing, said that he had not slept well and that he was still sleepy. He went to mass at nine o'clock; arriving at the chapel, he became faint, and, toward the middle of the mass, he was obliged to seat himself in his arm-chair; he became exceedingly pale, without however losing consciousness. The weakness left him after mass, and he returned quite gayly to his room, where he held a council over financial affairs; he did not dine; he only drank a cup of bouillon, and postponed his departure for Rambouillet until four o'clock in the afternoon, instead of leaving at one o'clock as he had planned. This was all that M. de Fréjus could persuade him to do. On reaching Rambouillet he had a chill and said that he had a headache; nevertheless he played a game of cards, but took a very light supper and retired at eleven o'clock.

"At night the fever developed and became violent; at nine o'clock he was bled on the arm; this relieved him somewhat and they took advantage of this moment of relief to take him back to Versailles where he arrived at four o'clock in the afternoon, but the fever having redoubled in the evening and his head feeling very oppressed, his foot was bled at ten o'clock. Thus passed Wednesday.

"Thursday, the fever continued, as well as the symptoms which accompany it, and he was given two grains of an emetic, but his stomach was so clogged that it had but small effect. This had been foreseen, still it was thought best to give him another dose of the emetic and an hour afterwards a dose of vegetable salts. About seven o'clock in the evening his stomach was relieved. Nevertheless on Friday, the fever and symptoms having continued, a second bleeding of the foot was determined upon and was performed at seven o'clock in the evening. The good effect of it was appreciable. The fever diminished. His head became clear and he passed a very quiet night. Saturday passed quite comfortably and the paroxysm was very slight. Yesterday, Sunday, evening, the headache returned. The doctors held a long consultation at seven o'clock but they could not agree as to the nature of the malady, and some blotches having appeared, the rumor was spread that he had smallpox, although there was no indication of it and the doctors did not even give it a thought. The night was peaceful and the fever having diminished he was purged in the morning. The fever did not increase and according to all appearances no dangerous results are to be feared, however, I am not very sanguine as yet.

"You can easily imagine the excitement of every one during all this. The Orleans people conducted themselves properly, at least in public.

"It was proposed to the king to allow M. le Duc to come to get news of his condition himself. He refused.

"All this news was immediately sent by couriers to Madrid and it was learned that the Queen of Spain made secret preparations to come to France. She felt herself so assured of attaining the French crown, that there was not a secret stairway, nor avenue, nor apartment, nor hallway of the château of Versailles that she did not know as perfectly, as if she had dwelt there all her life."

CHAPTER XXXVI.

Polet, confessor of Fleury.—Barjac, his valet-de-chambre.—His conduct toward the nobles who demeaned themselves to flatter him.

IT was the fate of France to be governed during the last years of the king by illegitimates, the confessor and the favorite of Louis XIV.

During the regency of the Duke of Orleans the élite of the debauchées, in concert with Law, Dubois and d'Argenson, got possession of supreme power.

Under M. le Duc a woman governed the state, ruined its finances, prostituted its offices and its positions and brought about bitter dissension between princes of the blood. France was tired of the rule of women and confessors.

Nevertheless under the ministry of Fleury, a confessor, a valet and a company of intolerant and bigoted priests, were to get possession of a part, at least, of the affairs of state. Polet, a parish vicar, superior of the Seminary of St. Nicholas of Chardonnet, desired Fleury, his penitent, to give over a part of the affairs to the confessional. The famous Barjac, his first valet-de-chambre, desired to have influence; and Saint-Sulpice, which had enemies to humiliate and a voice to be heard in the Gallican church, surrounded the prelate for the purpose of getting control of ecclesiastical affairs, according pardons to its pupils or its creatures, and favoring the propaganda of its order in and out of France.

order in all its designs; he had been its spy for the destruction of Port-Royal; he had put his hand to the acceleration this work and had helped d'Argenson, the lieutenant-general of police.

But his impetuous character, was at least, not like those political rages that intriguing, petty abbots affected when they desired to acquire prelacies. Polet, a man of good faith, was honestly devoted in mind and heart to his faith and doctrine. He refused the benefices, which the king offered him; he even refused a small pension. To direct the conscience of the nobles, of ministers, of court ladies, to persecute the Jansenists, were his delights and his amusements. He had disciples and instructed them in these sentiments; he inspired and imbued them with his opinions, he kept from Holy Orders every one who was not animated by the zeal with which he was burning, and recompensed those who showed fanaticism. Finally, his disinterestedness even went so far as to lead him to refuse the Parish of Saint-Nicholas, contenting himself with the duties of a simple vicar and the superior of young priests.

When M. le Duc was declared prime minister, Polet found that he did pay enough attention to the matters of the Bull and did not cease to goad on the ambition of the timid Fleury to get possession of supreme power. He told him of detailed schemes and plans of Mme. de Prie and caused him to take measures to remove M. le Duc, whom the Jesuits and the Sulpicians found too cowardly for their interests, which they identified with those of the church. Finally, it was said at that time, that in his quality of confessor, friend and councilor, Polet excited the old prelate to courage and to action and induced him to dismiss M. le Duc. He hoped to be able one day to direct the conscience of a prime minister, to give free vent to his active and persecuting genius, and to play the same rôle as did Father le Tellier under Louis XIV.

Polet, having become confessor of the minister, saw titled ladies and even ministers coming to him to solicit favors. They remained for hours in a little parlor on the ground floor of Saint-Nicholas in a room, cold, damp and scarcely twelve feet square. Polet, who, for himself, refused livings and even the curé of his parish, was fond of his influence in the choice of prelates of the Church of France, and of his title of Vicar of Saint-Nicholas. Seventy-four years of age in 1726, he was still of a noble and imposing appearance. He was an honest man, his habits were simple and austere. He carried out his Christian work as a matter of personal taste and through a love of virtue; he had protected his penitent, afterwards Cardinal de Fleury, while in his quality of preceptor of Louis XV.; and had induced Marshall de Villeroy to ask Louis XIV. for this favor. Fleury, very grateful, desired to make him confessor of Louis XV., when the regent banished the Jesuits; but he refused this place which Abbé Fleury held.

Polet, confessing the cardinal, who had become a minister, obtained from him as many *lettres de cachet* as he wished, to harrow the Jansenists, and he did this up to the very moment when Fleury wanted to reduce their life annuities. This simple vicar then said to the cardinal that he could by no means do this without committing an injustice, and the cardinal not wishing to abandon his plan, Polet replied that he could seek confessors of his own ilk and that he did not intend to damn himself for him. He not only refused him absolution, but declined even to listen to his confession, to the great pleasure of Couturier, a Sulpician, and of Chauvelin, the minister, who, because they wanted to govern under the name of the cardinal, were already very jealous of Abbé Polet.

Such was the character of the man who governed Fleury by confessing him. A valet, called Barjac, very easily dominated him in another way. Barjac, like Polet, was a man of common sense, of uprightness and even of virtue. For a long time in the service of Fleury in the quality of a valet-de-chambre, Barjac was formerly the confidant of his sorrows and his pleasures. The public knew it, and men in place did not blush to visit Barjac and to treat him like a noble. He maintained a magnificent household, and the cardinal who was not on his reserve with all courtiers sometimes told them when the table was too full: "Monsieur, kindly go and dine with Barjac." This valet accustomed himself so well to being caressed and courted without becoming insolent and without thinking himself above his place, that he acquired a powerful reputation, and even took part in the affairs of state, of finances, in the manner of a minister, and he often talked of the doings of the cardinal as the others did, never failing to say: "We have given to the Duke d'Antin such a commission. The Marshal de Villars came to see us this morning. . . yesterday at dinner we had a large company." Thus he imitated the cardinal.

In his letters he assumed the same tone, continually affecting equality even with the Marshals of France, to whom he did not always accord the courtesy, which custom and rank demanded, simply signing his name to the end of his letters, as the cardinal did, and without burdening himself with the customary finales. He knew so well how to imitate the simplicity of his master that his voice was not that of a valet; his manners were decorous; he knew the respect due to rank, title and to men in office; he caused courtiers, who forgot him, to remember who they were, by repelling them in a sort of affected respect when calling on him to talk of business affairs, and by using the imperious tone of a great lord or an important man.

But he did not wish to demean himself before the nobles, nor to allow the nobles to demean themselves before him. He always treated them with equality, without being disrespectful, and never withdrew from that rank in which they had placed themselves with him. He became respectful when he was treated with haughtiness or when one humiliated himself in his presence.

Barjac exacted visits, insisted on being consulted and was a factor in the distribution of all favors. Just in the favors he accorded, he always insisted upon knowing his protégés personally, excluding those from consideration who did not present themselves to him. When some personage was spoken of who did not visit him, he often laconically and coolly remarked: "I do not know him."

The cardinal, in his youth, had needs known to very few people and the valet had shown a devotion, a fidelity, and a discretion absolutely trustworthy. He had always served his masters in all the different stages of his career; he had acquired the cardinal's way, his little peculiarities of speech, his genial good nature, his sublety, his little tricky ways, in fact, his whole character. He exercised over him that power, which old valets are wont to exercise over their masters; but this power was respectful and friendly, as one must necessarily assume toward a cardinal minister and devout divine, and a man who had for a long time held in his hands the thread of his life conduct and of his early gallantries. Thus nothing was secret for Barjac in all the affairs of state; he spoke of them with an important air when he was with people initiated into the secrets, or with the ministers. He spoke of national problems as if they were the domestic affairs of the cardinal, and when he had been specially charged with some matter or when he had chosen those who were to negotiate it, he spoke in the most egotistic way, saying, "I did it, I concluded, I treated." And he spoke in this way concerning the principal affairs of state, which were all discussed in the home of the cardinal before they were taken to the council, while the king was amusing himself either with the famous sisters, or at Rambouillet, or on the hunt.

Barjac thus really guided the policy of France in certain matters; he nominated men to positions; he exacted from the superior officers of the army, from ministers and from prelates, whom he had served, the return service of employing some person whom he recommended; so that his protection was more important than that of the ministers, or even of the cardinal. He often had brevets, signed by the king and countersigned by a minister, brought to him, and the office given to others. He was always sure of obtaining a respite, or stay of execution. It must be confessed, however, that he had good tact, and he knew how to correctly estimate talents, character, merit, as well as the cardinal, who, acknowledging his uprightness and his good common sense, allowed him to have his way.

One had to be, therefore, well known to Barjac in order to advance, at least in the beginning of Fleury's ministry; for Chauvelin took the place of Polet and Barjac afterward; office-seekers had to pay a sort of homage to him, but it had to be done adroitly and shrewdly, for an unworthy action would have been reproved by him.

One day a titled noble of the court asked a favor of him which he most eagerly sought, and, passing the limits of the delicacy which he should have shown in the presence of Barjac, the courtier, in order to obtain it, treated him with respect, consideration, and in such a complaisant tone that Barjac was shocked. The noble went further and invited him to dine with him, familiarly placing himself at his right the first time he called on him, and scattered eulogies right and left on his virtue and on the brilliancy of M. de Barjac, attributing to him the prosperity of France.

Barjac, wearied with these demonstrations, arose, took his napkin from his buttonhole, placed it under his arm, took a plate from his valet, grasped the back of the chair of the duke and peer, and assumed the position of a servant at table. The latter, on the other hand, arose and told M. de Barjac that he would never permit it, and Barjac replied to him: "Although a peer of France has forgotten his station to please Barjac, Barjac should never forget his." He added that M. le Duc should not obtain the favor if he refused to be served by Barjac. The whole court, the king, the cardinal, laughed heartily over the facetiousness of Barjac. Thus the nobles learned, at their cost, that he must be approached with delicacy and with extreme shrewdness. Two letters written by him, which we give, will explain his character still better. He wrote to the Duke de Richelieu:—

"I assured M. de Monglas, secretary of His Eminence, with whom I am on good terms, that you should render all possible service to his brother. He begs me, sir, to impart to you his most humble thanks.

"M. de Marshal du Bourg is dead. This has meant for us since yesterday morning a deluge of company, men and women, relatives and friends, who wish to replace the deceased. All the marshals of France have slept at Versailles. M. de Coigny assumes all the airs; he claims that he has the promise of filling this place. M. Chauvelin and all the marshalls are asking questions.

"In regard to the premier, he is the enemy of M. d'Angervilliers and M. de Belle-Isle; this will continue, and will exact our careful attention.

"Our apartment is so full that I can scarcely move in it. I am writing to M. Menden asking him to come to Issy Thursday or Friday. The king is going to La Muette day after to-morrow. M. de Maillebois is here, and is preparing to leave for Corsica. I believe that they will give him sixteen battalions. I see M. de Firmacon very often; he almost excites my pity; he would like to go to La Muette, but there is no time.

"BARJAC."

His letter of the 23rd of February, 1739, shows to what extent Barjac penetrated at that time in state affairs.

"Here is the good deed I have just performed with reference to the marriage of the first lady with Don Philippe, but it may easily be believed that, for the dauphin, this will not go far. His Eminence continues Lent. M. de Saint-Florentin wished to give him the sheep you sent him, but he would have none of it. His Eminence is in extreme good health.

"You are interesting yourself, sir, in behalf of M. de Vicq in regard to a cordon; your protection is employed in behalf of a worthy man.

"M. de Boissieux is dead. His position will be given to M. de Contades, it is believed.

"M. de Maillebois took his leave yesterday.

"You will be surprised, sir, to see me having dealings with M. de Voltaire. I am ignorant, but I do not approve of what he does with a ferociousness that is not approved by any one. I have answered him; he will not be contented with my reply, but he is an undervalued man. I beg you, sir, to be persuaded of my respect and sincere devotion.

" BARJAC."

England, desiring to preserve our alliance and fearing the union of France and Spain as maritime powers, knew how to win the devotion of the regent, Cardinal Dubois, M. le Duc, Mme. de Prie and Cardinal Fleury. The ministers of Great Britain, in order to dominate our cabinet at Versailles, were shrewd enough to estimate the personal longings and the personal character of our ministers, of their mistresses and of all persons who might have influence in the affairs of state. They promised their assistance to the Duke of Orleans to aid him in securing the throne in case of the death of the young king; a large pension held Dubois in subjection; they bought Mme. de Prie for a heavy price and she, in turn, used her influence with M. le Duc. They won Fleury over by kind attention and making the most of his feeble and pacified nature. Thus France, for nearly ten years, had no real alliance, but was merely the subject of England, and we shall see by the terms of the instructions of Richelieu for the Vienna embassy, that he was not to act without consulting the minister from London.

This attention displayed by England in surrounding and winning over to her cause, whoever had the least influence in guiding French affairs, even went to the extent of treating with Barjac. It was known that he had influence over the cardinal, and, since Austria was interested in having us avoid a Spanish alliance—for she was treating with Spain at that time— her minister also negotiated with Barjac. Seeing himself courted by all the powers, Barjac very naturally assumed that important tone which he maintained in Fleury's home; nevertheless, always honest and veracious, Barjac said to the ambassador of Vienna, who desired to influence him: "Sir, the place is taken; two powers can't occupy it at once; I cannot devote myself to several at the same time; moreover, the interests of France are bound up at the present time with those of England."

It is seen by these anecdotes what a power the confessor and the valet-de-chambre of Cardinal de Fleury had over his mind. The priests of Saint-Sulpice also had a great influence over him; but in order to show what this influence was and what the Sulpicians stood for in the church, an instructive episode will not be out of place.

END OF VOLUME I.

CPSIA information can be obtained
at www.ICGtesting.com
Printed in the USA
LVHW081450150322
713379LV00007B/4